"The spiritual journey toward which Bruce Demarest is inviting you is deepening, exciting, and profoundly satisfying. It is grounded in classic Christian spirituality, and pertinent to contemporary needs."

—Thomas C. Oden, Drew University

"What an amazing journey Bruce Demarest has been on. While remaining solidly rooted in his own evangelical tradition, he has, with great honesty and courage, opened himself to the deep and vital spiritual life in Christian history that has much to offer us today. This book will be profoundly enriching to the Christian who desires something "more" in their union with God."

—Ralph Martin, president, Renewal Ministries

"If you want to feed your mind and nourish your heart then you will find this book to be a delicious, full-course meal. With the foundation of a biblical scholar, the intellectual rigor of a theologian and the heart of a fellow pilgrim, Bruce provides practical tools that encourage and challenge us to go further in our relationship with Christ."

—Gary J. Oliver, Ph.D., executive director of The Center for Marriage and Family Studies, and author of *Made Perfect in Weakness: The Amazing Things God Can Do with Failure*

pg 130 -

Dr. Bruce Demarest

RESTORING THE HEART *of* CHRISTIAN SPIRITUALITY

Satisfy Your Soul

BRINGING TRUTH TO LIFE
P.O. Box 35001, Colorado Springs, Colorado 80935

The Navigators is an international Christian organization. Our mission is to reach, disciple, and equip people to know Christ and to make Him known through successive generations. We envision multitudes of diverse people in the United States and every other nation who have a passionate love for Christ, live a lifestyle of sharing Christ's love, and multiply spiritual laborers among those without Christ.

NavPress is the publishing ministry of The Navigators. NavPress publications help believers learn biblical truth and apply what they learn to their lives and ministries. Our mission is to stimulate spiritual formation among our readers.

www.navpress.com

ISBN 1-57683-130-2

Cover illustration by David Carlson Design
General editor: Dallas Willard
Senior editor: David Hazard

Some of the anecdotal illustrations in this book are true to life and are included with the permission of the persons involved. All other illustrations are composites of real situations, and any resemblance to people living or dead is coincidental.

Demarest, Bruce A.
Satisfy your soul : restoring the heart of Christian spirituality / Bruce Demarest.
p. cm.
Includes bibliographical references.
ISBN 1-57683-130-2
1. Spirituality. I. Title.
BV4501.2.D44185 1999 99-19379
248—dc21 CIP

Printed in the United States of America
1 2 3 4 5 6 7 8 9 10 11 12 13 14 15 / 99

Contents

Preface

Christian spirituality can be controversial, perhaps even confusing. So many "brands" of it are offered today, and some are not Christian at all, as those of us who rest our faith in the Bible understand Christianity. A Christian spirituality would have to foster, as an irreducible minimum, a stronger connection to the God of the Bible and create in its followers a stronger resemblance in spirit to Jesus Christ. By this standard, some spiritual practices espoused today are not based in Christian spirituality at all. Some lead away from God altogether, into the spiritual darkness of this present age.

Today, for instance, Christians hear about meditation and contemplation. But they are as likely to hear some presentation of the Zen form of these practices as the true, beneficial Christian form. Do we know the all-important differences? Likewise, many are seeking spiritual direction. But is the one who is directing, guiding them closer to God in the humble, surrendered Spirit of Christ or in some form of spiritualized "actualization" that shrugs off any claims by any "deity" other than the *self?*

Given that there is confusion out there, isn't it *very* important to know, not only *what* a spiritual practice or path is supposed to do for you, but *who* is offering to guide you on it? To know their true aim and what they rely upon for their authority?

You've come to this book, most likely because you sense a need in the deepest part of your being—in your soul. Spiritual hunger, or even mild curiosity, puts you in a somewhat vulnerable position: You don't know, and you are looking to someone who supposedly does know. And because you are about to admit me—or at least my thoughts and words—into this important place, it is all to your benefit to know something about me, the man you are briefly admitting into your thoughts.

I approach the important topic of Christian spirituality as a Christian raised from childhood in an evangelical church. Today, and for the past thirty-five years, I've been married to one woman—a strong Christian and a leader in her own right. Together we raised three children to young adulthood, and the way that they and their spouses walk their Christian walk is most encouraging.

Because I wanted a firm grounding in the Bible, I was educated at Wheaton College and received seminary training at Trinity Evangelical Divinity School. After that, I earned a doctorate in biblical and historical theology at the University of Manchester in England. My mentor there for three years was, perhaps, the leading evangelical Bible scholar of the twentieth century, F. F. Bruce.

Thereafter, wanting to live as a follower of Christ, I spent a decade serving with two respected mission organizations: SIM International in West Africa and the International Fellowship of Evangelical Students (IFES) in Europe. I served IFES as Theological Secretary and assisted in the formation of university student groups in France, Lebanon, and Egypt. I've also been privileged to teach for various periods of time in seminaries in the United States, Canada, the Caribbean, the Middle East, and Asia.

As to church commitments, I am an ordained teaching elder in the Evangelical Presbyterian Church (EPC). As a member of the denomination's national Theology Committee, I write a regular column in the EPC's magazine, *Reflections*, and advise other Christian ministries.

My primary calling for the past quarter-century has been as a professor at Denver Seminary in Colorado, where I teach courses in theology, Christian spirituality, and mentoring.

Finally, I am an author of some ten books, and many articles, on various aspects of Christian theology and spirituality.

But beyond all personal history or credentials, you need to know this: I wholeheartedly subscribe to the essential truths of the historic Christian faith. These include the following core doctrines:

the Trinitarian nature of God;
the truthfulness and authority of inspired Scripture;

the fall of the human race in sin, through Adam;
the full humanity and deity of the incarnate Son of God;
Christ's substitutionary, atoning death on the Cross;
the Savior's glorious resurrection from the dead, and ascension to heaven;
salvation by grace, through faith in Christ alone;
the church as the body of the redeemed throughout the ages; and
Christ's literal second coming to judge the righteous, and also
the unrighteous for their entrenched obstinacy in disobeying the laws of God.

There are Christians of many persuasions. Where do I stand? I'm reminded of an incident that occurred during the Spanish Civil War prior to World War I. Leftists of Marxist persuasion were fighting against rightist followers of General Franco. When a woman was captured by the Franco faction, she was asked during questioning, "Are you from the left or from the right?" With firm conviction she replied, "I stand in the extreme center!" Theologically, I stand in the extreme center of the historic Christian faith. That is to say, I seek to avoid drifting to the left as well as to the right. Under God, the goal of my teaching and writing has been to defend orthodox Christianity against unbiblical challenges and to instruct and edify others in the gospel.

I also sense the importance of remaining alert to the fresh movements of God's Spirit in our day. Lack of vitality and power in churches is due to neglect of the life-giving ministry of the Holy Spirit and the things that foster growth in the character of Christ. We must take seriously Paul's command to "keep in step with the Spirit" (Galatians 5:25, NIV).

Dr. Vernon Grounds—whose distinguished service to Denver Seminary as president and provost spans nearly five decades—some years ago crafted an ethos statement that has become the hallmark of our school. It reads: "Here is no unanchored liberalism—freedom to think without commitment. Here is no encrusted dogmatism—commitment without freedom to think. Here is a vibrant evangelicalism—commitment with freedom to think within the limits laid down in Scripture." From the depths of my heart I take pleasure in this statement.

By giving you something of my background and attitudes, I wish to communicate my unswerving allegiance—by training, association, and ministry experience—to historic Christianity in its evangelical expression. Even as I personally probe fresh paths on which the renewing Spirit may be leading God's people today, I want to assure my readers that I stand with them "firm in one spirit, contending as one man for the faith of the gospel" (Philippians 1:27).

And in a very real sense, it is the life-renewing power of the gospel that we will focus on here. For the gospel is not a static message, it is dynamic. It leads us deeper into God and fortifies our hearts, minds, and bodies for the task of making His will known in the world, *if* we will follow Him and grow as "children of God" (John 1:12) and the "light of the world" shines in us (Matthew 5:14).

What we have all wanted, those of us who hunger to be children of the heavenly Father, is to know how to stay closer, grow deeper, stay more on course, find greater satisfaction in our life in Him, and recognize distractions and even spiritual traps.

To that end, I invite you to join me in discovering sound and true pathways to a more fulfilling life in God.

Acknowledgments

A constellation of kindly folk contributed to the conception and completion of this book.

First, my faithful wife, Elsie, introduced me to the people under God who would stimulate my explorations in the field of Christian spirituality. I am grateful for her encouragement and patience during the writing of this book. Thanks also to our wonderful children, Starr, Scott, and Sharon, and their spouses, Jeff, Sarah, and Jerry, for their love and support.

I am indebted to marvelous students at Denver Seminary who are catching the vision of a deeper relationship with Christ. Their encouraging words, both in and outside of the classroom, have spurred me on. I wish to thank faculty colleagues who read individual chapters of this book in their fields of expertise: Drs. Jim Beck, Steve Cappa, Vernon Grounds, Randy MacFarland, Gary Newton, and Bruce Shelley. I greatly appreciate the work of Janet Buntrock, who tracked down elusive quotations from spiritual writings from our Christian heritage.

I am indebted to our efficient seminary librarians, Sarah Miller and Jeanette France, for procuring books and articles necessary for the completion of the project. Faculty secretary Jeanette Frietag has been of great help with production of the copy. I particularly wish to thank Evan Howard, founding director of the Spirituality Shoppe, in Montrose, Colorado, for reading and commenting on the entire work. I alone am responsible for whatever deficiencies remain.

Heartfelt appreciation goes to community members of the Pecos Abbey, who have provided flesh and blood demonstration of the principles and practices presented in this book. Their incarnation of godliness, compassion, and spiritual wisdom speaks volumes to my life. They have been catalysts and role models for the development of some of my ideas and habits.

I also wish to thank David Hazard for his wisdom, good-natured encouragement, and editorial efforts. An author could not ask for a better editor to work alongside him. I appreciate the solid support from the NavPress administrative team led by Kent Wilson, publisher, and Sue Geiman, editorial director. They live the values commended in this NavPress Spiritual Formation Line.

I am grateful to the faculty, administration, and board of trustees of Denver Seminary for granting me a sabbatical leave. Release from regular responsibilities made the writing of this book a renewing experience.

Supremely, I offer thanksgiving to the Lord of the church who faithfully leads His people along paths of spiritual restoration and satisfaction, for His glory and the good of His chosen ones.

General Introduction

BY DALLAS WILLARD

The Spiritual Formation Line presents discipleship to Jesus Christ as the greatest opportunity individual human beings have in life and the only hope corporate mankind has of solving its insurmountable problems.

It affirms the unity of the present-day Christian with those who walked beside Jesus during His incarnation. To be His disciple then was to be with Him, to learn to be like Him. It was to be His student or apprentice in kingdom living. His disciples heard what He said and observed what He did, then, under His direction, they simply began to say and do the same things. They did so imperfectly but progressively. As He taught: "Everyone who is fully trained will be like his teacher" (Luke 6:40, NIV).

Today it is the same, except now it is the resurrected Lord who walks throughout the world. He invites us to place our confidence in Him. Those who rely on Him believe that He knows how to live and will pour His life into us as we take His yoke and learn from Him, for He is gentle and humble in heart (see Matthew 11:29). To take His yoke means joining Him in His work, making our work His work. To trust Him is to understand that total immersion in what He is doing with our life is the best thing that could ever happen to us.

To "learn from Him" in total-life immersion is how we "seek first his kingdom and his righteousness" (Matthew 6:33, NIV). The outcome is that we increasingly are able to do all things, speaking or acting, as if Christ were doing them (Colossians 3:17). As apprentices of Christ we are not learning how to do some special religious activity, but how to live every moment of our lives from the reality of God's kingdom. I am learning how to live my actual life as Jesus would if He were me.

If I am a plumber, clerk, bank manager, homemaker, elected official, senior citizen, or migrant worker, I am in "full-time" Christian service no less than someone who earns his or her living in a specifically religious role. Jesus stands beside me and teaches me in all I do to live in God's world. He shows me how, in every circumstance, to reside in His word and thus be a genuine apprentice of His—His disciple indeed. This enables me to find the reality of God's world everywhere I may be, and thereby to escape from enslavement to sin and evil (see John 8:31-32). We become able to do what we know to be good and right, even when it is humanly impossible. Our lives and words become constant testimony of the reality of God.

A plumber facing a difficult plumbing job must know how to integrate it into the kingdom of God as much as someone attempting to win another to Christ or preparing a lesson for a congregation. Until we are clear on this, we will have missed Jesus' connection between life and God and will automatically exclude most of our everyday lives from the domain of faith and discipleship. Jesus lived most of His life on earth as a blue-collar worker, someone we might describe today as an "independent contractor." In His vocation He practiced everything He later taught about life in the kingdom.

The "words" of Jesus I primarily reside in are those recorded in the New Testament Gospels. In His presence, I learn the goodness of His instructions and how to carry them out. It is not a matter of meriting life from above, but of receiving that life concretely in my circumstances. Grace, we must learn, is opposed to earning, not to effort.

For example, I move away from using derogatory language against others, calling them twits, jerks, or idiots (see Matthew 5:22), and increasingly mesh with the respect and endearment for persons that naturally flows from God's way. This in turn transforms all of my dealings with others into tenderness and makes the usual coldness and brutality of human relations, which lays a natural foundation for abuse and murder, simply unthinkable.

Of course, the "learning of Him" is meant to occur in the context of His people. They are the ones He commissioned to make disciples, surround them in the reality of the triune name, and teach to do "everything I have commanded you" (Matthew 28:20 NIV). But the disciples we make are His disciples, never ours. We are His apprentices along with them. If we are a little further along the way, we can only echo the apostle Paul: "Follow my example, as I follow the example of Christ" (1 Corinthians 11:1, NIV).

It is a primary task of Christian ministry today, and of those who write for this line of books, to reestablish Christ as a living teacher in the midst of His people. He has been removed by various historical developments: assigned the role of mere sacrifice for sin or social prophet and martyr. But where there is no teacher, there can be no students or disciples.

If we cannot be His students, we have no way to learn to exist always and everywhere within the riches and power of His Word. We can only flounder along as if we were on our own so far as the actual details of our lives are concerned. That is where multitudes of well-meaning believers find themselves today. But it is not the intent of Him who says, "Come to me . . . and you will find rest for your souls" (Matthew 11:28-29, NKJV).

Each book in this line is designed to contribute to this renewed vision of Christian spiritual formation and to illuminate what apprenticeship to Jesus Christ means within all the specific dimensions of human existence. The mission of these books is to form the whole person so that the nature of Christ becomes the natural expression of our souls, bodies, and spirits throughout our daily lives.

Introduction

BY DAVID HAZARD

When was the last time you *knew* you were in the presence of the Lord? When did you last sense His strong hand directing you? Hear the voice of the Spirit that speaks, in the words of the psalmist, as deep calling to deep?

As Christians we are promised the indwelling presence of God, by the Spirit. We hear of living water and bread from heaven, given to satisfy our souls. What we hunger for is an encounter, strong and genuine, with God . . . and more than that, a way to be filled from within every day, a way to know we are accompanied by Him and not left on our own.

But is that our experience? For many—possibly for you—it is not.

For centuries, Christians understood what it meant to "live by the Spirit" or "to walk in the Spirit," to experience "walking in the light as He is in the light" and "fellowship with God" in whom there is "no darkness at all."

Cyprian, the third-century bishop and martyr, writes of his encounters,

> A light fell upon me, as if from above. I was
> bathed in gentle peace. I was made clean.
> My heart was infused with His presence. . . .
> Presently, I was aware of the Spirit, the breath
> of the Father, coming into me from beyond this
> world. . . . In this way, I am growing daily
> in inward knowledge of Him, as I understand how
> to live in a way that nurtures this new life
> that is given to me.

Jonathan Edwards, the Puritan preacher so wrongly thought to be all anger and brimstone, also speaks of "beholding the beauty of God" with the eyes of his soul—of being freed from sin, receiving sure direction, knowing inward rest and comfort. There is far less in his sermons about sinners "in the hands of an angry God," and far more of spiritual wisdom and practices that keep the soul growing in the radiance of Christ.

What is the "knowledge" we need to walk with God, loving Him, working together with Him? How can we practice the type of contemplation that cultivates inward vision? And how can we stay on a truly Christian path when today there are so many false spiritualities offering us counterfeits and shortcuts that do not lead us to the Light of God, but to outer darkness?

As evangelicals, we need to remain firm in our grip on Scripture, so we are not misled. But it's possible that we play it more "safe" than we should with God, who breathed the Scriptures into the open hearts of those who wrote it down for us. We are not taught how to find the growing edge of our souls—where we hunger for God—much less how to take in "bread from heaven" or "living water." Who will teach us how to open our souls to receive Him who is our daily light, strength, beauty, and truth? Not all the "spiritualities" and "spiritual practices" offered to us today are biblical, or safe.

Bruce Demarest is a gentle person, gifted with extraordinary insight and ability in the care of the inner man. In his own soul, he has wrestled with questions about the deeper Christian walk. And with the mind of an accomplished and respected biblical scholar, he has thought through the careful distinctions between authentic Christian spirituality with its soul-building practices and the misleading counterfeits. Truly he is a spiritual mentor you may trust to guide you around the pitfalls and onto the path that will lead you deeper into the heart of God, in the character of Christ.

And so, NavPress is pleased to offer *Satisfy Your Soul* as part of our Spiritual Formation Line. The insights here will open up scriptural wisdom on the care and growth of the soul and give you solid biblical footing. And the practical instruction will give you simple, daily practices that will continually open you to the life and touch and direction of God. With these spiritual helps, you will indeed find satisfaction for your soul.

CHAPTER ONE

Path to Discovery and Transformation

"I have heard all about you, LORD, and I am filled with awe by the amazing things you have done. . . . Show us your power to save us."

HABAKKUK 3:2

"Spirituality . . . seems so boundless, so infinitely prone to human distortion. We need theological boundaries in order to maintain orthodox and scripturally sound views of redemption, yet we also need the experiential depth of a personal spiritual journey."

MARK R. MCMINN[1]

FROM COVER TO COVER, THE BIBLE portrays our God as living and active among human beings and in history. Scripture shows how our all-wise and loving God works, as theologians say, *preveniently*—or to put it plainly, He always makes the first move toward us. He awakens our spirits, then leads us on a path that sets us apart for Himself, at the same time satisfying our human soul. Theologians know this work as *grace*, the ongoing action of God in our lives.

Today the evangelical church has a tendency to limit grace to a single transaction—Christ's priceless payment for our sins with His blood so that we may be saved. As a group, we spend much of our energy cooperating with this first work of grace, focusing on evangelism, missions, and getting initial conversions. Beyond that, we spend tremendous energy to educate believers in their knowledge of the Bible. Once they are "saved," we want people to be acquainted with God's Word, indeed an important part in spiritual growth.

But when it comes to encountering God Himself, we are, frankly, a bit vague. And when it comes to such aspects of spirituality as growth in holiness, intimacy with God, and godly character, we can leave new believers very confused. *If Jesus paid it all, and it's the Holy Spirit's job to change us, then we should just read our Bibles and go to church. Right?* So many are left dissatisfied, without a sense that they really know God. And with the sense that, aside from where they spend Sunday mornings, they are not that much different from their "unsaved" neighbors, not when it comes down to it.

Now, it's true that evangelicalism vigorously addresses, for instance, the matter of sin and the need for holiness. But too often we do not know how to get at the root of sins that lie so powerfully in the heart's quiet, dark places. We recognize the problem of spiritual dryness, but often do not know how to open ourselves to God's Spirit so that the inner man may "draw water from the wells of salvation" (Isaiah 12:3). We sometimes tell new believers that they received all the "potential" to grow in spiritual character, or Christlikeness, at conversion. But do we tell them how to turn that potential loose in their lives?

Underneath it all, we seem to *assume* that spiritual growth will automatically result from knowing more about the Scriptures. But in fact, we encounter attitudes and resistance to God within ourselves, along with difficult, discouraging, or tempting circumstances outside ourselves, which seem to say there is no real power in the Christian life. We may even begin to wonder if what we've so faithfully read in the Bible is true at all, causing us to ask if Christianity has anything to offer, really, that will bring a life of growth and satisfaction to our souls.

As a seminary professor and Sunday school teacher in my church, I can tell you, many people are asking such questions.

Seeking Balance

What we need is an understanding of what encourages the growth of the soul *beyond* conversion, over the span of a whole life. We need to balance our understanding of what brings a soul to conversion with what keeps us on the path of growth in spirit. The truth is, we have not held these two together as we should. And for our help, we can turn to our Christian past—to men and women who understood how the soul finds satisfaction as we grow in God, and how His Spirit finds a more ready home in us.

From Pentecost on, Christians understood that conversion was just the beginning of a lifelong cooperation with God's work in the soul of the believer. The church and the individual played an active part in responding to God's grace, discovering that certain spiritual practices were highly effective in nurturing the inner man. These practices came to be known as the art and ministry of *spiritual formation,* a form of discipleship we are rediscovering today.

Spiritual formation is an ancient ministry of the church, concerned with the "forming" or "shaping" of a believer's character and actions into the likeness of Christ. The goals of this practice are such things as godliness, holiness, compassion, faithfulness, and obedience. The ancient church fathers, like Augustine (d. 430), spoke of the believer's growth in Christlikeness and communion with God as progressive—a "path" or an "ascent" on which the Christian experienced continuing, deep changes in heart that led to more evidences ("fruit") of the Spirit in the life. Conversion, the "new birth," was just the beginning, the head of a new pathway.

In contrast with today, then, Christians of the past looked upon repentance and regeneration as just the beginning. The shaping of the Christian was seen as a continuing process, during which the Spirit gradually restored and renewed the Christian's entire life through deepening relationship with his or her altogether lovely Lord Jesus. The church's role in the individual's life was a very active one, in which the believer was taught not only orthodox doctrine, but many practices that opened him or her to the presence and direction of God, and nurtured the character traits of Christ into fruition—traits such as humility, fortitude, and obedience. Where we assume that the great goal of spiritual training is to produce a Christian who boldly, verbally proclaims the gospel, earlier Christians saw gospel proclamation as but one result, or fruit, of something even greater. The real goal of spiritual training, or formation, is to produce a *life* that is being transformed from within and growing in the character of Christ. It was not assumed, however, that the believer could become perfect in this life. (The consummation of God's work in us will only occur when all believers are finally, fully transformed at the sight of the Savior, Jesus, when He returns in glory.) Nonetheless, a process of powerful inner change had begun and had to be rightly nurtured and directed.

This was not exactly my understanding of spiritual growth during the first decades of my Christian life. If I'd heard there was another approach or means to foster spiritual growth, I can't recall. And so I was somewhat surprised, and a bit hesitant at first, when I began to experience a deeper formative work of God in my life in the mid-1980s. In fact, it was to begin a quiet but utter transformation.

A Hesitant New Beginning

From outward appearances my life and ministry were above reproach and "successful." A flow of notes from seminary students and graduates expressed appreciation for my teaching and defense of the faith. With invitations in hand to participate in Christian ministries at home and abroad, I was on a roll, and life seemed rather rosy.

In retrospect, I admit I was a typical product of evangelical academic culture. The *grace* of God was something I'd experienced at the moment of salvation and relied on for my future with God in heaven. For now, though, God's continual outpouring of grace was fairly abstract to me. I'd been "saved" and that was that. Now it was up to me to work hard as a Christian, to succeed in higher education, and to prove myself to the watching world. My experience was not entirely foreign to that described by Robert A. Johnson, the Episcopal therapist and author, who wrote of "the standard American way of life, with the goals, the excessive work schedule, the constant feeling of pressure and deadlines, money to be made and people to be impressed."[2]

With this mindset, I could feel satisfied at the end of a day if I completed my ministry assignments, even if time alone with the Lord was squeezed out by the clock. (And "time with the Lord" meant a specific few moments set aside every day, not the growing, constant awareness of His presence, which the Bible speaks about.) I tended to view the Christian faith largely in terms of rational propositions, so I loaded (and probably overloaded) my mind with intellectual analysis. True, I could wax eloquent about the mysteries of the Trinity or theories about the Atonement, but I didn't relate that well to God on an everyday, affective level. I substituted knowledge of the Bible for knowing how to interact with God Himself, or a knowledge of His ways, as He makes Himself known to His sons and daughters. My evangelical culture and training led me to this belief: Personal experience is an untrustworthy pillar for Christian faith and life. Therefore you should relegate life and matters of the heart to an inferior place.

This approach to Christianity had formed the path of my life and my career. I felt no reason to alter anything until, in the late 1980s, an unexpected encounter opened my eyes to new possibilities—or I should say, some very old ones.

The God of Surprises

A renewal team from the Archdiocese of Denver was invited to our Presbyterian church to teach an eight-week course on Christian spirituality. The team made an immediate impression with our people, as they sang familiar gospel songs with gusto and prayed with refreshing fervor. Their teaching broke through intellectual barriers to touch hearts with unusual freshness in their love for God—and with impressive power in ministry. To be honest, I was quietly resistant because spiritual expressions that were this enthusiastic unsettled me.

Over dinner one Sunday, my wife, Elsie, told me that the course was unfolding aspects of the spiritual life that she'd never considered before. "They're teaching us how to do more than merely talk about God. They're showing us how to actually experience God in our hearts and lives—in a way that renews the soul. When you finish teaching your course," she said, "you really ought to attend this class."

Politely I replied, "I don't think I need this. My life and ministry are doing just fine."

In time, though, something in Elsie's new joy, her enthusiasm, piqued my curiosity. When I wrapped up my class, I joined hers.

Something was different here. And at first I sat there trying not to appear enthusiastic while the presentations were really resonating with my heart's longing. Didn't I *want* a deeper relationship with the living God? Didn't I want to know His presence and to sense His work in my life?

Beyond a look at Scripture, the class introduced me to Christian spiritual writers, both old and new. Some were only vaguely familiar, some were altogether new, but their words shed light on spiritual truth from the Bible. Spiritual insights from Thomas à Kempis (d. 1471), John of the Cross (d. 1591), and Henri Nouwen (d. 1996) began to work in my heart—in some cases convicting me, in other cases nurturing my soul, but always directing me to deeper trust in God. It was the first time in a long while that I had experienced the sense of actual growth in the inner man. And I had to admit that although some of the approaches were new to me, spiritual truth was being presented that was satisfying and transforming.

What was it in me that was coming to life, or at least opening up in new ways? I considered this question one Sunday, driving home after church. The workings of the mind, I knew very well. For years I had carefully crafted doctrinal formulations. I knew where I stood on matters like the divinity of Christ, salvation, the end times, and so on. But when it came to the inner man, the deep motives of the heart, I was on less steady ground.

What I was discovering was the *intuitive* way of engaging God; that is, learning how to open my *heart* as well as my *head* to truth. For the inner man has a capacity for knowing that is created by God Himself (see Ecclesiastes 3:11, John 1:9). In his letter to the Romans, Paul teaches that Gentiles who do not have God's Word acquire basic knowledge of His existence and character by an immediate intuition from the heart (see Romans 1:19, 2:14-15).

Knowing from the heart, in a daily, growing relationship, was my problem. When it came to relating to God with my inner being, trusting Him, letting His Spirit search my heart, allowing Him to clear a path in my spirit so He could change me from the inside out, in all honesty, this was foreign territory. I was surprised at the questions I still harbored inside—and the resistance. Who is God, really? Could I honestly reveal my inmost thoughts and feelings to Him? And when it came to real growth in my life, how did He really work to change my behavior in the face of everyday irritations and pressures?

And as for the idea the ministry team was promoting—relaxing in my expressions of praise and worship, showing some zeal or emotion—that did not come easy for me.

What was coming to life, or to light at any rate, was the inner man in Christ—the roots of my personality and the new character God wanted to form in me. I found that I'd let God have my mind and even my physical person for His service. The question was, Would I, after years as a Christian, give Him the depths of my heart?

Deeper

The more I attended the class, the more I delighted in this new way God was tuning the limp strings of my heart. No, I wasn't buried in a huge existential crisis, but I was longing for greater spiritual reality, for the constant connection of my spirit with God's Spirit as promised in Scripture. The presentations of these brothers and sisters in Christ echoed in the deep places of my heart, where my soul shouted back: *I want to know God.*

The ministry of this renewal team in our church proved to be God's *kairos*—a defining, redemptive moment in my life. Despite my initial resistance, I was beginning to experience more life from within than I'd ever known.

Over the next several years, I would meet for regular discussions with leaders of Christian renewal movements. I had come down from my attitude that I'd been a Christian so long that these people had nothing new to tell me. Taking the learner's seat, I allowed myself to be tutored in the principles and practices of Christian spirituality and formation. I was learning new spiritual habits, some of which were foreign. Yet, when I looked in Scripture and the classic Christian writings, they were there. Why had I missed or overlooked them? Practices such as *solitude, contemplating the presence and nature of God, keeping a spiritual journal,* and so on. A new awareness of God's being and work all around me grew. And a strong, quiet steadiness, like a rock of strength, seemed to settle within me. The promises of God I'd known in my head were settling down and becoming real in the core of my being.

Friends encouraged me to pursue this personal spiritual growth more actively, and so I attended spirituality seminars at

Christian retreat centers. The work of going back to basics was humbling for me, a seminary professor, but all of it was profoundly stimulating, freeing, and empowering.

Connections with the Past

During a sabbatical leave from my seminary a few years ago, I enrolled in a six-week residential program at the Benedictine Abbey—a renewal center in Pecos, New Mexico. They were presenting a course in spiritual formation and direction, teaching Christians how to cultivate the spiritual life and help others grow in the Lord.

Previously I would have felt out of place at a Benedictine abbey. To me, the Protestant Reformers of the sixteenth century separated from the Roman church over critical matters, such as papal authority, justification by faith or by works, the veneration of Mary, and praying to the saints. And like most other evangelicals, I had rejected the idea of receiving *any* spiritual instruction from the ancient church. But having gotten to know many wonderful, vibrant Christians in the Catholic renewal movement, I'd come to realize we had made an error. The Reformers and we their evangelical descendants, acting in reaction to medieval Rome, threw out a great deal of spiritual wisdom, insight, and important practices, along with the doctrinal and ecclesiological bath water.

As I traveled to New Mexico, I took stock of where I stood. God was leading me to honor what was true in my own tradition while welcoming back authentic Christian insights and practices from the older tradition. He was leading me to integrate the new and the old—to balance orthodoxy (right beliefs) and orthopathy (right affections) and orthopraxy (right actions). I had come to see that these are the three movements of the healthy, growing spiritual life. This balanced path of growth—changing the mind and heart in order to change the outward actions—keeps us from the deadly trap of self-deception in which we *believe,* but do not *grow, in Christ.* Or as the apostle James puts it, we deceive ourselves by being "hearers" of the Word but not "doers" of it (1:22-25).

For their part, the renewal folks I'd come to respect were downplaying obstructive doctrines in favor of a more evangelical approach to the Christian faith. In essence, they were moving toward me in certain important matters (certain doctrines) as I moved toward them in others (spiritual practices and understanding about soul growth). Now, eight years since getting my feet wet, I was much more open to their insights. They brought the Word together with my Christian past in ways that truly deepened my affection for God and my happy obedience to Him.

And so it was that, amid the New Mexican juniper and piñion in the Sangre de Cristo ("blood of Christ") Mountains, I joined forty other caregivers at the Pecos Benedictine Abbey. We were more or less evenly divided between Catholic charismatic Christians, renewal Anglicans, and free-church evangelicals like myself. To my surprise, many of these folks had connections to such evangelical bastions as Wheaton College, Bethel, Dallas, and Fuller seminaries; to stalwart ministries like The Navigators; and to Christian counseling centers across the country. Beyond our connections, we also shared this in common: *We wanted to reconnect with the ancient wisdom of the church.* Each of us—some with decades of ministry experience—were drawn to this place in search of a deeper connectedness with Christ; *and* we wanted to acquire skills for guiding others along the path to godliness.

This was like no program or retreat I had been involved in before.

Our days at Pecos centered around practicing God's presence, stimulated by three worship times per day: the morning Eucharist, afternoon prayers, and evening vespers. Again, as each day's lectures plumbed the heart of the spiritual life, I found myself stimulated and moved. Small group sessions encouraged sharing our lives with one another in prayer. Risky, but soul-bracing, too.

Each of us also received two hours of weekly spiritual direction. This meant we met with a spiritual counselor—someone gifted in touching on the tender, needy, or resistant places where God was at work in our lives—and then agreed to act on his or her directions in prayer, reading, and the first necessary steps toward change in actual life. I became as aware of God as I'd ever been, during quiet walks under pristine blue skies and rugged mountains.

At the end of the six weeks, virtually everyone—Catholic, Anglican, charismatic, and evangelical—testified to the many true ways the experience had transformed his or her spirit and life.

An Episcopal bishop had come, carrying the weight of serious problems in his diocese. During contemplative moments, he received several bolts of wisdom from the Lord, giving him insight to deal with the potentially explosive tensions. A pastor with thirty years of parish experience broke down in tears, telling us that problems long embedded in his life had come to light and been decisively resolved. A Christian therapist was convicted by the Holy Spirit that she was relying too heavily on psychological theories in her work. She saw that spiritual issues lay at the root of her own needs and problems, so she resolved to give the spiritual a more central place in her counseling work. Several who were involved in churches as deacons gained stronger vision for caring for the spiritual and emotional needs of hurting people.

Yes, the spiritual practices at Pecos acted upon me, but there was something broader and deeper, too—certain *qualities* to the spirituality there, which were old and rich. And refreshing.

Treasures from Ancient Christian Spirituality

After my time at Pecos, I considered what it was that made the six-week sojourn in a renewal monastery one of the brightest defining moments in my spiritual life. It wasn't just the place itself, of course, wonderful as it had been to me. It was the six weeks of soaking in spiritual traditions, views, practices, and insights as ancient and true as the church.

It was an encounter with God, shaped and formed by spirituality with great treasures to offer us all. Here are a few I discovered.

The first was a *Christ-centered orthodoxy.* At Pecos, for instance, everything centered around the simple core affirmation, "Christ has died; Christ is risen; and Christ will come again."

Over the weeks, I was affirmed in my spirit by the community's enthusiastic declaration and living of the gospel, and I gained a fresh vision of what it means to be connected to the mainstream of Christian faith and worship as it has existed for two thousand years. Our almost boggling number of evangelical denominations (275 varieties of Baptists in the United States alone!) are in some respects like newly formed tributaries to the central stream of historic Christian faith.

At the center of everything was worship, and at the center of the worship was Christ Himself and an awareness of His constant presence with us.

A second treasure was the *commitment to community, the recognition that together we comprise the body of Christ.* In American culture we're strongly individualistic; in evangelical culture we are committed to the Word and to service. Pecos treasured and embodied a togetherness-in-community that must have characterized the early church. Why is this important? Because God made us to be part of a body; I cannot know Him truly on my own. I encounter Him in the body of Christ, that is, in and through you. The men and women at the Abbey demonstrated such vulnerability and receptivity to God at work in each other that I was stunned. They wept with one another, set examples for one another, confronted one another, confessed their sins to one another, and they loved each other deeply, in Christ.

I had to ask myself, *Do I ever get close enough to another Christian that I can encounter Christ in him or her? How often do I, as an evangelical, confess my sins to someone else—even to the person I have wronged? Am I close enough to anyone else to weep with them when they hurt or to be really happy just because they are happy?*

In the spirituality of the ancients, it was understood that the closer we draw to one another in community, the closer we come to Christ.

A third treasure from the past was the *practice of spiritual disciplines.* We Protestants are a largely undisciplined people. Reacting against late medieval regimens, the Reformers minimized the role of spiritual exercises as a path to growth. They interpreted the spiritual disciplines practiced by priests, monks, and nuns as "works" intended to gain points with God. But the classic Christian disciplines were known to be an effective means of grace, tools used by God to renew us from the inside out.

Richard Foster, an evangelical Friend, says it well:

> The Disciplines . . . put us where [God] can work within us and transform us. . . . They are God's means of grace. . . . God has ordained the Disciplines of the spiritual life as the means by which we place ourselves where he can bless us.[3]

Fourth, I learned a significantly different view than I had held of the spiritual leader's primary role. In my experience, a leader's part is to "give a good teaching." But in the view of the ancients, it's *to lead others into the presence of God.* This was made plain to me in the daily worship at Pecos. The leaders never attempted to get an emotional reaction or to entertain us. With extraordinary sensitivity they led us into God's presence, relying on the simple beauty of ancient liturgies, so that the Holy Spirit was freed to move us with awe, wonder, and love. Never in my Christian experience have I encountered such reverence, grace, and a connection with God in worship, thanks to the power of a Spirit-inspired Christian liturgy, which dates back two millennia.

Fifth, I discovered a *balanced approach to honoring the place and work of the Holy Spirit.* My church experience has provided few viable models of what responsible exercise of the Spirit's work and gifts should look like. Alarmed by certain Pentecostal excesses, we have swung the pendulum to the opposite pole of neglecting the Holy Spirit's mighty working in our midst.

My time at Pecos, and other experiences, gave me a healthy model of New Testament *charismata*—the Spirit gifts described in Romans 12:6-8, 1 Corinthians 12:28-31, 1 Corinthians 14, and Ephesians 4:7-13—exercised with sensitivity and grace, and validated by lives that are growing in the beautiful character of Jesus Christ. I witnessed Spirit-directed displays of wisdom, power, and love that I had seldom seen in other churches. A brother quoted a Scripture that addressed a specific need in another person's life. A sister shared an insight from the Word that gave the community a needed sense of direction. Christians ought not fear, ignore, or be confused about the Holy Spirit. We must allow the Paraclete to shape us into the likeness of Christ so that He may flow through us to bless others. Faithful exercise of the Spirit's gifts keeps orthodoxy open to the Transcendent in practice as well as in theory.

Last, it was truly a treasure to *connect with the classic understandings of Christian spirituality—especially through the spiritual masters of history.* Protestants often neglect much that is edifying in Christian writers such as Bernard of Clairvaux (d. 1153), Francis of Assisi (d. 1226), Teresa of Avila (d. 1582), and Brother Lawrence (d. 1691). We act as if between St. Paul in the first century and John Calvin in the sixteenth the Christian's spiritual life was rote drudgery and ritual. But I found it exhilarating to enter into the Christ-centered experiences of church fathers, desert mothers, ancient martyrs, scholastics, and responsible Christian mystics through the centuries.

Admittedly I found that certain beliefs and traditions remained foreign to me, being based more on tradition than solidly on Scripture. All denominations have their blind spots. But I also found that, once I got past my old prejudices and misunderstandings, I accepted more than I rejected.

Discovering these perspectives and practices of an older Christian spirituality has led me into the most transforming time of my four decades as a Christian. They have taught me to be more present to Christ, who is always present to us, His redeemed children. I've come to understand the invitation of the risen Lord, who continually says, "Look! Here I stand at the door and knock. If you hear me calling and open the door, I will come in, and we will share a meal as friends" (Revelation 3:20).

TESTING THE FRUIT

All told, my discoveries began to teach me at the heart level what the personal experience of Christ really means and how it comes about. Consequently, I was able to grasp some words from Augustine, which I had read but not fully understood. The fourth-century church father, a giant of our faith, exclaims in his classic autobiography, *Confessions*:

> I entered into my inmost self with You, Lord, as my guide; and this I was able to do because You were my helper. I entered in and saw with the eye of my soul, the unchangeable Light, very different from earthly lights. . . . Those who know the truth know this Light, and those who know it know eternity; it is love that knows it.[4]

Augustine, once a pagan philosopher, realized that the very questions that exercised his soul were God-inspired. Even in all his early confusion and lostness, God was shining a light on the deep questions of his heart, which the Word would later answer. He was awed that God had always been present to him, even when he was completely blind to God. You can hear the wonder and satisfaction pouring from him as he exclaims, "Lord, You are the Light of my heart, and the Bread in the mouth of my soul."[5] He'd seen, at last, that the Bread of the Word provided answers to the probing questions of his soul—questions planted there, and brought to light, by the Spirit.

I, too, realized that questions and longings had existed in me for some time. I had either ignored them (as Christians we *have* the answer, as we like to say) or labeled them irrelevant (feeling disconnected or distant from God, or "overworked for God," doesn't matter because *feelings* don't matter). Now I realized how important it is to give place to human longings and questions—how to allow the Spirit to use them, focused by the spiritual disciplines, to draw your soul into more intimate knowledge of God and, ultimately, into peace and rest in Him.

After the time at Pecos, I wondered whether others were looking for the spiritual bounty I had begun to find. I had not been back at the seminary long, when students asked, "What was a good evangelical theologian like you doing in a Benedictine monastery?" Through the surface incredulity, I detected a heartfelt interest in spiritual growth, as if they were asking, *Is it all right to try a different spiritual path to knowing Christ?* Very soon, a number of students were coming privately to hear what I had found.

Soon, because of the interest, I began a spiritual formation group and developed elective courses in Christian spirituality, eager to share the insights and graces I had received. As my experience of Christ changed, I found that even my work was being transformed. It was no longer enough to teach students *about* God. I wanted to help them open up and experience the touch and reality of God in their lives.

Suddenly, the classes came to life.

Jay, a bright young professional effective in lay Christian ministry, enrolled in one of these courses to test whether seminary was for him. At the end, he admitted with a broad smile, "I'd heard seminary can kill your spiritual life. But if this is what seminary is about, I want it!" Another pastor-in-training confessed he'd grown weary while experiencing so little of God's reality.

Today, as an outcome of these courses, students who are now pastors have made spiritual formation the main thrust of their ministries.

What convinced them they were on the right track with God? Jesus left us a simple but foolproof test for distinguishing what is true from what is false. He said, "The way to identify a tree or a person is by the kind of fruit that is produced" (see Matthew 7:20, compare verse 16). The litmus test of spiritual reality is a transformed life—one that manifests the fruit and graces of the Spirit in a way that radiates Christ's reality to others. If I had any doubts, they were dispelled for good after walking this path for a couple of years when a colleague pulled me aside to ask what was going on with me. He wanted to know what was going on because, in his words, "You are the most spiritually changed person on campus."

For perhaps the first time in my life, I thought these words might really be true of me.

Reason for Concern

As eagerly as I've shared my discoveries, I cannot begin this book—introducing Christians to old and rich practices of spirituality—without stating the fact that I also have serious concerns. *Spirituality* is a buzzword in our culture, covering the waterfront from African voodoo to Zen Buddhist practices. Not everything that stirs the soul is from God.

As a result of this "glut" of spiritual practices in our culture, Christians have been wise to be wary. Which experiences are from God and which are counterfeits leading away from God? Because of the general confusion, I will help you examine Christian versus nonChristian approaches to spirituality. From the outset, I want to emphasize that by Christian spirituality I mean *the shaping of our inner character and outer conduct, in cooperation with the work of the Spirit, so that we are gradually being conformed to the likeness of Jesus Christ.*

Yes, we are bombarded with exotic spiritual practices, such as yoga and forms of meditations that supposedly lead a person back through past lives. Why not stay away from such practices as contemplation altogether and avoid the problem? Shouldn't we just keep it simple, reading the Bible, praying, and attending church? What's all this about practices that "open" your heart to an awareness of God? The reason we need the full range of spiritual practices stems from truths we hate to admit as evangelicals. When we're honest, we have to acknowledge that our Bible reading is frequently dry and ineffective. Too often when we pray, we can't remember what we've said, or our prayers bounce off the ceiling. Church can be programmed and lifeless.

We need to have all spiritual disciplines at our disposal—the way a workman needs various tools—to keep us alert and tender to the presence, work, and direction of our living God. Knowing God means more than processing information about Him. We can learn how to open up to His living presence, to sense and enjoy Him with our whole being.

Christians are also right to worry about "error" and wrong doctrine. But buried among some inferior theologies of the past are valuable resources for spiritual growth. We need to know what many of our forebears knew about the life with God. And so we'll explore insights from godly church fathers, medieval saints, Reformers, Puritans, charismatics, and other kindred spirits. You may be very surprised at the treasures of wisdom that have been forgotten along the way. Lost, I say, through overreaction. For that reason, I like to think of this exploration as part of evangelicalism's much-needed search to recover our balance—biblically, historically, theologically, and spiritually.

Beneath it all, my purposes in writing this book for the NavPress Spiritual Formation Line are these: I want to help you as a Christian to determine which features of spirituality are biblically faithful and which are not. To do so, we'll take a careful look at biblical, theological, and historical resources to help you identify what is truly edifying and what is not.

I want to offer you simple steps that will help you move deeper in your understanding and experience of God. At the end of each chapter, I will offer fruitful exercises that you can do on your own or with a group to help you personally apply new understandings and practices.

My one prayer as we enter into this study together is that you will "grow in the grace and knowledge of our Lord and Savior Jesus Christ" (2 Peter 3:18).

Try It Yourself

We grow as we explore the personal implications of what we have read. And we've just read that in spiritual terms we grow as we admit our questions and longings, and as we seek God out of gut-level honesty. What *are* your questions and inner longings? When do you know God's closeness? When do you feel far from Him, or even abandoned and on your own? Journeys of discovery begin when we admit there is more that we need to know.

1. Describe your spiritual journey.

Reflect on your Christian life and experience, and identify the high and low points. Recall the times when you knew strength and joy as a Christian, and also when you were indifferent or cold to spiritual things.

- How do you describe your spiritual highs? Were your spiritually satisfying experiences rational and cognitive as you studied the Bible? Or were they intuitive, coming from a heartfelt experience?
- What does this tell you about the types of spiritual experiences that have been most significant in your life?

- Speculate as to what kind of spiritual experiences would be most enriching and redemptive for you in the future.

2. Draw a line diagram that depicts your spiritual journey.

Let the horizontal axis represent time, and the vertical axis your level of spiritual satisfaction and maturity. Like this:

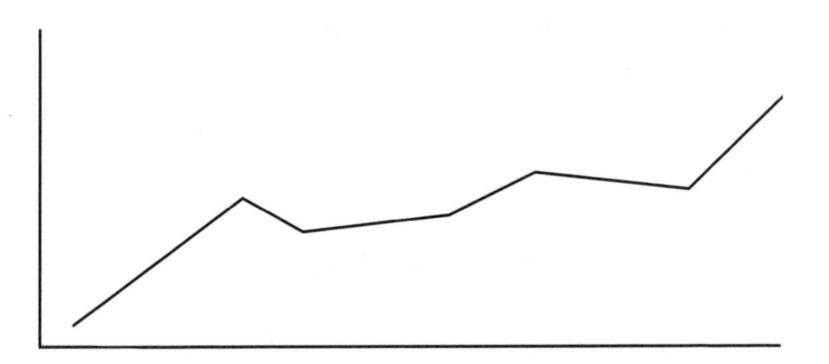

Save this diagram, as you will use it again for an exercise in chapter 8.

3. Reflect on your concerns and hopes.

- Where are you currently in your relationship with God?
- Is God's presence a reality you experience in your life right now?
- If relationship with God is lacking, are you aware of any way in which you have failed the Lord?
- Do you feel that God has disappointed you in some way?

4. Spend time in prayer, talking honestly with the Lord about these matters.

You also may want to discuss your spiritual life with a trusted friend or pastor.

Suggestions for Further Reading

Collins, Ken J. *Soul Care: Deliverance and Renewal Through the Christian Life*. Wheaton, Ill.: Victor, 1995.

Downey, Michael. *Understanding Christian Spirituality*. New York: Paulist, 1997.

Houston, James. *The Transforming Friendship*. Oxford: Lion, 1989.

Lovelace, Richard F. *Renewal as a Way of Life*. Downers Grove, Ill.: InterVarsity, 1985.

CHAPTER TWO

Spiritual Hunger

"As the deer pants for streams of water, so I long for you, O God. I thirst for God, the living God."

PSALM 42:1-2

"The deepest desire of our hearts is for union with God. From the first moment of our existence our most powerful yearning is to fulfill the original purpose of our lives—'to see Him more clearly, love Him more dearly, follow Him more nearly.' We are made for God, and nothing less will really satisfy us."

BRENNAN MANNING[1]

TODAY, ORGANIZED RELIGION IS "OUT" but spirituality has become a "hot item." People who are not interested in religious commitment per se are going on retreats, attending seminars, and following "spiritual paths," hoping to find inner satisfaction and, when necessary, repair their broken lives.

A smartly dressed real estate executive in Phoenix leaves his office and his cell phone behind and goes to a "wild man" weekend to smear himself with mud and beat drums with forty other professionals. A school principal and several teachers journey out of town to attend a Celtic spirituality weekend that features dancing, bards, and Druidic spring rituals. All this to connect with the spiritual world.

A California newspaper article entitled "A Spiritual Tuneup in Colorado Solitude" features a dozen retreat centers and monasteries in the state, where the public may go for spiritual refreshment.[2] *Newsweek* magazine reports that people are buying more books on meditation, prayer, and spirituality than on sex or self-help. And on the Internet, with the click of a mouse, the cyber-surfer can go modem-to-modem with the latest "guru" or with the pope in the Vatican.

George Gallop states, "If the focus of the twentieth century has been on outer space, the focus of the twenty-first century may well be on inner space."[3] Martin Marty, the respected American church historian, observes that "Spirituality is back, almost with a vengeance."[4]

SPIRITUAL CULTURE VULTURES

It appears the culture that brought us "the American dream"—with its mega-malls, 150-channel cable TV, and weekend flings in Cancun and Las Vegas—has failed to fill the void in the human heart. The more consumer gadgets people accumulate, the more restless their spirits become. Harvey Cox observes that people may not want "to live in a monk's cave," but they are most definitely "fumbling for a new consciousness."[5]

In this restless reaching, waves of people are seeking significance by turning to the spiritual world, which they sense instinctively. At the root of it all, they know life is spiritual, and they long to touch the transcendent. God—however vaguely they conceive deity—is getting a second hearing.

Christian theology explains this universal spiritual hunger in terms of the *imago Dei.* As creatures made in the image of God, fallen humans have a void deep in their souls that only the Three-in-One can satisfy. Yet in their disillusionment with Christian churches, people have turned to Eastern sages, to the occult, or to self-styled New Age practices to satisfy their cravings. The yuppie "culture vultures" of the 1980s have become the spiritual eclectics, open to just about anything, as the new millennium dawns.

Signs of "designer spirituality" are everywhere. Consider the current popularity of home altars and shrines. A recent poll conducted by *House & Gardens* magazine reveals that 82 percent of respondents have set aside in their homes "a quiet place for meditation or spiritual contemplation."[6] The sacred space may be in a closet, on a mantle, or in an unused fireplace. The altar or shrine typically contains icons, incense, flowers, aromatherapy candles, and meditation pillows. The purpose of the sacred space is to allow the peace and joy that comes in the presence of the divine to flow into the harsh and draining reality of daily life.

Instinctively we seem to understand that authentic contact with God *should* affect us in some meaningful, even palpable, way. And it seems we're willing to go far beyond our Christian-based culture to seek meaning.

Some turn to Islam, a potent and rising force in the world. An April 1997 edition of the ABC television news magazine Nightline featured a well-educated American businessman who recently converted to Islam. The man was interviewed during a *hajj* on a Mecca hilltop, overlooking two million other Muslim pilgrims clad in white robes, thronging the *Ka'abah,*

Islam's main mosque. This distinguished-looking Western professional boldly testified before the watching world: "We come to Mecca to engage the presence of God in a life-changing way."

Interest in Buddhism, Hinduism, and the religions of Africa and the Orient is rapidly on the rise throughout Western culture.

In America especially, interest in Native American spirituality is exploding, appealing to Western fears about the environment and teaching that Anglo-European materialism fails to recognize the divine connectedness of all creation. Through prayer, ceremonies, and meditation, followers of Native American religion seek spiritual meaning in a physical world.

Return of the "Old Gods"

Along with this interest in other traditions, new forms of spirituality are taking hold, resurrecting the old gods of pagan religions.

Recently a pagan spirituality has developed around Gaia worship and also re-creations of the Wiccan and Druid religions. Gaia is the Greek name of the Mother Goddess of the Earth. Gaia followers believe that planet earth is a large, living organism. All the forms of life (trees, rocks, streams, man) are interconnected and creative. Gaia worship intends to recapture the sense of one's divinity as part of earth's living organism. Olivia Newton John's album *Gaia* celebrates these ideas. Wicca is the religion that worships the Mother Goddess and offers personal power through the "white magic"—a cleaned-up version of witchcraft. It bears some similarities to the resurgence of interest in Druidism, with its worship of masculine and feminine nature deitics. Followers are urged to open the channels of the divine life-force within by taking part in ancient rituals, casting "magic circles," and divination, which will direct them in the use of spells and charms.

Alternative, or complementary, medical practices—though beneficial in certain ways—also have components that delve into nonChristian esoteric practices. For instance, some go beyond the exercises of yoga, occasionally employed in alternative healing for musculoskeletal problems, and delve into the spiritual path of a yoga in search of spiritual ascent. ("Yoga," as a spiritual practice, offers "union with the divine.") Those who seek spiritual ascent hope to open psychic energy centers called *chakras*, through which the soul is believed to reconnect with the creative Power, leading to self-realization.

The "dabbler" is not left out, either. For the occasional seeker, there are New Age psychic readings, offering to help you discover your true identity and purpose as a spiritual being. Popular author Alice Bailey commends hypnotherapy, energetic healing, and spiritual counseling to advance people on their soul's path. She and other New Age teachers, like Hollywood guru Marianne Williamson, preach that the world is poised on the verge of a great spiritual awakening, if only enough souls will shake off the chains of traditional spiritualities and achieve individual enlightenment—*perfect selfhood*.

And so we come down to it: Contemporary spiritualities aim at helping the individual realize that he or she is *divine*.

In order to achieve this realization—that "I am God"—people are willing to go, literally, to the ends of the earth. A Denver newspaper recently featured a full-page article entitled "Seeing the Sacred." A former travel agent, now a self-styled "planetary acupuncturist," photographs sacred sites around the world. Places include the pyramids, Stonehenge, and the Golden Temple in Amritsar, India. He writes, "Sacred places have a density of holiness that saturates and surrounds the place. . . . These places connect people to the essence of the earth and life." This man's spiritual mission is to "translate the spirit language of these places" for the "transformation of consciousness."[7] In hopes of achieving this "God-consciousness," streams of spiritual pilgrims travel the globe.

Besides visiting "sacred sites," these seekers spend millions attending events as diverse as Native American sweat lodges and "channeling workshops"—each in its own way promising to open you to your "higher self" or to a spirit guide who can convey power and messages from the other world. As one practitioner puts it, "Channeling is for anyone looking for a quantum leap in their spiritual growth." More than four million tourists each year visit Sedona, Arizona, a small town one hundred miles south of the Grand Canyon, which boasts a full menu of psychics, holistic healers, and shamans. A study commissioned by the Chamber of Commerce showed that 65 percent of the visitors to Sedona seek some kind of a spiritual experience. Sedona claims to be "the only town in the world with 1,500 channels and no TV station"!

These and other quests for spiritual reality are not new; they are as old as humanity itself. For as long as they have walked the earth, people have searched for the meaning of life and for personal satisfaction. I think of the hunger for God that Augustine experienced before becoming a Christian. He wrote, "I sought for something to love, for I was in love with love. There was a hunger within me from a lack of inner food, which is none other than Yourself, my God."[8]

A Hungry Church

The Christian community scoffs at such flamboyant practices and the great lengths to which people will go in their spiritual search. But we need to beware and be more honest about the hunger in our own ranks.

The craving for spiritual reality and an encounter with the Transcendent are very strong among committed Christians who would never think of experimenting outside the Christian faith. Why?

Many ordinary believers struggle—often unsuccessfully—to live clean and godly lives that are pleasing to God. Amid these efforts to "behave" and give a good Christian witness, many admit they are missing a sense of spiritual reality—in terms of heart engagement, intimacy, and warmth—in their relationship with God. Many of us rank-and-file Christians who listen to sermons and pay our tithes ask, "Is this all there is to Christianity? Where is the presence and working of God in my life and in my church? Where is the personal satisfaction that ought to accompany knowing the God of the universe?"

Are you feeling empty, spiritually dry, lost in a sea of questions? You are far from alone. Many who have been respectable Christians for decades acknowledge that they feel adrift from their soul's real home in God. Henri Nouwen (d. 1996) writes,

"One way to express the spiritual crisis of our time is to say that most of us have an address but cannot be found there. We know where we belong, but we keep being pulled away in many directions, as if we were still homeless."[9]

Many of us know our Bibles, and our theology is sound. But when we're honest, joy, peace, and power seem to be missing. We hunger for a sense of God's presence and long for a connectedness with Him that will make us come alive at the core of our being. Some bridle at such talk—but if we are all honest, we must admit that it is entirely possible for a Christian to lose touch with God, while believing correct doctrine. A. W. Tozer writes, "For millions of Christians, God is no more real than He is to nonChristians. They go through life trying to love an ideal and be loyal to a mere principle."[10]

For many of us, the problem stems from the fact that we have forfeited God in the busyness of life's activities—even church work. A recent study of two dozen conservative Christians who left the church found that while most were actively involved in church programs, they were starving on the inside.[11]

A man I know well—a competent pastor with a doctor of ministries degree—put it this way: "Toward the end of seminary my spiritual life reached an all-time low. Seminary sent my prayer life into hibernation, and my first church nearly killed it altogether." A mission administrator said, "I see fellow missionaries whose level of spirituality is sufficiently low to concern me."

If pastors and missionaries struggle with the quality of their spiritual lives, so do the rest of us. Brothers and sisters in Christ, let us be honest among ourselves: We freely speak about God, but so often the reality of God's transforming presence and power is absent. As conservative Christians, we have done a superior job defending doctrine and evangelizing the unsaved. Have we done as good a job of building spiritually mature disciples? Dallas Willard, along with other evangelical leaders, suggests that the church needs to turn its efforts to producing Christlikeness in its people. "What Christians [are] normally told to do, the standard advice to churchgoers, [is] not advancing them spiritually."[12]

The tension between outward respectability and inward satisfaction that many Christians feel is widespread. It's a tension that is driving some to seek inner fulfillment by "borrowing" from or even slipping into other spiritualities, such as Buddhism. In the United States alone, an estimated one million professing Christians are experimenting with Buddhist spiritual practices. In 1997, some twelve hundred groups of spiritual seekers, known as *sanghas*, were known to practice Buddhist meditation. Many in these groups—often mature professional people—retain ties with Christian churches. Why are these professing Christians attracted to the rigors of Buddhism? "People feel Buddhist practices offer them a credible alternative to mainstream churches, because they focus on particular spiritual methodologies which they feel can help them in their daily lives."[13] Among followers of Buddhism is former Chicago Bulls coach, Phil Jackson, who was raised in a fundamentalist Christian environment. Today he calls himself a "Zen Christian."

Spiritual hunger within the church reflects the natural desire on our part as Christians to connect with God and, ultimately, to satisfy our souls' need for purpose, peace, and an encounter with love. But the Christian's search for these things diverges from other spiritualities at the most fundamental level. *We do not seek to become God or to achieve awareness of our "godhood."* Self is not God.

The path of authentic Christian spirituality recognizes that the fallen self, apart from God, is imprisoned and cannot receive spiritual light or life at all. And so our path of growth will always require us to go beyond the self to connect with our Source, who is God. Paradoxically, this self-forgetfulness opens us to the presence and will of the Other, who is God Himself. Only the living God can satisfy our deep hungers because He is the One who planted the urge and longing for Himself in our hearts.

What He has planted is, in fact, our longing to be healed of the wound that was rent in the spirit of the human race when we rebelled and pulled away from God. It is the longing to be whole again.

Striving for Wholeness

As we've said earlier, evangelicalism attempts to change the individual by changing the mind through the teaching of right doctrine. But doesn't it stand to reason that a search for satisfaction must enlist the whole person and embrace everything that we are and do before God?

With many people searching, and many leaving the church, we would do well to reexamine what it means to cultivate spiritual growth and change. Surely the first thing we must examine is the very soul of man.

The Bible describes us, men and women, as immaterial souls or spirits alive in a material body. Made in the image of God, we have vast capacities for living—intellectually, volitionally, emotionally, morally, relationally, and functionally. When we become Christians, it follows that we should grow spiritually as we grow in each of these God-given capacities. Since Jesus Christ has given us the example of a life lived perfectly in connection with the Father in all these ways, our "path of spiritual growth" is the way that leads us in greater Christlikeness. For the Christian, the path of connectedness to God involves the development of a Christlike *mind, will, affections (or emotions), character, relationships,* and *actions.* When any of these capacities is undernourished, our spiritual growth will be stunted.

An undernourished soul can suffer great pain in several ways.

First, the soul suffers *intellectually* when we fail to use our minds to know God, His Word, and His world, or when we believe the heart can be satisfied merely by *right thinking* about God.

Growing Christians must use their God-given minds to explore truth in the Bible and across the entire field of human learning. Unfortunately, anti-intellectualism is widespread in American culture today. Recent educational studies show that American high school students rank ninth in academic test scores worldwide—behind several European countries, as well as behind Russia, Singapore, and India. Intellectual flabbiness has pervaded the church. Remember that all three Synoptic Gospels record Jesus' command, "You must love the Lord your God with all your . . . mind" (Mark 12:30, compare Matthew 22:37, Luke 10:27). We urgently need a renewal of the Christian mind (see Ephesians 4:23, 1 Peter 1:13) so that the growing, spiritual person will know how to apply truth wisely (see Proverbs 23:23, Colossians 1:9).

Strangely enough, while conservative Christians have distrusted human intellect, we have relied heavily on the teaching of Bible doctrine to produce mature Christians. It hasn't worked, and now we're getting the picture: The soul begins to die when we view the faith chiefly as a set of intellectual propositions.

Just as the thought of food will not satisfy an empty stomach, *cognitive truth alone is not sufficient to form and nourish the Christian soul.* What the inner man longs for is knowledge of God that comes from encountering, grappling with, participating with God in all levels of human experience—mind, body, and spirit. We were made to crave God with our whole being.

Howie wonders why, after teaching a men's Bible study for a decade, he feels so empty inside. All he can do to combat the growing deadness is to tell himself, *I shouldn't feel this way.* But it doesn't help. Howie feels empty, at least in part, because like so many other Christians he was trained to know God largely through the intellect. Unfortunately, the result of an intellectual approach to the faith is that we become detached from God Himself, and He becomes a set of propositions. Spiritual vision and passion fade.

Second, the inner man suffers *volitionally*; that is, our inner man can become weak and unable to stand up for the Christian convictions we so strongly espouse. Our faith was meant to work into the bone and blood of our very being, as we make godly choices, so that God's heart, mind, and will are realized in us. But deepening the heart relationship with God is not achieved by mustering the will to make external adjustments to our behavior. And decisions to amend our conduct do not necessarily strengthen our hearts spiritually. An important quality of the growing Christian is the ability to bring his will into harmony with God's will.

Third, the soul can suffer from *emotional deadness.* This happens when we fail to cultivate godly affections, such as compassion, pity, and sorrow, or when our emotions get out of control. Christian growth includes developing our capacity to feel appropriate emotions deeply. A Christian who cannot feel life as Jesus felt it—feeling pity for the lost, anger at the self-righteous, compassion for the poor and sick—is a stunted Christian. Likewise, the Christian whose affections toward God are inhibited—in praise, worship, and repentance—is spiritually stunted.

On the other hand, the soul also suffers emotionally when it gives free rein to such emotions as rage, jealousy, lust, or hysteria. Many Christians are being told that to deny emotions is unhealthy. Recognizing and admitting our feelings, as opposed to living in denial of them, is indeed part of mental and emotional health. But owning up to our true feelings is not the same as allowing them to run rampant and to dictate our words and actions.

Let's be clear: *Our culture tells us that our feelings are the true measure of reality.* But the Christian knows that this *overattachment to emotional experience is a danger to be avoided.* An important quality of the Christian who is growing in spirit is that his emotional life is coming into balance under the help and direction of the Holy Spirit.

Fourth, our soul suffers *morally* when we fail to keep God's wise commandments and we violate conscience (see 1 Timothy 4:2). We also suffer morally when we give in to legalism, believing that Christlikeness comes from rigidly following a set of rules.

A growing, healthy Christian gives heed to God's wise commands in the Bible. On the other hand, legalism is a chronic affliction for too many of us. Sadly, many believers go through life spiritually crippled by the false belief that they please God by fulfilling the letter of human regulations. The Anglican evangelical Alister McGrath calls this lingering legalism "the dark side of evangelicalism."[14] An important quality of the spiritual person is that he is growing in obedience to God's commands *because he loves God so deeply he does not want to cause any break—through guilt or shame— between himself and the love he experiences in closeness to God.* Keeping the commands is not a burden then, it is freedom from heaviness and the sense of spiritual separation.

Fifth, the soul suffers *relationally* without mutually enriching relationships with God and with others. Augustine expressed his deeply nourishing connectedness to God with these words: "O Lord my God, You alone do I love; You alone do I follow; You alone do I seek; You alone am I prepared to serve."[15]

The human soul withers, becoming self-absorbed, when we isolate from others. Western Christianity struggles with an unhealthy individualism, and our spiritual journey can become a trek into narcissism (God is tailored to our needs and wants; we are not reshaped and transformed in Christ). But God made us to need healthy relationships—to be present to Him and others in satisfying interpersonal connectedness. An important quality of the spiritual person is his ability to relate lovingly to God and to others.

Finally, our souls suffer *functionally* when we fail to do what is right in service to God and our neighbor. On the other hand, the soul suffers when we succumb to hyperactivism, never knowing when we've done enough or done the right thing.

The "performance syndrome" traps the Christian who thinks he can measure his worth by how much he accomplishes for

God. Something inside says that if he does the correct things and does them long enough, he'll be spiritually mature. And so he errs on the side of *doing*, often ignoring the character quality of the person he is *becoming*.

It has been said that God made us *human beings* and not *human doings*. All clichés aside, it's true that when we are physically and emotionally depleted, we are less available to God as vessels for His habitation. In his excellent book, *Abba's Child*, Brennan Manning asks if our kind of activism *without relationship* is not a "heresy of works."[16] An important quality of the spiritual person is his ability to know when and how to serve others, and when and how to rest, letting God's Spirit replenish both body and soul.

Facing Ourselves

If we evangelicals face the truth about ourselves as a spiritual culture, we see that we suffer imbalances caused by intellectualism, emotionalism, legalism, individualism, and hyperactivity. An imbalance in any of these areas hinders growth to spiritual maturity.

McGrath makes the following observation: "Evangelicalism, particularly American evangelicalism, is failing the modern church. Evangelicals have done a superb job of evangelizing people, of bringing them to a knowledge of Jesus Christ as Savior and Lord, but they are failing to provide believers with approaches to living that keep them going and growing in spiritual relationship with Him."[17]

Addressing deficiencies in our spiritual training, Canadian theologian John Stackhouse writes, "There is widespread discontent in North American Christianity. Many of us are being asked by churches to settle for life-support Christianity instead of thriving Christianity. We should be saying, 'Are we missing out on something?'"[18]

Resisting Inner Growth

Unfortunately, many Christians feel stuck. Many of us have recognized our need for help with authentic, healthy spiritual growth. But who will direct us beyond the basics of Bible study, church attendance, and service? Who will teach us about interior growth? And who will we trust—who *can* we trust—to guide our souls in the direction of growth in Christ?

Unfortunately there can be thick walls between us and any idea that is new and unfamiliar. Each one of us encounters life and new thinking through a "grid" that has been put in place by our experiences plus cultural and religious training. As rational beings, we expend considerable energy organizing into a coherent pattern the vast amount of data from life experiences.

When we encounter new experiences or new thoughts, we check them against our grid. And this is where our wariness and resistance to things new and different begins. When an idea doesn't immediately fit our understanding of the world, we tend to resist and reject it. Unfortunately, we can even reject new ideas, at first, even when they could help us. At times, an encounter with new and challenging ideas can prompt an angry response.

For example, a pastor or counselor might need to lead a guy we'll call Jeff to see a truth about himself. Perhaps it's a tendency to blame other people and never shoulder personal responsibility. To this point, Jeff hasn't seen, or he has refused to accept, this piece of the truth about himself. Let's face it, seeing yourself as immature and irresponsible is, at first, a negative experience. So he hasn't incorporated "irresponsible" into his view of himself. His view—that he is mature and others are always to blame—is part of the "grid" that protects his inner man and keeps him from having to make the effort to change.

Now, the counselor confronts Jeff with a new view of reality—the fact of his irresponsibility in passing off blame. But Jeff doesn't want to face this uncomfortable piece of reality and he resists, first by making more excuses, then with anger. Why? Because of the anxiety he feels when his old, comfortable view of himself starts to crumble.

I have taken some pains to describe how difficult it is to grow in our inner being. Why? Because moving into unfamiliar territory doctrinally or spiritually often causes anxiety. Even though a measure of disquiet necessarily accompanies spiritual growth, *we don't like it!* The truth is, we will never change unless we're sufficiently challenged with new ideas. But it is a fact of human existence that, when confronted with the new, our natural tendency is to defend our old position from behind a wall of resistance, sometimes even when our old position is draining the life out of us.

I suspect that some of you may encounter resistance in yourselves, even as you crave a new encounter with God and long for new life within. This may be one reason for the anxiety we feel when we first meet the wisdom of Christians from other, older traditions. We look for *our* ideas, *our* comfortable phraseology, and we don't find it. Or we find other views of Scripture, prayer, and the path of holiness. Biased by our own beliefs, we resist. And our minds close.

In his introduction to Athanasius's classic work, *The Incarnation of the Word of God*, C. S. Lewis (d. 1963) addresses this problem—personal biases that result in a closed mind. Lewis writes, "Every age has its own methods. It is specially good at seeing certain truths and specially liable to make certain mistakes. We all, therefore, need the books that will correct the characteristic mistakes of our own period." As Lewis saw it, we must be open to the best scholarship—the wisdom of the ages—to keep us on track and free from errors caused by our limited, culturally influenced views. Admittedly, Lewis said, the person who explores new ground and carefully weighs new possibilities puts himself at risk. For when he proposes new insights or approaches, he is likely to be misunderstood and resisted.

Perhaps Lewis had a twinkle in his eye when he wrote, "If you then venture to speak, you will have an amusing experience. You will be thought a Papist when you are actually reproducing Bunyan, a Pantheist when you are quoting Aquinas."[19]

This brings us back to the matter of *spirituality* and especially to the matter of spiritual progress in Christ. If you're a Christian, it's very likely you have already formed certain opinions about spiritual experience and growth. For example, you may not care to listen to a spiritual writer who lived prior to the sixteenth century. Or you might dislike written prayers, say, in the Anglican *Book of Common Prayer.*

Many of us are discovering that if we would continue our growth in Christ, we can find help if we are willing to move beyond our prejudices and open up to God in ways that have been known to the church for centuries. *Growth requires an open heart and a receptive mind to every overture of the Spirit.* Charles Hummel warns, "If we refuse to accept the possibility that God is indeed acting in unexpected ways, opening the eyes of his people to scriptural truths long overlooked or misunderstood, we run the risk of smothering a fire that is being kindled by the Holy Spirit."[20]

The truth is, if we do not open up to ideas beyond ourselves, we run the risk of shaping God to our views and our ways—making God in our image—and never allowing Him to shape us in His. Centuries ago, Augustine (d. 430) uttered the following prayer: "Lord, Your best servants are those who wish to shape their life on Your answers rather than shape Your answers on their wishes."[21] May this be the prayer of our hearts as well.

May we also be like the Berean Christians who "searched the Scriptures day after day to check up on Paul and Silas, to see if they were really teaching the truth" (Acts 17:11). Throughout this book, we will explore means of spiritual growth that may seem foreign to you. And so I have worked to connect Scripture with the spiritual practices described. Please check the Scriptures yourself.

Toward the Future with Confidence

In light of the growing interest in spirituality today, many believe that we may be entering a new era in God's work to reach and revive His people.

In Old Testament times there were great spiritual revivals led by Elijah (see 1 Kings 18–21), Hezekiah (see 2 Kings 18:1–7, 2 Chronicles 29–31), Josiah (see 2 Kings 22–23, 2 Chronicles 34-35), and among the people of Nineveh under Jonah (see Jonah 3:4-10). In New Testament times the revival that began in Jerusalem at Pentecost (see Acts 2, 4:4, 5:14, 6:7) spread explosively through much of the Roman world. The book of Acts and the New Testament letters tell the exciting story of the expansion of God's kingdom rule.

In the centuries that followed, God gave additional seasons of refreshing through Bernard of Clairvaux (d. 1153), Francis of Assisi (d. 1226), and John of the Cross (d. 1591). The spiritual impact of the sixteenth-century Reformation in Europe shaped the course of Western civilization. The First and Second Great Awakenings in America and Britain (1730s and 1790s) and the Welsh Revival early in the twentieth century brought great blessing to multitudes. Beginning in the 1960s, the charismatic renewal in the Catholic church and mainline Protestant denominations has also powerfully impacted lives.

The stream of life—the life of God that is the Holy Spirit—has flowed through Jewish and Christian history. At times it has become obscured or lost. But God's Word promises that revival once again will bless the nations. Psalm 104:30 says, "When you send your Spirit, new life is born to replenish all the living of the earth." We know that in the future refreshing, many Jews will believe and enter the kingdom (see Ezekiel 37:1-14, Romans 11:24). Paul was so confident of this that he wrote, "All Israel will be saved" (Romans 11:26).

Might the signs of interest in Christian spirituality today erupt in a renewal of faith and life? Might we be on the verge of a new spiritual awakening that will revive God's people and sweep multitudes into the kingdom? From all appearances, God's Spirit seems to be leading us today to time-honored, spiritual resources that can nourish and empower us.

In the chapters that follow, I aim to examine leading issues of Christian spirituality to determine which are safely Christian, for the satisfaction of our spiritual hunger and for fruitful Christian living. I encourage you not only to read but to participate in the practices presented here. Seize the challenge by pursuing other readings, attending workshops, making retreats, and talking to competent people in the field. Respond to the welcoming invitation of the psalmist: "Taste and see that the LORD is good. Oh, the joys of those who trust in him!" (Psalm 34:8).

TRY IT YOURSELF

1. Search your soul.

Theologians identify the collection of opinions, convictions, and beliefs a person holds as she undertakes a new endeavor as her "entry point." For example, a person raised in a charismatic church likely will have strong opinions about prophecy and tongues-speaking. Your entry point will influence the way you perceive and process new information. Undoubtedly, you have already formed convictions and opinions about Christian spirituality or spiritual formation.

Read again the section on pages 55-58 entitled "Resisting Inner Growth."

- What teachings in the book thus far are you inclined to dismiss? What biblical evidence do you have to support your opinion?
- What teachings about Christian spirituality do you resist? Identify the reason(s) you resist or belittle these teachings. How might these factors relate to your cultural or denominational "grid"?
- Identify the life experiences, presuppositions, or assumptions that form your point of entry into the faith. Can you see how these factors influence your response to new teachings, say, in theology and spirituality? Reflect prayerfully on these before the Lord.

- What do you learn about yourself from an honest look at the kind of Christian spirituality you practice? (For instance, you may "feel more comfortable working hard for God and relying less on prayer," or you may "feel more comfortable praying more and letting God work things out." Either approach tells you something about yourself and your spiritual preferences, which God may be working to change in some way.)

2. 'Purposeful' conversation.

Make spirituality a topic of conversation among your friends, neighbors, and coworkers. You might begin by commenting on the great interest in spirituality today.

As you talk with nonChristians, your main purpose will not be to try to convert them, not at this point anyway, but to sense their spiritual aspirations and hungers. With Christians, you can talk more frankly about their relationship with the Lord.

God knows the hearts of the people you speak with, so be open to the leading of the Spirit. It may help to use some of the following questions along with your own.

- Do you ever wish there was something more to life?
- What do you believe about prayer, miracles, the afterlife?
- Do you believe in a supreme God who created us and loves us?
- How do you satisfy your inner needs? Do you have any spiritual practices that are helpful to you and bring you closer to God, such as prayer, meditation, or silent walks in nature?
- Do you believe this God is capable of satisfying your spiritual needs? How?
- What prevents you from trusting God to satisfy your innermost needs?
- What is your assessment of the spiritual hunger and longings of the people you have talked with? How great are the spiritual needs of the nonChristians? Of the Christians?

- When you consider the above questions yourself, what are your answers?

Suggestions for Further Reading

Jones, Peter. *Spirit Wars: Pagan Revival in Christian America.* Mukilteo, Wash.: Winepress, 1987.

Manning, Brennan. *Abba's Child: The Cry of the Heart for Intimate Belonging.* Colorado Springs: NavPress, 1994.

McGrath, Alister. *Spirituality in an Age of Change.* Grand Rapids: Zondervan, 1994.

CHAPTER THREE

The Need for Discernment

"Dear friends, do not believe everyone who claims to speak by the Spirit. You must test them to see if the spirit they have comes from God. For there are many false prophets in the world."

1 JOHN 4:1

"You can be straight as a gun barrel theologically and as empty as one spiritually."

A. W. TOZER[1]

THE WORD *SPIRITUALITY* IS LIKE THE word *love*. It lends itself to various meanings, some good, others not so good. And just like love, spirituality also leads to a variety of practices, some of which are uplifting and totally transforming, while others are destructive.

Some people believe they are pursuing spiritual growth by meditating in a trancelike state for hours at a time. Others believe they are doing so by withdrawing into a cloister and renouncing all contact with the outside world.

Among evangelicals, we tend to think that spiritual growth is what happens at given events or turning points, like when we get together with other believers at retreats, seminars, or huge stadium events such as Promise Keepers gatherings. Often we are not sure what to do with the spaces between these events, which are filled with the grind of everyday living. And so our "growth" may happen in fits and starts. And our struggles in between can leave us limping until the next "event."

Our task in this chapter is to distinguish true Christian spirituality from nonChristian forms that compete for hungry hearts in search of greater connection with God.

USE AND ABUSE OF THE WORD *SPIRITUALITY*

Because of abuses such as those we saw in the previous chapter, there's a tendency to approach this topic cautiously. After all, the word *spirituality* is freely used by nonChristian prophets, humanists, New Agers, and occultists, as well as by orthodox Christians. In some types of spirituality, the word *God* is not even mentioned. Confusion reigns when any term is shrouded in mist.

At the most basic level, the word *spiritual* refers to what is immaterial—the soul or spirit—as opposed to what is material—

the body. In this sense, *spiritual* describes the inner person in its activities of thinking, willing, and feeling. *Spiritual* also can mean "pertaining to the sacred," whether this be the true and living God, the Great Spirit, or a menagerie of lesser spirits. In this sense, a spiritual person shows interest in some higher power. Many people view the spiritual in these two ways. *Spiritual* also can describe qualities produced in a Christian by the Holy Spirit of God. Scripture describes the believer as spiritual in the sense that he or she knows God with the heart and is being renewed by the Spirit in holiness and love (see 1 Corinthians 2:15, 3:1, Galatians 6:1).

The word *spirituality* indicates the condition of being spiritual. From a Christian perspective, spirituality refers to the shaping of our lives in relationship with Christ for the glory of God and the good of others. (I'll offer a more complete definition later in this chapter.) Suffice it to say, spirituality has to do with the godly quality of a believer's life as he grows, worships, and serves in relationship with Jesus. Spirituality begins with the renewing and satisfying of the soul, and extends to every aspect of the Christian's life before God and others.

Across the Great Divide

In the Middle Ages, man's view of life split. Until that time, the spiritual and material worlds existed side by side, interacting with each other. With the dawn of the Enlightenment, a break occurred between the spiritual and material worlds. As a result, the concept of *spirituality* narrowed and came to mean only the inner life of the Christian.

In reality, spirituality encompasses all that we are and do—our Christian beliefs, heart connection to the Lord, relationships to others, how we use our money, our concern for the environment, and so on.

In many ways, we have been trying to close the "great divide" between the spiritual and material worlds ever since the Middle Ages. And as we've seen, the expressions of spirituality in the world today are mind-boggling. To get a handle on things, it's helpful to divide these many forms into three categories. The first category we'll call *nonreligious* or *generic spirituality.* These forms of spirituality convey the human search for personal fulfillment. The second category is *religious spirituality.* These forms represent the human response to a Supreme Being or beings, expressed through the nonChristian religions. Religious spirituality reflects what John Calvin (d. 1564) called the "sense of divinity" or "seed of religion" implanted in all persons as image-bearers of God. The third category is *Christian spirituality.* This represents the believer's Spirit-directed response to God's revelation in Jesus Christ and the Scriptures, leading to self-surrender, worship, and service.

So that we may recognize the genuine article and reject the spurious, let's take a closer look at each of these three forms of spirituality.

Generic Spirituality

Much that goes by the name of spirituality today focuses on human self-fulfillment with little or no regard for God. In 1775, Dr. Samuel Johnson, the English literary scholar, defined spirituality as "acts independent of the body, pure acts of the soul; mental refinement." Consider, too, Gordon Wakefield's definition: "[Spirituality] is a word which has come much into vogue to describe those attitudes, beliefs, practices which animate people's lives and help them work towards supra-sensible realities."[2] Samuel Johnson's definition clearly is nonreligious. Wakefield's is sufficiently vague to describe almost any aspect of spiritual concern. We often find nonreligious spirituality in newspaper "personal ads," where a male seeks a female companion (or vice versa) with interests in candlelight dinners, classical music, and spirituality.

How do you recognize generic spirituality when you see it? It will bear some of the following features.

First, it is *highly eclectic,* picking and choosing from a wide range of beliefs and practices.

Second, it often *focuses on the self,* and its driving passion is the satisfaction of felt, personal needs. In the *Screwtape Letters,* Screwtape urges Wormwood to keep the man in his care focused on himself. "The Enemy [God] wants to turn the man's attention away from self to Him and to the man's neighbors."[3]

Third, generic spirituality is *indifferent to religious beliefs.* There is little focus on Christ, the Bible, or the Christian lifestyle. If the word *sacred* is used, it can mean almost anything.

Finally, nonreligious spirituality often centers in *social or environmental issues.* It may involve a crusade to raise literacy levels or save the spotted owls. These are good causes, for sure. But disregard for the God of the Bible is a fatal flaw of generic spirituality.

Thomas Moore, the best-selling author of *Care of the Soul* (1992) and *Soul Mates* (1997), promotes a generic spirituality. Moore's popular writings contain some valuable insights. But by his own admission, the spirituality he presents is fashioned out of human materials alone. "What I am presenting is not specifically Christian, nor is it tied to any particular religious tradition."[4] His spirituality has little to do with salvation as Christians understand it. He writes, "Dropping the salvational fantasy frees us up to the possibility of self-knowledge and self-acceptance, which are the very foundation of soul."[5] In developing his generic spirituality, Moore appeals favorably to soul-yoga, alchemy, spiritualism, astrology, and Zen.

A person becomes spiritual, according to Moore, in a variety of ways. One way is to cultivate depth of feeling and imagination through poetry, painting, sculpture, and music. Another is to develop one's playful "inner child." Third, one should pay attention to the messages conveyed through one's dreams. A fourth way is to cultivate pleasurable sensations, for example, through massage therapy. Or you can recover the living tradition of the religion into which you were born. For Moore, spirituality is the art of living from the depths of our inner being, simply as it presents itself to us.

Jesus would disagree. New life does not spring forth from fallen human nature. "No one puts new wine into old wineskins. The new wine would burst the old skins, spilling the wine and ruining the skins. New wine must be put into new wineskins" (Luke 5:37-38).

Nonetheless, generic spirituality has wide appeal. Why? Because it makes people feel good about focusing on self and their own goals, desires, and achievements.

Religious Spirituality

Religious spirituality involves the search for transcendence and purpose by appeal to a Higher Power, or powers.

The teacher writes that God "has planted eternity in the human heart" (Ecclesiastes 3:11). Because we are fashioned for eternity, humans instinctively long for a reality above and beyond their finite selves. The universal hunger for spiritual satisfaction confirms Augustine's famous declaration, "You have made us for Yourself, O Lord, and our hearts are restless until they rest in You."[6]

Religious spirituality is a potent force in the nonChristian religions, such as Islam, Hinduism, and Buddhism. It drives such Christian heresies as Gnosticism. And it empowers quasi-religious systems such as yoga, Transcendental Meditation, and the New Age. It is also the sparkplug embedded in self-help movements like Alcoholics Anonymous, which plainly states that its aim is to nourish a "religious" spirituality by seeking relationship with a Higher Power.

The many forms of religious spirituality reflect common characteristics. Primarily, religious spirituality possesses a *well-defined form* that can include a creed, dogma, prayer, and rituals. Religious spirituality is *often relativistic*, claiming that there are many ways to achieving the soul's goal. Third, it always *elevates works above grace* in the quest for salvation, promising that we can "ascend the ladder to God" by our human effort.

Christians respond that religious spirituality negates salvation by grace through faith in Christ. For the risen Lord says, "I am the way and the truth and the life. No one comes to the Father except through me" (John 14:6, NIV).

One well-known example of religious spirituality is that espoused by Mahatma Gandhi (d. 1948), the late Indian politician and spiritual leader. The title Mahatma ("Great Soul") indicated that Gandhi was a virtual messiah for his people. Gandhi stated that God is Life, Truth, Light, Love, and the Supreme Good. He believed that prayer leads to purity of soul and peace of heart. The goal of Gandhi's life was "self-realization," which means being freed from the cycle of birth and death (*Moksha*). Inspired by the Hindu holy book, the *Bhagavad-Gita*, Gandhi believed in the unity of humankind under one God. He argued that as there are many paths leading to the top of a mountain, so there are many ways to God. Throughout his life Gandhi preached ethical principles from Hinduism, Islam, and Christianity.

Another example of religious spirituality is the brand espoused by financier and humanitarian Sir John Templeton. A Presbyterian influenced by the Unity School of Christianity, Templeton left the financial world to devote himself to advancing the spiritual dimension of life. Templeton testifies that great wealth does not satisfy the human heart for very long. Templeton's spirituality is an amalgam of Christianity, Buddhism, Hinduism, and Islam. The committee that awards the Templeton Prize for Progress in Religion consists of representatives from the world's major religions. The 1997 Templeton prize was awarded to a wandering Hindu guru named Pandurang Shastri Athavale, who founded a spiritual self-knowledge movement that has spread to one hundred thousand villages in India and many other countries. Athavale's philosophy recognizes the inner presence of God in all people. It claims that all human beings are brothers and sisters in God's family.

In our culture, religious spirituality has become popular through writers like Deepak Chopra, an Indian-born physician and holistic medicine guru. Chopra's books have sold more than ten million copies. Frequently seen on American television, Chopra promotes a religious spirituality from the perspective of pantheistic Hinduism. His deity is Cosmic Mind or Quantum Energy Field. All of us, he claims, are gods and goddesses in embryo form—"conscious energy-spirits" in the guise of persons on a cosmic journey. Our task, says Chopra, is to discover the divinity hidden within us and allow it to blossom like a beautiful flower. This will occur if we follow "The Seven Spiritual Laws of Success" ("the law of detachment," "the law of karma," and so forth) and observe "The Ten Keys to Happiness" ("listen to your body's wisdom," "live in the present," and so on). Central to his teaching is the practice of meditation using a mantra, similar to that in Transcendental Meditation.

Chopra promotes these principles through an organization known as The Global Network for Spiritual Success.[7] At this writing, he has gathered a large following in the West, including movie star Demi Moore, ex-Beatle George Harrison, Michael Jackson, and ex-financier Michael Milken. Says Chopra, "I satisfy a spiritual yearning without making [people] think they have to worry about God and punishment."[8] Chopra's brand of Eastern spirituality enables people to dabble in the spiritual world without having to confront the offense of the Cross (1 Corinthians 1:18). It is a religious spirituality a world apart from biblical and Christian norms.

Christians must not allow themselves to be taken in by charismatic gurus who promote a spirituality that is religious but not Christian. Remember John's warning: "Dear friends, do not believe everyone who claims to speak by the Spirit. You must test them to see if the spirit they have comes from God. For there are many false prophets in the world" (1 John 4:1). We must carefully discern the work of God's Holy Spirit from the many unholy spirits abroad.

Authentic Christian Spirituality

Christian spirituality concerns the shaping of our inner beings into the likeness of Jesus Christ. Certainly it involves human effort, but it trusts in the work of the indwelling Holy Spirit, which prompts and empowers us to live out of the Savior's values, in service to others. It involves cultivating a healing, renewing, and satisfying relationship with Christ, deepening love for Him, and giving flesh to the new life through obedient and fruitful living. Christian spirituality describes our growth in those familiar pursuits, *godliness* and *piety.*

What distinguishes Christian spirituality from the many nonChristian alternatives in our world?

The following characteristics will help growing disciples to "hate what is evil" and "cling to what is good" (Romans 12:9, NIV).

First, biblical and Christian spirituality is unashamedly *Trinitarian*. At the heart of Christian spirituality is a satisfying relationship with the living God who exists as Father, Son, and Holy Spirit (2 Corinthians 13:14). Anything less than this is false and destructive.

Second, Christian spirituality is also *revelational*; that is, it is framed and nourished by the Word of God rightly unfolded by sound principles of interpretation. Christian spirituality believes that God is not silent, that He has spoken through the messages of prophets and apostles recorded in the Scriptures. It teaches that God has spoken from outside time and nature to reveal truths we could not have discovered on our own: His existence as three divine persons; our fall and need for salvation; God's plan to redeem and restore us to friendship with Himself.

Third, Christian spirituality is *Christ-centered*. It is grounded in the person of Jesus Christ, the Savior. The fullness of life we crave is found only in heart-to-heart relationship with Christ, in growing in His character, and in being directed by His Spirit. In this way, we experience the life and will of God lived out, in, and through us. Jesus Himself says, "I have come that they may have life, and have it to the full" (John 10:10, NIV).

Fourth, Christian spirituality is also *creational*. A faithful spirituality affirms that the material world created by God is good (Genesis 1:4,10,12), not evil. Christian spirituality encourages responsible self-discipline, but not a severe asceticism that holds the body or the material world in contempt.

Fifth, Christian spirituality is *salvational*. It is the gracious gift of life that flows from God's heart of love. True spirituality begins with conversion to Christ through repentance and faith; it is established by the miracle of the new birth; it enlarges through growth into the likeness of Jesus Christ; and it will finally consummate with the perfecting of body and soul at the Savior's second coming (see 1 John 3:2). Theologians call this spiritual growth to maturity *progressive sanctification* (see 2 Corinthians 3:18, 2 Corinthians 4:16, 1 Thessalonians 5:23).

Sixth, authentic Christian spirituality is both *individual and corporate.* It involves nourishing the spiritual life of each believer as well as the Christian social unit. Christlike character develops through the encouragement, challenge, and support of fellow believers in local churches who themselves are growing in Christ. True spirituality flourishes in what is called the "communion of the saints." Growing Christians learn the ways of Christ from other committed believers from a variety of ethnic, cultural, and denominational traditions.

Finally, Christian spirituality is *pneumatic*, meaning that it is empowered by the Holy Spirit *(pneuma)*. The Spirit testifies to Christ, heals deeply ingrained woundedness, and restores our souls. Through the Spirit believers enjoy intimacy with God, crying from the heart, "dear Father" (see Galatians 4:6, compare Romans 8:15). Many believe that Christian spirituality embraces the gifts of the Spirit (see Romans 12; 1 Corinthians 12,14; Ephesians 4). But all Christians agree that it requires evidence of the fruit of the same Holy Spirit (Galatians 5:22-23).

Taking the broadest view of Christian spirituality, we see that it embraces *knowing, being,* and *doing.* It involves the lifelong integration of the disciple's head, heart, and hands. We value the mind, which wrestles with the teachings of Scripture, the ancient creeds, and the writings of faithful theologians. Moreover, we believe in the transformation of the believer's inner being. Through deepening relationship with the living God, inwardly we become more like the lovely Lord Jesus. Then from the foundation of heart that is renewed and empowered, we reach out in compassionate service to the world, for the salvation of the lost, the building of new converts, and for just social causes, such as human rights and integrity in government.

From the Head to the Heart

Some who read the above description of Christian spirituality will think, *I know these things already. But knowing them hasn't given me the satisfaction in life I've been hungering for.*

That's because we're talking about a different kind of knowing—the kind that only comes from taking the truths we are given and going out into the world to understand them in experience. Because in the midst of life, where the commands and promises of God often do not appear to make sense, the deepest questions of our hearts are revealed. And we are challenged to open our lives to God in ways we did not think possible.

David was a keen young disciple when he became a Christian, devouring books on theology, apologetics, and the like. He developed a great knowledge of the faith, but after a number of years he sensed that something was missing in his life. At first, it was hard to admit. If "Jesus lived in his heart," as he was taught to say, how could he feel an emptiness inside? How could he have any questions?

Then David was stricken with a serious illness that triggered deeper questions: Where was God? Why had He allowed this illness? What was God's purpose in his life? David realized that God had seemed distant to him, really, for a long time, and that he'd neglected crucial issues of the heart, like trusting God and willingness to surrender to Him in all things, no matter what. He could argue doctrine with the best, but did he, in his heart of hearts, *really know* God?

David realized he was at a watershed point in his life. He had given himself to God in his youthful strength. He had enjoyed health, independence, vitality. But he had never gotten to know God by surrendering to Him, depending on Him in a time of real limitation. Doctrine and apologetics were good, but didn't help him much here.

David began to read the works of writers of the past—some of whom had come to know God in times of terrible persecution, opposition, or illness. He began to incorporate the spiritual disciplines they spoke of, for instance, silent contemplation. For perhaps the first time, he wasn't just "talking at" God in his prayers, he was stilling himself long enough to listen, too. In this way, he began deepening his relationship with Christ.

Soon after, David enrolled in courses on spiritual formation and mentoring at a nearby seminary. His spiritual vision and passion grew, leading to greater satisfaction in God. Soon he was teaching courses on the spiritual life in local churches. Eventually he purchased an attractive piece of land and built a retreat center on it. Since then he has helped hundreds of hungry Christians to strengthen their satisfaction in God.

When all is said and done, the core of Christian spirituality is *a loving, deepening relationship with the living God.* From a biblical perspective, all values, commitments, and actions flow from within us, from either our spiritual poverty or abundance. Though our evangelical emphasis has been on producing good works—witnessing, teaching, missions—in fact, the fruit of our lives is no better than the quality of our hearts. As Jesus said, "A good person produces good deeds from a good heart, and an evil person produces evil deeds from an evil heart" (Luke 6:45, compare 1 Timothy 1:5). Francis Schaeffer wrote,

> The areas of true spirituality . . . are not basically external; they are internal, they are deep; they go down into the areas of our lives we like to hide from ourselves. The inward area is the first place of loss of true Christian life, of true spirituality, and the outward sinful act is the result. If we can only get hold of this, that the internal is basic, the external is always merely the result, it will be a tremendous starting point.[9]

Christian spirituality concerns the shaping of our inner beings after the likeness of Jesus Christ by the indwelling Spirit and the living out of Jesus' values in service to others. The marks of Christian spirituality presented above draw a clear line in the sand between the genuine article and the confusing maze of nonChristian alternatives.

Leading Voices

The current movement by evangelicals to a deeper spirituality is not "brand new," it has been growing for some years, fomented by some leading voices. Men like Henri Nouwen,

Richard Foster, Dallas Willard, Richard Lovelace, and others have encouraged exploration of the church's ancient perspectives and practices. Michael Horton stands out as an opponent of the spirituality movement. Because there is variation in their thought and approach, it's helpful to know how these representative leaders have understood Christian spirituality. So that you can understand where they are coming from, I'll place these authorities in one of three categories: progressive, moderate, and conservative.

Progressives

Among the progressives is the Roman Catholic spiritual writer Henri Nouwen (d. 1996), who taught at Notre Dame, Yale, and Harvard. Nouwen testified that during his years in academia he believed all the right things with his thinking mind, but work overload crushed his spiritual heart. In search of healing, Nouwen joined the L'Arche Community of Daybreak in Canada, which ministers to the handicapped and disabled. Nouwen testifies that his soul was restored in that caring community. His dozens of popular books (for example, *In the Name of Jesus, The Path of Freedom, Return of the Prodigal*) reveal a man of deep dependence on God, great compassion, and honesty regarding his own spiritual struggles. Two overarching questions for Nouwen were "What does it mean to live a spiritual life?" and "How do we do it?" Nouwen was solidly Christian in that he affirmed the core doctrinal convictions of the faith. Secondary points of doctrine, however, took a backseat to his burning passion to see people related to the Father through Jesus, in the power of the Spirit.

Themes that loom large in Nouwen's writings include listening to God in solitude, responding to God in prayer, a life of faithful discipline, the Spirit who draws us into intimacy with God, deep devotion to Jesus, the grace of Christian community, and self-sacrifice for others. I add holy indignation against racism, sexual exploitation, and war. Nouwen's passionate hunger for God is reflected in a typical prayer:

> Let me recognize you at that virginal point in the depth of my heart where you dwell and heal me. Let

> me experience you in that center of my being from which you want to teach and guide me. Let me know you as my loving brother who holds nothing—not even my worst sins—against me, but who wants to touch me in a gentle embrace.[10]

Nouwen's literary masterpiece is *The Return of the Prodigal Son: A Story of Homecoming* (1993). Inspired by Rembrandt's painting by the same name, the book movingly depicts humanity's rebellion against God, moral ruin, and the remorseful return to the Father's embrace. Nouwen's reflections on Christian spirituality are widely read and appreciated by evangelical Protestants. His is a Christian spirituality from a moderate Catholic perspective, emphasizing experiential love from Christ and the Christian's grateful response.

Other examples of progressives in the field of Christian spirituality include the Southern Baptist E. Glenn Hinson, the Presbyterian Howard Rice, and the Episcopalian Morton Kelsey.

Moderates

Richard J. Foster, a spiritual theologian from a Quaker background, is an example of a moderate. Foster is the author of best-selling books on the spiritual life, including *Celebration of Discipline* (1988); *Prayer: Finding the Heart's True Home* (1992); *Devotional Classics* (1993); and *Streams of Living Water* (1998). Foster is also the founder of RENOVARÉ, a ministry dedicated to spiritual renewal in the church. RENOVARÉ's program for renewal brings together six Christian traditions: the *Contemplative,* which seeks spiritual depth through prayer and intimacy with God; the *Holiness,* which pursues a life of righteousness and virtue; the *Charismatic,* which displays the enabling Spirit's grace and power; the *Social Justice,* which labors for the broken and oppressed; the *Evangelical,* which upholds the Word of God and the imperative of evangelism; and the *Incarnational,* which calls for kingdom living in the world.

Foster believes that many Christians who desire to serve Christ experience painful failure because of lack of heart-relatedness to Him. He believes that spiritual maturity is far more than a quick fix. The cultivation of Christlike qualities demands diligence and discipline (see 1 Timothy 4:7). Foster commends spiritual disciplines such as meditation, fasting, simplicity, solitude, and confession as means of deepening relationship with Christ. Foster's major themes are friendship with Christ, hearing God's voice, resting in His presence, and serving others in Jesus' name.

Foster arguably has done more than any other contemporary evangelical to unfold the treasures of Christian spirituality for the church. He ranges widely in spiritual literature, drawing insights from church fathers, medieval monks, Eastern mystics, Western ascetics, Protestant Reformers, Russian Orthodox, Quakers, and neo-orthodox churchmen. In the original edition of *Celebration of Discipline* (1978), Foster proposed a meditative experience, using the imagination, intended to help the reader open up to God. When questioned about the exercise he removed it from the revised edition (1988) of *Celebration.*[11] This shows that, while passionate to help Christians grow spiritually, evangelical spiritual writers are concerned to preserve biblical orthodoxy.

Evangelical church historian Richard Lovelace is another example of a moderate spiritual writer. Lovelace is indebted to Augustine, the Reformers, Puritans, and Pietists. He takes a wholistic approach to spirituality, viewing it as a three-legged stool that involves personal spiritual growth, church renewal, and social transformation. Lovelace believes that evangelical spirituality has significant strengths. These include a high view of Scripture, doctrinal precision, and the priesthood of all believers. But he also senses that evangelicalism suffers from blind spots and distortions that beg to be addressed.

Weaknesses of evangelical spirituality include a tendency to read the Bible through a skewed cultural lens—for example, favoring the health-and-wealth gospel, with lack of concern for social justice. Recent evangelicalism has emphasized a moralistic code of behavior—an arbitrary list of behavioral do's and dont's. In addition, it has a weak sense of the holiness of God and of individual and collective sinfulness. Some evangelicals harbor active distrust of personal experience as an essential ingredient of spiritual wholeness.

Lovelace insists that we must listen attentively to the Word of God rightly interpreted. The core doctrines of the Christian faith—particularly justification by grace through faith alone—determine the integrity and vitality of our spirituality. Sympathetic to truth in other models of Christian spirituality, Lovelace says that we should learn from responsible voices from the past: "The early fathers, the medieval mystics, the spiritual doctors of the Reformation and Counter-Reformation, the leaders of the awakening eras, the uneven prophets of liberal social reform—all of these can force us back toward biblical balance and authentic spirituality."[12]

I also place in this centrist, or moderate, category spiritual writers such as James Houston, Eugene Peterson, J. I. Packer, Dallas Willard, Peter Toon, and Alister McGrath.

Conservatives

Among conservatives on the right, consider the position of Michael Horton, described in his book *In the Face of God* (1996). Horton claims that the greatest threat to the gospel is the ancient Gnostic heresy. Gnosticism is a dualistic system—meaning that the good realm of spirit opposes the evil realm of matter. The Gnostic Jesus was not God incarnate; he was a man on whom the Christ-spirit descended as a dove. Salvation, according to the Gnostics, is all about freeing the spirit from the material world by a secret *gnosis* (knowledge) and by direct and private religious experiences.

Horton claims that much of Christian spirituality—from medieval monasticism to many evangelical expressions today—borders on the heretical. He argues that "the entire religious landscape—New Age, liberal, evangelical, or Pentecostal—is essentially gnostic in nature."[13] A good deal of evangelical spirituality, he insists, elevates private experience above the revealed Word. It attempts by meditation and other disciplines to climb the ladder to capture the glory of God. He writes,

> We want to have direct, intuitive supernatural experiences. But God has determined that we derive all of our knowledge of Him, not through direct encounters, but through the written Word, the Bible, and in the Person and work of His incarnate Son.[14]

Horton protests against the "gnostic impulse" in a long list of Christian traditions—including medieval Christian mysticism, Arminianism, the Anabaptist sects, Quakerism, Pentecostalism, the Keswick "higher life" movement, fundamentalism, (non-Calvinistic) evangelicalism, the neocharismatic movement, Southern Baptist piety, and the Vineyard. He sees dangerous gnostic emphases in the writings of Thomas Aquinas, Julian of Norwich, Thomas à Kempis, Menno Simons, William Law, John Wesley, C. I. Scofield, R. A. Torrey, Charles Kraft, John Wimber, Peter Wagner, Clark Pinnock, Richard Foster, Robert Schuller, Pat Robertson, and Henry Blackaby and Claude King—the authors of the popular contemporary workbook *Experiencing God* (1997). All of these, Horton claims, promote a dangerous shift from the objective to the subjective, from the historically given gospel to the private mystical quest.

The Reformers, on the other hand, present a faith centered in the preached Word, celebrated in the sacraments, and contained in the church's creeds. What is important, Horton argues, is the objective event of Christ's life two thousand years ago—not what happens in our personal experience today. In the many forms of "false" spirituality, he claims, "The God and the Christ outside of us (the Reformation emphasis) is replaced with God and the Christ within us in the individual's heart (the medieval and Gnostic influence)."[15] Horton states that God does not stand at the heart's door waiting to enter (but see Revelation 3:20). Rather, He is a judge about to execute wrath.

Is Evangelical Spirituality Liberal or Gnostic?

We need to evaluate the claim that evangelical spirituality today is a bedfellow of the ancient Gnostic heresy.

Again, I say for the record: I am absolutely committed to the timeless essentials of the Christian faith. The saving life, substitutionary death, and bodily resurrection of the Son of God, received by faith, are the sole means of salvation from sin. The search for God apart from personal conversion, the teachings of the Word of God, and the ministry of the Spirit is a futile enterprise. The great historical facts about Jesus the Christ, preserved in the gospel, must never be compromised. Christians must be prepared to die, if necessary, for these great truths of the faith.

However, the conservative claim that the current revival of evangelical spirituality succumbs to the ancient Gnostic heresy, I find to be false. Follow me carefully as I explain my reasons.

First, the description of Gnosticism by current critics of Christian spirituality is broad to a fault.

It is anachronistic to pin the Gnostic heresy label on the Christian expressions of spirituality outlined above. Evangelical spiritual writers such as Houston, Lovelace, Peterson, Willard, Foster, and others of like faith are a world apart from the ancient Gnostic heresy. These spiritual writers do not accept the authority of extra-canonical Gnostic writings, such as the *Gospel of Truth*, the *Acts of Peter*, or the *Apocryphon of John.* They do not hold to a cosmological dualism that identifies two divinities—the transcendent God and the demiurge. Evangelical spiritual authorities do not subscribe to a moral dualism with its chasm between good spirit and evil matter. They do not devalue the Old Testament in favor of the New. To the contrary, many spiritual disciplines—such as quietness before God (see Psalm 46:10, 131:2), resting in the Lord (see Psalm 62:1,5), and practicing the presence of God (see Psalm 130:6)—draw heavily on the Old Testament.

Furthermore, evangelical spiritual authorities certainly do not deny the incarnation of Christ and His physical suffering on the Cross, as did the Gnostic heretics. Nor do they deny the resurrection of the physical body. They never suggest that salvation comes by some secret knowledge that violates the Word of God. And evangelical spiritual writers do not elevate experience over doctrine. They insist that both our thought life and our religious experiences must be subject to the rule of Scripture.

The widespread defection from the church today should rouse all Christians to anchor themselves in a true, wholehearted relationship with God as never before. Unfortunately, one of Satan's strategies is to deceive people by clothing error with the appearance of truth. The enemy makes occultic, New Age, and other pseudo-spiritualities resemble the genuine article. Therefore, Christians are duped into discarding it. Believers must be careful not to throw out the baby of truth with the bath water of imitation. Let's remain alert "so that Satan will not outsmart us. For we are very familiar with his evil schemes" (2 Corinthians 2:11).

It's dishonoring to the Holy Spirit to assign the current revival of Christian spirituality to the ancient Gnostic heresy. The former clearly is of God; the latter plainly is of the Evil One.

Second, conservatives claim that the spirituality commended by many Christian authorities during the past two thousand years attempts to ascend the ladder to glory by human effort alone.

Let's consider the meaning of "ascent" to God—a figure widely used by ancient Christian writers such as Origen (d. 254), Gregory of Nyssa (d. 395), Augustine (d. 430), John Climacus (d. 649), Bernard of Clairvaux (d. 1153), Walter Hilton (d. 1396), and John of the Cross (d. 1591). These church authorities viewed "ascent" symbolically to describe the Christian's spiritual journey to the heavenly home. They saw believers following the pattern of Christ, who, after His descent to earth, ascended to heaven's glory (see Ephesians 4:8-10). These writers emphasized that the "ascent" to God through salvation is the very opposite of the tragic "descent" of the race by the Fall (see Genesis 3). The language of "ascent" symbolizes the Christian spiritual journey, involving conversion, growth in godliness by the practice of holy virtues, and final perfecting at the sight of Jesus' return. Their imagery of "ascent," in fact, was taken directly from the Bible.

The account of Moses' life shows the leader of Israel climbing Mount Sinai to receive revelation from God and commune with Him (see Exodus 19:3,20; 24:1-3). The imagery of "ascent" was further encouraged by Jacob's vision of an angel-filled stairway extending from earth to heaven, at the top of which stood the Lord Himself (Genesis 28:12-17). The stairway, with angels ascending and descending, symbolizes the upward path to heaven. For Jacob said, "What an awesome place this is! It is none other than . . . the gateway to heaven!" (verse 17). The New Testament tells us that Jesus is the stairway to heaven (see John 1:51). The Old Testament also describes the "ascent" of the godly to Mount Zion for worship and prayer. "Come, let us go up to the mountain of the LORD, to the Temple of the God of Israel. There he will teach us his ways, so that we may obey him" (Isaiah 2:3, compare Micah 4:2). Notice how often in the New Testament Jesus ascended a mountain to commune with his heavenly Father (see Matthew 14:23, Luke 9:28).

The Christian writers mentioned above never suggested that the "ascent" to God is achieved by human works or that it gives the believer godlike status. John of the Cross wrote, "The rising is here understood, spiritually, as an ascent from the low to the high, which is the same as to go out from oneself—that is, from one's own low way of life and love of self to the high love of God."[16] John suggested that Christians ascend to God after the manner of Jesus, who ascended by descending—that is, by assuming our humble, lowly place under the government and direction of the Father, in the manner that Jesus demonstrated for us when He came as Son of Man. Our "ascent" is enabled by God's grace, as well as by faith and perseverance. John of the Cross very directly said, "The soul . . . ascends by faith."[17]

∞

Third, it is not Gnostic or heretical for followers of Jesus, grounded in the Word, to seek intimacy with their Lord.

We should not tar with the same broad brush nonChristians seeking a vague transcendence or a means of becoming "divine" and Christians who are pursuing a love relationship with God in Christ. Growing Christians need not choose between faith in biblical truths and life in God's presence. Both are essential. The Son of God suffered on the Cross for sins and rose from the dead. But He also lives out His life in believers through the indwelling Spirit. The God who customarily addresses us through the written Word also whispers directly to the believing heart. So the psalmist says of the Lord, "My heart has heard you say, 'Come and talk with me!' And my heart responds, 'LORD, I am coming'" (Psalm 27:8). The teaching and testifying ministry of the Spirit is a powerful, inner reality. "The Holy Spirit . . . lives within you, so you don't need anyone to teach you what is true. For the Spirit teaches you all things" (1 John 2:27, compare 3:24, 4:4).

Christians who delight in theological orthodoxy (myself included) must attend to the gentle promptings of the Spirit and join fellowship with Christ. In the sanctuary of the heart, the twice-born "draw close to God" (James 4:8); they allow themselves to be embraced, loved, and nurtured by Christ. At the personal level, Christian spirituality is about "living in the light of God's presence" (see Psalm 16:11) and enjoying sweet communion with Him (see 1 John 4:12). According to the book of Revelation, Christ gently whispers to the believing heart, "Look! Here I stand at the door and knock. If you hear me calling and open the door, I will come in, and we will share a meal as friends" (Revelation 3:20). The spirituality that is being recovered by evangelicals today enables those who know Christ as Savior to find Him as Friend and Lover. It offers believers proven principles by which to "grow in the special favor and knowledge of our Lord and Savior Jesus Christ" (2 Peter 3:18).

Fourth, overreacting evangelicals betray an excessive rationalism that limits faith to the cerebral zone between the ears.

Opposing liberalism's theological adventurism and Pentecostalism's emotionalism, some evangelicals have overloaded the intellectual side of the faith. The spiritual path utilizes right thinking, but it also engages the heart with its life-giving energies of spiritual passion and vision. Blaise Pascal (d. 1662), a creative scientist and mathematician, challenged the sovereignty of reason promoted by Descartes and others in his day. Pascal claimed that reason establishes only an abstract God. Authentic Christianity involves the experience of God in the heart. John Wesley (d. 1791) likewise believed that a person may elevate correct beliefs into a religion, while failing to relate to God with one's affections.[18]

At a recent chapel service at our seminary, Dr. Neil Anderson of Freedom in Christ Ministries said, "We have made knowledge and doctrine an end in itself, whereas according to the Great Commandment the biblical goal is love. It is possible to know a lot about God, but not know God Himself." A rigorous system of formal propositions, elevated above truth experienced in the heart, borders on idolatry. Head knowledge of God does not automatically translate into spiritual vitality. As the Puritan Stephen Charnock (d. 1680) wrote, "A man may be theologically knowing and spiritually ignorant."[19]

How are the functions of heart and mind related? Simply put, *the heart discovers and experiences God; reason demonstrates and explains God.* Right-thinking must be wedded to personal experience of God in the core of one's being. The mind cannot adequately motivate us volitionally (by the exercise of willpower) to overcome deep resistance to God so that we can follow and serve Him with joy. That's why Scripture commands us to love God with the whole heart, mind, and strength (see Deuteronomy 6:5, Mark 12:30). For a starter, read Psalms and Proverbs, and notice how often these Scriptures focus on the heart. Brennan Manning concludes that "the engaged mind, illumined by truth, awakens awareness; the engaged heart, affected by love, awakens passion."[20] The church that continues to live primarily in the head is a people yet in bondage in Egypt. Follow me as I unfold a helpful and interesting insight from Christian missions specialists.

Evangelical missiologists state that there are three principal ways of gaining knowledge: the *intellectualist or conceptual* way common in the West, the *intuitional or mystical* way used in the East, and the *concrete, relational* way followed by tribal peoples worldwide. Because it is in this arena of *knowing* that we run into conflict among Christian thinkers and leaders, let's examine these three ways of knowing more closely.

The Western way emphasizes critical thinking and logical consistency. Western thinking seeks to define, analyze, categorize, and system-build. It seeks exact and precise answers to theological questions. This kind of thinking occurs in the Pauline doctrinal treatises in Romans, Ephesians, and Colossians.

The Eastern mind, however, pursues truth through intuition and experience. This approach pays less regard to logic, theories, or dogmas. For the Eastern mind, truth is perceived through a flash of intuition or a sudden insight born out of contemplation. Biblical parallels include knowledge communicated through dreams, visions, or direct impressions by the Spirit on the heart.

Tribal people worldwide, as mentioned, present a third way. They seek knowledge concretely through symbols, parables, proverbs, and storytelling. During missionary service in Africa, I was impressed how this very earthy way of thinking differed from our Western intellectualist approach. Instead of making a propositional statement, Africans tell a story laden with pictures from their surroundings.

Old Testament poets, prophets, and sages used sensory-rich word pictures to impart spiritual truths. So did Jesus, in His highly concrete and symbolic teaching through parables.

Missions specialist David Hesselgrave says, "The human tendency toward idolatry is present in all three types of thinking." But he adds, "In the early history of Christianity, conceptual thinking fashioned the *mental* idols of Gnosticism which were every bit as offensive to God as the *metal* images of the cult of

Diana in Ephesus."[21] Isn't it ironic that Gnosticism was a heresy created by the mind?

Hesselgrave asserts that although one particular form of knowing may predominate in a given culture, each approach becomes unbalanced unless informed by the other two ways of knowing. Therefore full-orbed knowledge will employ *all three* methods: the intellectualist, the intuitive, and the concrete-relational. Intellectual system-building, on its own, which characterizes evangelical thinking, becomes unbalanced if it neglects crucial aspects of truth in the biblical sense.

Let's be clear: The strength of the intellect is its ability to define issues with precision and closure. From its inherent logic, the intellect portrays matters as either black or white. But the transcendent and majestic God, as well as the spiritual life of the Christian, contains at least a granule of gray. Hear the apostle Paul: "Now we know only a little" (1 Corinthians 13:9) and "Now we see things imperfectly as in a poor mirror, . . . All that I know now is partial and incomplete" (verse 12). Our knowledge of God and His ways is only fragmentary.

As Christians, therefore, we must be prepared to live with a measure of ambiguity. By this I don't mean absence of theological conviction; I refer to that measure of uncertainty that characterizes the finite life we are in before our welcome into the full presence of our infinite God. In the invisible, spiritual realm, the sensing and feeling heart—the right brain—functions in complementary ways to the logical intellect—the left brain. In short, God created us with both left and right sides of the brain, and so He is the one who gave us the ability to know in our heart—that is, to "sense" what is right and true—sometimes before we can "logically explain" or "defend" it.

We must face the fact, some of us, that with our logical bent, intuitive-type Christians can be threatening. In the past when I met a believer whose spirit seemed more alive than my own, I sometimes felt inadequate. A correct response would have been to say, "Look at what I have been missing all these years. I want to rededicate myself to pursuing a deeper walk with Christ." Instead I tended to retreat to the stronghold of my logical mind. It was more comfortable, and less risky, to dwell in the domain of the dogmatic than to engage experiential realities.

It takes strength and courage to move out of our comfort zones and claim new ground spiritually. And in fact, our greatest potential for growth lies in our areas of weakness. When truth remains in the head, we shrivel up and become spiritually lifeless. But when the head engages the heart, new life is brought forth.

Listen to an Oxford-trained, evangelical pastor from Britain:

> Evangelicals have rightly stressed the use of the mind in listening to God, but sadly they have not always realized that God's words must penetrate more deeply than the mind, to affect conscience, heart and will as well. The result has been a generation of evangelicals with a good knowledge of Christian doctrine, but with a shallowness in spirituality and little realization of the depth of fellowship and intimacy with himself to which God calls us. . . . We need to learn again how to bridge the gulf between intellectual understanding and heart-warming devotion.[22]

Hingley asks, "What should be the evangelical response to the modern interest in spirituality?" Then he replies, "My belief is that it should be one of qualified welcome. It is as foolish to dismiss it all as a perversion of the gospel, or a manifestation of the New Age movement, as it is to accept all that it teaches uncritically."[23] Sincere Christians can be too cautious and critical about life-giving, spiritual resources.

Fifth, the criticisms levied against the renewal of evangelical spirituality today reflect a lack of humility and charity.

The excoriation of many Christian movements and leaders communicates the messages that "I alone have the truth" and "the majority of faithful Christians today are wrong." A Reformed missionary statesman recently commented to me that such protests "show very little love for brothers and sisters in Christ with whom we will spend eternity together in Christ's presence."

In the final Judgment, we may be embarrassed that we have maligned fellow believers to whom Jesus will say, "Well done, my good and faithful servant. . . . Let's celebrate together!" (Matthew 25:21,23). We need to practice, not merely preach, the rule of love. "Dear children, let us stop just saying we love each other; let us really show it by our actions" (1 John 3:18). Satan breeds distrust among God's people. Let's not give him any opening to divide and conquer the body of Christ.

Rediscovering Christian Spirituality: A Case Study

The following true account (with names changed) casts light on one couple's discovery of authentic Christian spirituality. Ben was a typical believer, preparing for Christian ministry in a leading evangelical seminary. After taking courses and participating in the life of the seminary, he came to the conclusion that the faculty were good people, expert in their fields, and theologically orthodox. But he sensed something missing in the life of the school. Ben couldn't escape the conviction that while the seminary taught him *about Jesus*, it did not reflect to him the *person of Jesus.*

Ben and his wife, Candy, began to attend a Catholic retreat center in another city. They entered into experiences of silence, prayer, uplifting worship, and spiritual direction. Their understanding of the Christian life expanded as they learned how to love and obey Christ more fully through the Scriptures. Over time, this experience produced a marked deepening of their personal relationship with Christ.

Ben and Candy, however, recognized a potential problem. They struggled with the fact that the theology of their mentors at the center was not as conservative as their teachers at the evangelical seminary. Some sisters held a lower view of biblical authority. A few subscribed to critical theories, such as the documentary hypothesis of the Pentateuch. The couple was torn between two options. Should they follow the way of a more precise orthodoxy, which appears to embody a less vital spirituality? Or should they walk the path of a slightly weaker theology, joined to a more vibrant spirituality?

After committing the matter to the Lord in prayer, Ben and Candy made their decision. They would be discriminating and selective. They would choose the better part from each tradition. They would preserve and honor the strict theological orthodoxy of the evangelical seminary. But following the leading of the Spirit, they would open their hearts to the spiritually enriching way of life they discovered at the renewal center. They believed this choice would maximize their growth in doctrine, in conduct, and in devotion to Jesus Christ. God blessed this decision, and today they are spiritually mature servants, fruitfully serving Jesus Christ.

I offer this testimony to encourage you in your exploration of Christian spirituality. Let it guide you in two ways. First, make a renewed commitment to knowing the Bible. Read, study, and learn the Word of God. And at the same time, be willing to pursue new ways to sense God's presence, direction, and work in your life. What you stand to gain is a deeper encounter with the God who lives in believing hearts.

Try It Yourself

1. Knowing your own "grid," or comfort zone.

- What spiritual practices make you feel uncomfortable? Raising your hands and singing loud praise songs? Sitting in silent contemplation? Group prayer?

- What Christian groups, denominations, or spiritualities make you uncomfortable? Conservatives? Catholics? Charismatics?
- What makes you uncomfortable with these groups or their teaching? (I'm not asking what you *disagree* with, but what it is that makes you feel anxious or uncertain about them.)
- Do you think you might gain by relaxing and opening up to their views and practices?

2. Evaluating evangelical spiritual authorities.

Consider three or four evangelical spiritual writers you may be familiar with, whose views were not developed (for lack of space) in this chapter. Where would you place them on the spectrum of Christian spirituality? Why do you believe they belong where you have placed them? Names to consider might include Francis Schaeffer, Brennan Manning, Ken Gire, Max Lucado, John Piper, and Philip Yancey.

Suggestions for Further Reading

McDermott, Gerald R. *Seeing God: 12 Reliable Signs of True Spirituality.* Downers Grove, Ill.: InterVarsity, 1995.

Schaeffer, Francis. *A Christian View of Spirituality.* Westchester, Ill.: Crossway, 1984.

Toon, Peter. *What Is Spirituality?* London: Daybreak, 1989.

CHAPTER FOUR

Knowing God . . . As Intimates

"O God, you are my God; I earnestly search for you. My soul thirsts for you; my whole body longs for you in this parched and weary land where there is no water. I have seen you in the sanctuary and gazed upon your power and glory."

PSALM 63:1-2

"God wills that we should push into His presence and live our whole life there. This is to be known to us in conscious experience. It is more than a doctrine to be held; it is a life to be enjoyed every moment of every day."

A. W. TOZER[1]

"The knowledge of God is the most glorious treasure anyone could possess, yet in most civilized countries there is but one institution engaged in promoting that knowledge, and even that institution is not working very hard at it."

A. W. TOZER[2]

One of the hallmark claims of evangelical Christian spirituality is this: We promise the new believer a heart-connectedness to God through Christ. This promise comes straight out of the gospel, which offers both a doctrine to believe *and* a restored relationship with the God of the universe to enjoy. Besides the Scriptures, we also appeal to question 1 of the Westminster Shorter Catechism (1648) which asks, "What is the chief end of man?" The answer given is, " . . . to glorify God and to *enjoy Him forever*" (emphasis added).

It should disturb us then, when a Christian has a decent understanding of the faith and faithfully serves God, but Christ's presence is missing from his or her life. We find it easier to *perform for* God, rather than to learn how to *be aware and work along with* Him.

In this chapter we explore the deeper relationship God wants with us, His redeemed and reconciled children.

Connecting with Christ

In any relationship, it's easy to get caught up doing things for someone, rather than learning to *communicate*, *understand*, and *cooperate with* him or her in any endeavor. For instance, a mother may think it's too frustrating to get her child to make his bed, so she makes it herself—thereby cutting out all the relationship-building steps that train the child to cooperate with her *and* learn responsibility. True, the work gets done, but at the expense of a relationship that's growing in love and training in cooperative obedience.

In the same way, we too often get caught up in *doing* for God. Is it any surprise that all our striving, apart from a daily, directed, in-step relationship with Christ, leaves us feeling full of "wood, hay, or straw" in our souls (see 1 Corinthians 3:12)? Great saints of old, such as Isaiah, Paul, and Augustine, encountered God, spoke to God, and were led by God with their hearts as well as their minds. For many Christians today, however, God is a fuzzy and distant vagueness. Do they attend church, give money, and serve God? Yes. But do they know they are conforming to Christ's image by walking closely with Him? Too many admit the answer is no.

We are often like the disciple Philip, to whom Jesus said: "Have I been with you all this time . . . and you still do not know me?" (John 14:9, NRSV). God's people will not be fulfilled and fruitful until they engage God's heart and live in His presence.

"Have I Been with You All This Time?"

"I just don't sense God at work in my life. I know I'm not supposed to depend on feelings, but is this plodding repetition all there is to the Christian life? Or this feeling that I'm not really pleasing God because I fail Him so often?"

Have you ever felt this way? The truth is, God is always at work in our lives (see John 5:17), trying to communicate with us through events and other people, and waiting to ignite His written Word within our hearts. God always seeks us out before we seek Him.

We see this in Genesis, when God reached down to Abram, an obscure Chaldean in the land of Ur. As God awakened Abram to His presence, He gave awesome promises and invited Abram's obedient response (see Genesis 12:1-3). Moses, likewise, was minding his business, tending sheep in the wilderness, when the angel of the Lord (God Himself) appeared to him in a fiery bush (see Exodus 3:1-6). God called to the prophet-to-be Jeremiah while he was yet a fetus, saying, "Before I formed you in the womb I knew you, before you were born I set you apart" (Jeremiah 1:5, NIV).

The same pattern continues in the New Testament. Jesus reached out to Simon and Andrew (see Mark 1:16-17), James and John (see Mark 1:19-20), and Matthew (see Mark 2:14) and called them to be His disciples. Paul, en route to Damascus to crush the fledgling church, was struck blind by the glorified

Christ (see Acts 9:3-9) and later wrote about God's intervention in our lives, saying, "Now that you have found God (or should I say, now that God has found you . . ." (Galatians 4:9).

It is clear that God is seeking us in both subtle and surprising ways, all the time. And as C. S. Lewis put it, "When you come to knowing God, the initiative lies on His side. If He does not show Himself, nothing you can do will enable you to find Him."[3]

How astonishing that the infinite Creator of the universe should seek out undeserving people for heart-to-heart relationship. But this is what He does! Let's consider what satisfying connectedness with the living God means for our lives.

Relationship, Not Frenetic Activity

Do we understand what it takes to build a relationship *at all*, let alone a relationship with God?

The Bible affirms the virtues of "faith, hope, and love" (1 Corinthians 13:13), and to that many Christians add a fourth virtue: *busyness* for God. Many find that the crush of daily life prevents them from really relating even to their spouse or children. Communion with the God of the universe? Who has time for that? And then from the pulpit we're challenged to roll up our sleeves and get busy for God. The pastor of the church in which I was raised urged us to "burn out for Jesus!" as if a total breakdown makes you a good Christian!

In his informative book, *Exit Interviews*, William Hendricks questioned Christians who voluntarily left evangelical churches. His research shows that believers who withdrew from membership failed to find *God* in the maze of programs. Hendricks concludes that many spiritually starved Christians are exiting the church to search for God outside its walls.[4]

The badge of busyness we so proudly wear is a demon of our times. Our competitive, survival-of-the-fittest culture is unabashedly performance-driven. And so are we in the church. We find our identity and measure our worth in what and how much we accomplish.

Listening to God? Whatever for? Don't we already have the

marching order—"Go into all the world . . . teach . . . make disciples"? Learning to be open and directable—isn't that a waste of time? Learning to "rest" our spirits in God—isn't that an excuse for not obeying God? The demon of busyness whispers in our ears, also blinding our eyes to the fact that our pressured lives leave us irritable, uncaring, vulnerable, and guilt-ridden when we see that we haven't accomplished everything on our spiritual "to do" list. Compassion grows numb, God gets put on hold, and the flesh quenches the Spirit.

Do you see how the hyperactivity that crowds God out actually kills the soul?

A fulfilling and empowering connection with God cannot develop in busyness. It comes in quietness and prayer, and as we act under His peaceful guidance in concern for others. Nourishing the inner man comes through relationship (being). The inner man is drained as the result of compulsion (legalism) and hyperactivity (doing). The life empowered to obey God only flows from a heart relationship with Him, in the manner of Christ. With this in mind, we can understand Jesus' words: "Yes, I am the vine; you are the branches. Those who remain in me, and I in them, will produce much fruit. For apart from me you can do nothing" (John 15:5). Only as we are graced with God's peaceful presence are we really equipped to serve Him.

Intimacy, Not Amassing Information

Some Christians seek spiritual satisfaction through intellectual pursuits. So they seriously devour books on church history, theology, and the like. Followers of this path learn a great deal *about God;* but they may know less about *God Himself.* Following the intellectual path, we accumulate facts with which to refute theological foes and impress fellow believers. But our knowledge may be brain-deep rather than life-deep. As a legacy of the eighteenth-century Enlightenment, evangelicals often extol "reason" as the key that unlocks knowledge of God. Theology then becomes an intellectual undertaking—an activity *of* the mind, *for* the mind.

Morton Kelsey observes that "In Protestantism, God became a theological idea known by inference rather than a reality known by experience."[5] Through a "left-brain" approach to the faith, God easily becomes an abstraction removed from lived experience. A. W. Tozer noted that even as many scientists lose God in His world (for example, Carl Sagan), so many theologians lose God in His Word.[6]

Intellectual truth forms the framework of a biblical spirituality. But gaining head knowledge of God without engaging the heart of God brings dryness to the soul. Lack of God-consciousness through personal encounter explains why some seminarians complain of spiritual deadness amidst perfectly orthodox studies. The goal of Christian spirituality is not information, it is transformation into the likeness of Christ. On the subject of food sacrificed to idols, Paul wrote,

> You think that everyone should agree with your perfect knowledge. While knowledge may make us feel important, it is love that really builds up the church. Anyone who claims to know all the answers doesn't really know very much. . . . So because of your superior knowledge, a weak Christian, for whom Christ died, will be destroyed. (1 Corinthians 8:1-2,11)

Christians need to view God less as a *proposition* to be scrutinized and more as a *Person* to be engaged with the heart.

Heart knowledge means loving God with all our faculties of thinking, intuiting, willing, feeling, and relating. It's a knowledge formed by personal connection and lived experience, not by intellectualizing alone. We are to deepen in knowledge of God through our hearts, without losing our minds. We must remain doctrinally orthodox, but we must also press on to know God with immediacy in the core of our being.

Heart knowledge encompasses the wisdom and insight of *encounter*. The biblical root words behind our word to *know* signify that, in addition to gaining information, there is an intimate knowing through active personal engagement (see Matthew 7:23).

It's the knowledge a married couple acquires through sexual union (see Genesis 4:1, Luke 1:34). It's the terrible knowledge Adam and Eve acquired when they disobeyed God and it sank in, too late, that grasping for the forbidden knowledge of good and evil separated them from God (see Genesis 3:5,22).

Knowing God, therefore, requires us to engage all our created capacities and energies. So Yahweh says to His people, "I don't want your sacrifices. I want you to know [me]" (Hosea 6:6). Listen to the apostle Paul: "I want to know Christ and the power of his resurrection" (Philippians 3:10, NIV). Paul was deeply committed to truth *about* Jesus as well as to the truth *of* Jesus.

As I mentioned before, in times past I tended to live in the atmosphere of pure thought. But after experiencing conversion as a matter of the heart, I began to be consumed with *Christ Himself*, as a living reality in the core of my being. I know far better now what Paul meant when he said, "Yes, everything else is worthless when compared with the priceless gain of knowing Christ Jesus my Lord. I have discarded everything else, counting it all as garbage, so that I may have Christ and become one with him" (Philippians 3:8-9).

Heart knowledge comes from interacting with God, allowing Him to powerfully transform us (see Isaiah 60:16; Hosea 6:6; Galatians 2:20; 1 John 4:7,13). This kind of transformation comes when you open yourself at a deep level with another person. It requires closeness, vulnerability, disclosure, shared history, and *complete trust.*

This is where our hearts turn to jelly. Why? Because surrendering all that's in us to God is threatening. First and foremost, it means giving up our tendency to insist on our own way. It means giving over our will to God and ceasing in our efforts to control others—even, at times, God Himself.

Yet, somewhere within, haven't we always known it? That intimacy with God will only grow as we become open and present to the One who is always present to us (see Exodus 3:14, Revelation 3:20)? Haven't we always sensed that life would indeed change for the better, if only we would overcome our own resistance to Him and allow Him to do what comes naturally, that is, to embrace, nurture, and lovingly correct our course?

The spiritual master Bernard of Clairvaux (d. 1153) beautifully depicted intimacy as casting our heart into God (see Colossians 3:1). When we become intimate with God, our emptiness and loneliness vanish like mist before the rising sun. Christians must not stop at the word God speaks, but press on until we encounter the God who speaks the Word.

Face to Face

Some Christians feel uncomfortable with this talk of intimacy with God. Intimacy conjures syrupy images of sweethearts on a romantic moonlit walk. But the joint chiefs of staff are "intimate" with the president of the United States in that they share opinions, views, and strategies that the rest of the nation and the world are not privy to. They know each other's minds and innermost attitudes and, perhaps, each other's personal hot-buttons, soapbox agendas, and quirks.

Intimacy is not to be confused with moons and Junes and mere *infatuation* (from the Latin word meaning "to make foolish"). Augustine described infatuation as falling in love with love.[7] You may know people who became infatuated with God in a sudden burst of energy that soon burned out. This kind of energy comes from being attracted to another for selfish reasons. It makes you feel good, but fails to genuinely engage the other person's soul; it fails to recognize the *face* of the person's inner being.

Learning to dwell in the presence of God requires us to step out from behind our shame and pretense, also our head knowledge and our good works, to show God who we really are on the inside. And then to look long and hard into the face of who He is. The Hebrew word for *presence* also can mean "face," suggesting that we can have a face-to-face (presence-to-Presence) intimacy with the Lord through the Spirit. The Bible tells us that angels (see Luke 1:19), wisdom (see Proverbs 8:30), and Christ (see John 8:38, Hebrews 9:24) abide in God's holy presence. The infinite God of the universe invites every believer to abide in His awesome presence. David wrote, "You will show me the way of life, granting me the joy of your presence and the pleasures of living with you forever" (Psalm 16:11). Again: "Happy are those who hear the joyful call to worship, for they will walk in the light of your presence, LORD" (Psalm 89:15).

What can be clearer than these assertions from Scripture that we *can* live in God's presence here and now? That is, we can let the truth about our inner man—with all our struggles, hopes, failures, dreams, and needs—come out into the light of God's nurturing presence. Only in His light, open and surrendered, can we *know* forgiveness, redirection, and transformation that changes us day by day until the distinct pureness, sweetness, and obedience of Jesus Christ—those invisible but distinct lights of glory that evidence His presence in us—begin to show themselves in our lives.

The chorus of the song, *In His Presence*, includes these uplifting words:

> In Your presence, that's where I am strong.
> In Your presence, . . . that's where I belong.
> Seeking Your face, touching Your grace,
> In the cleft of the Rock, in Your presence, O God.[8]

As I have alluded elsewhere, it is God who "fathers" these changes in our inner being. Or else they do not come at all; we cannot drum them up. But we expect to grow in such strong heart-bonds to God that His qualities "flow," like the nourishing fluids in a vine, to us. And so, eternal life is not only *imputed* to us; because of Jesus' astonishing blood sacrifice that life also *becomes real* in us.

Abraham Kuyper (d. 1920), a great Reformed theologian and prime minister of the Netherlands, wrote, "When we know God Almighty as a presence on the paths of our lives, when we have entered into a personal, particular relationship with him, then and only then does he become our Father in heaven." Kuyper added, "What we're talking about here is a relationship so personal and intimate that it can't be described in words. If you don't understand, you don't *know* God at that level. But if you deeply desire to know him in that way, then you're already on the right track."[9]

It is rightly said that God has no favorites, but He does have His intimates. Do you long to experience the passionate flame of His loving and renewing presence?

Communion, Not Metaphysical Union

To know God's presence within. That's a tough one, isn't it? Many Christians find it easy to think of the Lord as dwelling outside of them. But it's more difficult to grasp what it means to know Him as a Lover who dwells in us.

In his letters, Paul used the expression "in Christ" (also "in him," "in the Lord") 164 times. This phrase encompasses an extraordinary truth: Christ dwells in the Christian (see Romans 8:10, Galatians 2:20, Colossians 1:27), and the Christian dwells in Christ (see 1 Corinthians 15:22, 2 Corinthians 5:17). Jesus brings these two relations together, saying, "When I am raised to life again, you will know that . . . you are in me, and I am in you" (John 14:20, compare 15:4).

What does this mean?

The union of Christ and the believer is, first, a *positional union.* Prior to our conversion, God reckoned us as situated in Adam (see 1 Corinthians 15:22)—that is, totally fallen, lost, and blind. But justified by faith, He reckons us as positioned in the sphere of Christ's saving work (see Romans 8:1, 1 Corinthians 15:22).

Let's be clear, though: The union between us and God, in Christ, is *not an essential union.* My finite being does not unite with God's infinite being. Gnostics and certain mystics falsely claim that spiritual Christians become absorbed into the divine life, thereby losing their individuality. Communion with Christ involves a meeting and a marriage, but not a merging or melting of our humanity into His divinity.

Still, our union with Christ is an *experiential union.* We are indwelt, nourished, and empowered by Christ through the Spirit.

Jesus said, "All those who love me will do what I say. My Father will love them, and we will come to them and live with them" (John 14:23). Think of it this way. What the Evangelists recorded in the Gospels was the sweat, blood, tears, and elation they experienced with Jesus. Fishermen and tax collectors came to Jesus, listened to His teachings, witnessed His works, and observed His devotion to the Father. The Evangelists' *theology* of Jesus in the Gospels is rather thin. But their *experience* of Jesus is rich—so strong and convincing, in fact, that it prompted them to lay down their lives for Him. Experience changed them from timid, lukewarm followers into tenacious, blazing disciples of the risen Lord.

Paul's writing makes it plain that Christians *will* experience the living God because they are His dwelling place. He wrote, "Don't you know that your body is the temple of the Holy Spirit, who lives in you and was given to you by God?" (1 Corinthians 6:19, compare 1 Corinthians 3:16, 2 Corinthians 6:16). Paul likened our bodies to the inner sanctuary *(naos)* of the temple in Jerusalem, where the Divine Presence uniquely rested. How awesome that the infinite and majestic God of the universe literally indwells our mortal bodies!

What we have lacked as conservative Christians is a practical theology of experience. No, experience is not the *summum bonum* of the faith, but it is a necessary means by which we know God in such a way that we grow in conviction and present a convincing witness to the world by the power of our lives. Through experience, the teachings of Scripture come to life in the very chambers of our heart. It is the heart that detects God's gentle whisper. The Lord said to Isaiah, "Whether you turn to the right or to the left, your ears will hear a voice behind you, saying, 'This is the way; walk in it'" (Isaiah 30:21, NIV). To many Christian authorities, "human experience is the very 'stuff' of spirituality."[10]

True Encounters

What does Christian encounter and experience of God look and feel like? Let me suggest several features of authentic, spiritual experience.

First, we can expect that an encounter with God, in the humble spirit of Jesus Christ, will produce a deep sense of *connectedness* with Him through the Spirit. With John Wesley, we may find our hearts "strangely warmed" by the indwelling Holy Spirit. We may sense this warmth as beloved children of the Father even in encounters when God deals with us about sin, because we know He is exposing corruption not to shame or degrade us, but to free us from its deadly effects.

Second, Christians are likely to experience a strong sense of *God's undeserved love* for them. "See how very much our heavenly Father loves us, for he allows us to be called his children" (1 John 3:1). Tears of joy, expressions of awed worship, may flow spontaneously from awareness of His majesty, sovereignty, goodness and righteousness, all encompassed in boundless love.

Third, we also perceive that *God accepts us* in spite of our painful imperfections. As Paul wrote to flawed and struggling believers, "accept each other *just as Christ has accepted you*" (Romans 15:7, emphasis added).

Fourth, our identity in Jesus is another characteristic of real encounter with God. In His accepting and affirming presence, we know our status as children of the Father by creation and redemption (Galatians 4:6). We are transformed as we learn to let go of our old need for external validation of our worth, because our soul finds validity as a son or daughter of the living God. We find a new steadiness within, knowing that we are people of eternity, even in the midst of life's trials and afflictions (see Job 2:7, Acts 9:16, James 1:2, 1 Peter 1:6).

Fifth, Christians deeply feel a range of spiritual affections born of the Spirit. These include *joy* (mentioned 235 times in the Bible: Psalm 21:6, Romans 14:17, Galatians 5:22); *peace* (see Psalm 29:11, Isaiah 26:3, John 14:27); *gratefulness* (see Ephesians 5:20, Colossians 3:16); *tenderheartedness* (see Proverbs 4:3, Ephesians 4:32); and *spiritual desire* (see 1 Peter 2:2).

America's greatest theologian, Jonathan Edwards (d. 1758), claimed in his classic book *Religious Affections* that true religion must include the cultivation of the heart's affections. A person who does not possess affections that stir the soul is not growing in Christ.

Experience is not the means by which finite man reaches upward to lay hold of God. On the contrary, experience is an important avenue by which God reaches down to touch us. Virtually everything we know about God has come through believing other people's experiences—from Moses, David, and Isaiah to Paul and John. Our experiences must be checked against Scripture, but the Christian's experience of God is not as problematic as some allege. C. S. Lewis helps us out again:

> What I like about experience is that it is such an honest thing. You may take any number of wrong turnings; but keep your eyes open and you will not be allowed to go very far before the warning signs appear. You may have deceived yourself, but experience is not trying to deceive you. The universe rings true wherever you fairly test it.[11]

Our hunger for relationship, intimacy, and communion with God is not self-absorption, irrational escapism, or some sort of Gnostic esotericism. It is a God-given desire for a fulfilling, lived experience of the Lover of our souls—Jesus—who welcomes us into fellowship with Himself. By all means, let's understand the truth God has revealed in His Word. But Christians who do not find authentic connection with God in their churches are vulnerable and are likely to succumb to transcendent experiences offered by Eastern religions, the New Age movement, and the occult. The hunger you cannot satisfy at home may drive you to find satisfaction elsewhere.

Our God offers to fill us within with the experiential knowledge that comes from a heart encounter with Him, in Christ.

Encounters with God in the Word

The Bible is not timid when it paints the nature of our relationship with God. Its images are bold and engaging. Although our present knowledge of God is still a distant cry from what it will be (see 1 Corinthians 13:9,12), four images ignite excitement in my heart as they reveal the height, breadth, and depth of our relationship with the Father, in Christ.

God-Chosen People

The Old Testament teaches that by a holy covenant, Yahweh became Israel's God and they became His special people (see Genesis 17:7, Exodus 6:7, Ezekiel 11:20).

The New Testament represents the Jewish-Gentile church as the new people of God (see 1 Peter 2:9, Revelation 18:4). Scripture abounds with statements about God's heart-bond with His people.

God loves His people *unconditionally*. Moses said to Israel, "The LORD did not choose you and lavish his love on you because you were larger or greater than other nations, for you were the smallest of all nations! It was simply because the LORD loves you" (Deuteronomy 7:7-8, compare Deuteronomy 33:3). God's covenant with His believing people is "a covenant of unfailing love" (Deuteronomy 7:12).

The people of God are *specially chosen*. The Lord said to Israel, "From among all the families on the earth, I chose you alone" (Amos 3:2, compare Deuteronomy 7:6, 10:15, 14:2). God has graciously chosen believers in Christ, individually and corporately, to be His unique people (see Colossians 3:12, 1 Peter 2:9).

As chosen people, we are *pleasing to Him*. Paul wrote that "our lives are a fragrance presented by Christ to God" (2 Corinthians 2:15). Clothed with the righteousness of Christ, believers find favor in His eyes (2 Corinthians 5:21).

And *God dwells among His people*. As saints, we are the privileged habitation of God. The Lord says, "I will live among you, and . . . I will walk among you" (Leviticus 26:11-12). How marvelous it is that the savor of God's presence goes with us wherever we go.

Parent-Child

This biblical relationship describes our intimacy with God using both father-son and mother-child images. On the paternal side, Yahweh is Israel's Father (see Deuteronomy 32:6, Isaiah 63:16) and Israel is His son (see Exodus 4:22-23, Isaiah 1:2-4, Hosea 11:1). The Lord said to David, "I will be his father, and he will be my son. . . . my unfailing love will not be taken from him" (2 Samuel 7:14-15). By the miracle of the new birth, Christians call God "our Father" (see Matthew 6:9, 1 Thessalonians 3:11), even "Father, dear Father" (see Romans 8:15, compare Galatians 4:6). Every believer in Christ is God's specially adopted child (see Romans 8:14-17,19,21,23).

Of His maternal passions, the Lord says, in a figure, "Can a mother forget her nursing child? Can she feel no love for a child she has borne? But even if that were possible, I would not forget you!" (Isaiah 49:15). Should a mother's love fail, God's love will not falter in the slightest. Here's another insight, from the Psalms: "I have stilled and quieted myself, just as a small child is quiet with its mother. Yes, like a small child is my soul within me" (Psalm 131:2). A nursing infant can be agitated in its quest for nourishing milk, but God's tender care gives our soul such satisfaction that we experience greater security and intimacy—and rest—than that child in its mother's arms.

The parent-child likenesses in Scripture are other expressions of what our soul may encounter in quest for fullness in God. We can know that we're recipients of the Father's special love (see 1 John 4:9-11) and care (see Deuteronomy 1:31, Luke 11:11-13). We are not lone wanderers in an empty universe; we bear a new name and belong to a new family as "God's children" (1 John 3:2). As spiritual sons and daughters, we experience the glory of God's Spirit in us (see Romans 8:15, Galatians 4:6). And we enjoy the privilege of free access into the Father's holy presence (see Hebrews 4:14-16).

Lover-Beloved

The love relationship between husband and wife offers a human picture of the bond of affection between Christ and the believer. The Old Testament pictures Yahweh as Israel's faithful husband (see Isaiah 54:5, Hosea 2:16) and Israel as His wife (see Isaiah 62:4, Hosea 2:2). Yahweh steadfastly loves

His people (Jeremiah 31:32) and takes great delight in them. "God will rejoice over you as a bridegroom rejoices over his bride" (Isaiah 62:5). And in spite of Israel's constant rejections, Yahweh refused to abandon His "wife." In love and faithfulness He called her back and renewed the marriage covenant (Hosea 2:14, 3:1), saying, "I will make you my wife forever, showing you righteousness and justice, unfailing love and compassion" (2:19). Moved by this act of grace, the bride repents and clings to her husband (see Jeremiah 2:2). The prophet speaks for the beloved: "I am overwhelmed with joy in the LORD my God! . . . I am like a bridegroom in his wedding suit or a bride with her jewels" (Isaiah 61:10).

The New Testament portrays Christ as the church's bridegroom (see Matthew 25:1-10, 2 Corinthians 11:2), and God's people as His betrothed (see 2 Corinthians 11:2; Revelation 21:2,9). The Puritan preachers treasured the image of the mystical marriage between Christ and His people. The Bridegroom tenderly cares for His bride as His own body (see Ephesians 5:29). The beloved is satisfied and reciprocates when she senses that she receives the Lover's gift. So great is the Bridegroom's love that He surrenders His life for His bride (see Ephesians 5:25).

Do we hear our heavenly Spouse say, "I love you"? Do we respond with love for Him? Here is a marriage that will never be broken. Lover and beloved will enjoy perfect communion throughout eternity (Revelation 21:2-3).

May our response be that of the prophet Hosea, who exhorts the beloved: "Oh, that we might know the LORD! Let us press on to know him! Then he will respond to us as surely as the arrival of dawn or the coming of rains in early spring" (Hosea 6:3).

Shepherd-Sheep

Sheep are wayward creatures of habit that require more care than most any other domestic animal. Scripture pictures Yahweh as the shepherd (see Psalm 23:1, Ezekiel 34:12) and Israel as His flock. The Lord says to His people, "You are my flock, the sheep of my pasture" (Ezekiel 34:31). Similarly, Christ is the "good shepherd" (John 10:1-18, compare Hebrews 13:20), and His people are the "sheep" or "lambs" (John 21:15-17). The *rō 'eh yiśrā'ēl* (shepherd of Israel) is a type of the Lord Jesus—a patient and loving caretaker of the sheep.

God's patient love for us becomes clear as we understand the relationship between this Shepherd and His sheep.

The Shepherd *knows each of us intimately.* "He calls his own sheep by name and leads them out" (John 10:3).

He *nourishes us.* "I will give them good pasture land on the high hills of Israel. There they will lie down in pleasant places and feed in lush mountain pastures" (Ezekiel 34:14).

The Shepherd *searches for us when we wander from the fold.* Yahweh says, "I will find my sheep and rescue them from all the places to which they were scattered" (Ezekiel 34:12, compare verse 16). "'Not a single one of them will be lost or missing,' says the LORD" (Jeremiah 23:4).

The Shepherd *stands constant guard over us.* "He will carry the lambs in his arms, holding them close to his heart. He will gently lead the mother sheep with their young" (Isaiah 40:11). And David declares, "We are the people he watches over, the sheep under his care" (Psalm 95:7, compare Psalm 78:52).

The Shepherd *communicates with us, and we are taught to listen to His voice* (see John 10:3, compare verse 16). The Shepherd sings over us, and as we experience His gentle peacefulness, our souls are made to rest quietly within us (see Ezekiel 34:15).

Finally, in the ultimate act of love, the Shepherd *lays down his life for us* (see John 10:11, compare verse 15). Jesus is our "good shepherd." In goodness and mercy He leads us through life's rugged terrain and provides for our deepest needs.

Obstacles to Really Knowing God

Of course we know relationships don't develop smoothly. They go through delightful highs and painful lows.

We're baffled when we don't experience God's presence, when prayer is dry dust, or when the sense of God's love is cold. There are two main obstacles that block our loving communion with Him.

Unconfessed Sin

Sin that we refuse to uncover corrodes our connection with the Lord. In Psalm 15 David muses, "Who may worship in your sanctuary, LORD? Who may enter your presence on your holy hill?" (verse 1). His answer? "Those who lead blameless lives and do what is right, speaking the truth from sincere hearts" (verse 2).

Sin is a plant with a broad root system. One root of sin is *self-centeredness.* Love turned in on itself chokes off love for God. J. B. Phillips observed that "the sins which do most damage and cause most suffering are those which have the highest content of self-love."[12] Another root of sin is *unbelief.* When Christians abandon faith in God, they relinquish the basis for fellowship (Hebrews 11:6). John wrote, "We are lying if we say we have fellowship with God but go on living in spiritual darkness. We are not living in the truth. But if we are living in the light of God's presence, . . . then we have fellowship with each other, and the blood of Jesus, his Son, cleanses us from every sin" (1 John 1:6-7).

A Christian psychiatrist who has practiced for nearly forty years reports that the first question he asks each patient suffering an emotional problem is this: "Are there any unconfessed sins in your life?" He's well prepared to use standard techniques of psychiatric evaluation and treatment, but from long experience he's concluded that unresolved sin is the immediate cause of much emotional disturbance and illness.

Breakdown of Communication

God is faithfully present to His children through the Spirit (John 14:16,23). But there are times when we willfully distance ourselves from Him. One Christian mystic observes how prone we are to wander from God: "God is in, we are out; God is at home, we are strangers."[13]

Growing intimacy requires that I pay careful attention to the other person. When that other is God, it's necessary to still my own voice and listen in quietness. Then I can detect the gentle whispers of the Spirit. Too often we fail to hear God speak because we are not attentively listening.

Relationship suffers due to lack of dialogue. God waits for us to express our love for Him as well as our loneliness and confusion. As we become more comfortable expressing our feelings, affective connectedness to God will grow. Spiritual directors Barry and Connolly observe that "a person who begins simply and wants to share his feelings will gradually find that he has deeper feelings to share."[14]

We may talk with God honestly from our hearts as David did: "I pour out my complaints before him and tell him all my troubles" (Psalm 142:2). James 4:8 (MSG) reads: "Yell a loud *no* to the Devil and watch him scamper. Say a quiet *yes* to God and he'll be there in no time." This Scripture suggests that right now you and I can be as close to God as we choose to be.

The Experience of God

I've noted that some Christians resist experiencing God—perhaps because they fear it will lead them away from the Word into a maze of subjectivity. But many faithful Christians of old spoke vividly about their personal experience of God. Here are a few examples of saints who can teach us in this area.

The Puritans

Famous for their doctrinal orthodoxy and devotion to Jesus Christ, the Puritans were Reformed Protestants in Britain and North America. Leading Puritans include William Perkins (d. 1602), John Owen (d. 1683), Richard Baxter (d. 1691), and John Bunyan (d. 1688). The Puritans had a rich intellectual life, reading the great authors of Christendom as well as the secular classics. But they also enjoyed a robust spirituality, emphasizing the heart knowledge of God through lived experience. These disciplined lovers of Christ saw themselves as people on a spiritual pilgrimage to the New Jerusalem. At the heart of the journey was a passion for communion with God. They took great delight in God, and they knew that God delighted in them.

The spirituality of the Puritans embraced three pillars: *intellectual knowledge, Spirit-directed religious experience,* and *practical obedience.* The Puritans knew the truth with their minds, felt the truth in their hearts, and obeyed the truth in their lives. The Puritan preacher was reluctant to explain a godly truth without having first experienced it in his own heart. Spiritually mature Puritans savored the sweetness of their union with Christ through the five senses. "Taste and see that the LORD is good" (Psalm 34:8) was a favorite Puritan text.

An important part of Puritan spiritual discipline was daily soul examination. The Puritans scrutinized and tested their personal experiences of Christ. They recorded their spiritual struggles, answers to prayer, and experiences of God in diaries and spiritual autobiographies. They gladly shared the fruit of their soul-searching with others for their edification. The Puritans relished the words of the psalmist, "Come and listen, all you who fear God, and I will tell you what he did for me" (Psalm 66:16).

Today, we commonly examine a person's doctrine before admitting him or her to church membership. Puritan candidates also were asked to give *experiential evidences* of the work of grace in their souls. By balancing biblical doctrines with personal experience of the truth, the Puritans avoided a frigid rationalism.

Blaise Pascal (d. 1662)

Pascal was a French mathematician and scientist who, after his conversion, became a powerful apologist to educated unbelievers. For Pascal, reason alone failed to produce full-orbed knowledge of God. The eye can see color and the ear can detect sounds within only a limited wave band. So there are many things (natural and supernatural) that are beyond reason's scope. It is the heart's capacities for "faith, hope, and love" (1 Corinthians 13:13) that most adequately engage God. Pascal treasured the verse from Solomon, "Above all else, guard your heart, for it affects everything you do" (Proverbs 4:23). The heart apprehends God at a glance; the intellect articulates in words and concepts what the heart instinctively knows.

The following short excerpts from Pascal's *Pensées* illustrate his understanding of the relationship between the head and the heart.

"It is the heart which perceives God, and not the reason. That is what faith is: God perceived by the heart, not by the reason" (#424).

Those "who are accustomed to reason from principles, have no understanding of matters involving feeling, because they look for principles and are unable to see things at a glance" (#751).

"What a long way it is," Pascal insists, "between knowing God and loving him!" (#377).

The Christian who by grace has experienced God cannot formally prove this to doubting rationalists. A God whose existence could be proven would not be the God of the Bible. Hence Pascal's most famous saying, "The heart has its reasons of which reason knows nothing" (#423).

Pascal rejected the autonomous reason of the skepticswhile seeking a responsible integration of the head and heart. Some truths about God can be established and explained by reason; others can only be discovered and understood by the heart, which knowledge does not "offend" reason. Pascal was committed to the careful integration of head and heart. He wrote, "If we submit everything to reason, our religion will be left with nothing mysterious or supernatural. If we offend the principles of reason, our religion will be absurd and ridiculous" (#173).

Peter Kreeft nicely summarizes Pascal's position on the believer's knowledge of Christ through the experiencing heart.

> Christ is our God. Experience is not our God. . . . Yet we need to experience Christ, meet Christ, touch Christ, not just believe correct theology about Christ. What we need is not experience without Christ, nor Christ without experience, but the experience of Christ; not psychology or theology but religion, lived relationship.[15]

A. W. Tozer (d. 1963)

The Canadian-born pastor wrote passionately about the believer's relationship with God in the heart. A man of strict biblical orthodoxy, Tozer read widely in the classics of Christian spirituality. Tozer was well ahead of his time in communicating the riches of a contemplative and mystical spirituality to evangelical Christians. Tozer's writings grip the intellect, stir the emotions, and energize the passions.

Tozer identified three sources for knowing God: *knowledge furnished by reason, by faith,* and *by spiritual experience.* These three correspond to the outer court, the holy place, and the holy of holies in the Levitical tabernacle. First, *reason,* working on the data of creation, yields basic knowledge of God's existence, character, and moral demands. Such knowledge does not save. Second, *faith* in the revealed truths of Scripture imparts the knowledge of God that is necessary for salvation. And third, *spiritual experience* affords an immediate knowledge of God in the heart.

Only through personal experience is God's presence known and felt. Tozer wrote, "Through the indwelling Spirit the human spirit is brought into immediate contact with higher spiritual reality. It looks upon, tastes, feels and sees the powers of the world to come and has a conscious encounter with God invisible."[16] Jesus validated experiential knowledge when He said of those who love and obey Him, "I will reveal myself to each one of them" (John 14:21).

Tozer insisted that our formal understanding of God must be drawn from the Bible, but he stressed the interior nature of religion—"Christ in you, the hope of glory" (Colossians 1:27, NIV). Through the Spirit, Christ takes up residence in the believing heart and discloses Himself in a face-to-face meeting. By abiding in Christ, the Christian beholds the Lord, not with physical eyes, but with spiritual sight. The believer senses the tug of the Spirit on the heart and is drawn deeper into the life of Christ. According to Tozer, "The objective Reality which is God must cross the threshold of our personality and take residence within."[17] Through quietness and prayer, the Christian practices the "God-conscious life."

Is Christianity Mystical?

Because many Christians equate "mystical" with "heretical," it's important to raise the question: *Is Christianity mystical or not?* Can biblical people subscribe to some form of mysticism?

In jest it's said that mysticism is something that begins in mist and ends in schism. The term *mysticism* is used by nonChristians as well as by Christians. NonChristian forms of mysticism reject logic, promote dualism, and in some cases promote the loss of individuality through fusion with the divine. Unbiblical forms of mysticism must be rejected, as well as *extreme expressions* of so-called Christian mysticism.

Mysticism is related to the New Testament word *mystērion,* which means "secret" or "mystery" (see 1 Corinthians 2:7; 4:1; Ephesians 1:9; 3:4,9). The God of the Bible is transcendent and infinite Spirit. He "lives in light so brilliant that no human can approach him. No one has ever seen him, nor ever will" (1 Timothy 6:16). In the words of Job, "God is exalted beyond what we can understand" (36:26). Our knowledge of God, therefore, always involves a measure of mystery. Reason alone cannot fully describe realities such as beauty, love, or passion. Common sense tells us that intangibles such as these are "better felt than telt." As C. S. Lewis grasped this, and as he put it, "The best is perhaps what we understand least."[18]

For example, I may say that last fall the turning of the aspen forests near my home in Colorado was beautiful. But if you were to sit with me on a rock outcropping at ten-thousand-feet elevation, facing a mountainside whose aspens were burning like golden fire under the setting sun, you'd speak about it with an awe and passion in your voice that gave authority to your words. *Because you had seen beauty, you could convince others it was real and that you knew where to find it!* Similarly, it's one thing to explain grace as a theological concept, but it's another when your life is revolutionized by the actions of God's grace!

Some authorities, therefore, describe Christianity as "suprarational"[19] or "trans-rational."[20] Great Christian realities, such as intimacy with God, spiritual passion, and prayer, must be framed by the mind *and* experienced by the heart.

Christian mysticism, simply put, is the believer's direct experience of God in the heart.[21] A more complete definition might be: *the believer's unmediated experience of God, ministered to the heart by the Holy Spirit, which facilitates Christlike character and empowers for kingdom service.*

This kind of spirit-to-Spirit encounter with God usually gives rise to expressions of joy and praise. So there is a legitimate mysticism in the devotional life of growing disciples. We see this proper mysticism in the lives of Moses, David, Isaiah, Jesus, Paul, John, and other biblical characters. Likewise, in the lives of Augustine, Bernard of Clairvaux, Martin Luther, Thomas à Kempis, John of the Cross, Teresa of Avila, John Wesley, and A. W. Tozer.

Augustine, for instance, believed that Christians must relate to God with their *minds*, *emotions*, and *wills*. To really progress in spirit, we must move beyond the conversion experience to enjoyment of God and delight in His beauty. Passionately Augustine prayed, "Let me enter into the secret chamber of my heart and sing to you songs of love, which are largely sighs: my attempts to express what cannot be expressed."[22]

Responsible Christian mysticism does not demean reason or logic. And it does not mean a secret knowledge that gives you more power or fervor, or that makes you "better" than others. It simply requires that doctrines formed by the mind unite with the experienced presence of Christ in the heart.

We Need an Evangelical Mysticism

Referring to evangelical mysticism, Donald Bloesch observes that "Reformed Protestantism has been too quick to deny its universally true and abiding insights."[23] He sees a guarded Christian mysticism as a healthy corrective to evangelicalism's leanings toward cold rationalism. As a lawyer, Chuck Colson admits to being a product of the age of reason. But in his walk with the Lord, he testifies to having had remarkable spiritual intuitions and experiences of God's presence. Colson writes, "So I no longer distrust the mystical. No. I've had plenty of experiences with it."[24]

What can we expect in a real encounter with God?

Peace—A Rock to Stand Upon

We do not need to seek mystical thrills or shimmery feelings up the spine. We have only to ask God to make His presence real to us, and He is likely to begin with a subtle knowing, a *conviction* or a *calm awareness,* that resolves the tensions of *not* knowing whether we are alone or accompanied. This sense that we are on firm footing and that nothing ultimately can harm our eternal soul is what we call the *peace of God.*

Yes, we can and should expect God to make Himself known to us through the indwelling Spirit. The Spirit's ministry in testifying to the assurance of salvation is one example of this. Paul wrote, "His Holy Spirit speaks to us deep in our hearts and tells us that we are God's children" (Romans 8:16). Or as John put it, "We know he [God] lives in us because the Holy Spirit lives in us" (1 John 3:24, compare 4:13).

On his deathbed, Samuel Wesley, a devout Anglican, said to his son John, "The inward witness, son, the inward witness, that is the proof, the strongest proof of Christianity."[25]

Because the Spirit of God knows no bounds, we can enjoy heart-to-heart communion with God at any time, at any place, and under any circumstance (see Psalm 139:7-10, Hebrews 4:16).

Alex is a dedicated Christian leader living in the Ukraine. In the former Soviet Union, Alex was arrested by the KGB and imprisoned for seven years. During this difficult time of isolation and physical abuse, he was deprived of formal Christian worship, receiving the Lord's Supper, and even reading the Bible. But Alex testifies that during these years of imprisonment, when the external means of grace were denied him, he met Christ in his heart and experienced the peace of God in mystical experiences similar to those of Paul during his imprisonment.

Fascination—The Burning Bush

While Moses was tending sheep on Mount Sinai, God revealed Himself in the form of a flame of fire in a bush (see Exodus 3:1-4). Moses erected no wall around his soul to shield himself from this extraordinary encounter. Rather he responded to the theophany, or visible appearance of God, with rapt fascination (verses 2-3). "'Amazing!' Moses said to himself. 'Why isn't that bush burning up? I must go over to see this'" (verse 3). Only after Yahweh saw that "he had caught Moses' attention" and that Moses was receptive to the glorious Presence, did He speak to him in words (verses 4-6). A genuine meeting with the majestic God exerts on human hearts a compelling attraction. Christians who experience the glory of God in Jesus Christ are fascinated, and they long to know more (see Psalm 34:8). Many Christians are jaded and spiritless because they lack fascination with God. Churches that attempt to relieve spiritual boredom with entertainment vainly mimic the ways of the world.

Wonder—The Transfiguration

A Christian friend with a good knowledge of the Bible admitted, "It's been a long time since I've felt a profound sense of astonishment and wonder before God." Some of us may have similar feelings.

Wonder in the presence of God is seen in the account of Jesus' transfiguration on Mount Hermon (see Matthew 17:1-9). Peter, James, and John (perhaps because they had a close relationship with Jesus) were astonished at the revelation of Christ's glory. Before their very eyes, "Jesus' appearance changed so that his face shone like the sun, and his clothing became dazzling white" (verse 2). How struck with wonder they were when Moses and Elijah appeared and talked with Jesus (verse 3)! Peter's terse response to this startling event was, "Lord, this is wonderful!" (verse 4). When the voice of God sounded from heaven saying, "This is my beloved Son, . . . Listen to him" (verse 5), "the disciples were terrified and fell face down on the ground" (verse 6). This wonder-evoking experience must have greatly encouraged the disciples, who had just learned that Jesus must soon suffer and die (see Matthew 16:21).

Charles Wesley expresses this sense of wonder before God in one of his hymns.

> Changed from glory into glory,
> Till in heaven we take our place.
> Till we cast our crowns before Thee,
> Lost in wonder, love, and praise.[26]

Awe—The Exodus and Pentecost

Following Israel's miraculous escape from Egypt, Moses sang a song of deliverance to God. "Who is glorious in holiness like you—so awesome in splendor, peforming such wonders?" (Exodus 15:11). Later David experienced awe, or godly fear, in the presence of the Lord: "With deepest awe I will worship at your Temple" (Psalm 5:7, compare 111:9). When Isaiah encountered the Lord exalted on His throne, surrounded by adoring angels, he cried out, "Woe to me! . . . I am ruined! For . . . my eyes have seen the King, the LORD Almighty" (Isaiah 6:5, NIV). Daniel similarly prayed, "O Lord, you are a great and awesome God! You always fulfill your promises of unfailing love to those who love you and keep your commands" (Daniel 9:4).

Consider also the early church. In the first century the church lived and died in an atmosphere of awe. We read that "A deep sense of awe came over them all, and the apostles performed many miraculous signs and wonders" (Acts 2:43). In Hebrews we find these words: "Let us be thankful and please God by worshiping him with holy fear and awe. For our God is a consuming fire" (Hebrews 12:28-29). Growing Christians should view God less as a proposition to be scrutinized and more as a glorious Person to be engaged in moments of loving awe and wonder.

Ecstasy—Paul's Glimpse of Heaven

Ecstasy comes from the Greek word *ekstasis,* meaning "taken out of" oneself. It's a state of spiritual exaltation in which the Christian temporarily loses himself in God's love. Paul writes about an experience of ecstasy in 2 Corinthians 12:1-7. The apostle's opponents claimed to have received visions and revelations from God. Paul replied that he had a genuine ecstatic experience from God that was truly glorious. "I was caught up into the third heaven fourteen years ago. Whether my body was there or just my spirit, I don't know; only God knows. But I do know that I was caught up into paradise and heard things so astounding that they cannot be told" (verses 2-4). This extraordinary experience of heaven's glory fortified Paul to complete his mission in the face of relentless persecution. Tozer comments that "The Spirit-filled man may literally dwell in a state of spiritual fervor amounting to a mild and pure inebriation."[27]

Ecstasy is not the end or goal of the spiritual life. But if the Lord be pleased to grant this rare gift in the course of our obedience, ecstasy will be another means of satisfying our souls in Christ and strengthening us for service!

Charles Wesley wrote another hymn, in which he describes ecstasy as an appropriate Christian response to the unveiling of God's glory to the soul.

> Show me that happiest place,
> The place of Thy people's abode,
> Where saints in an ecstasy gaze,
> And hang on a crucified God.[28]

Orthodox . . . and Mystical

We evangelicals pride ourselves on being orthodox Christians. But the word *orthodoxy* comes from two Greek words meaning "right glory."

Israel encountered the Shekinah glory many times in their experience, for example, during the Exodus (see Exodus 13:21-22), at Sinai (see Exodus 24:16-18), in the tent in the wilderness (see Numbers 9:15-23), and in the temple (see 2 Chronicles 7:1-3). The apostle Paul claimed that the glory of God is the birthright of every believer in the age of the Spirit. "We, who with unveiled faces all reflect the Lord's glory, are being transformed into his likeness with ever-increasing glory, which comes from the Lord, who is the Spirit" (2 Corinthians 3:18, NIV).

When we, with great saints of old, experience God's glory, we become radiant personalities that attract others to the Lord.

A. W. Tozer was comfortable with this kind of orthodox mysticism. He wrote that the mystic

> differs from the ordinary orthodox Christian only because he experiences his faith down in the depths of his sentient being while the other does not. . . . He is quietly, deeply and sometimes almost ecstatically aware of the presence of God in his own nature and in the world around him. His religious experience is . . . immediate acquaintance with God by union with the eternal Son. It is knowing that which passes knowledge.[29]

A Christian mystic need not be a recluse or a hermit. That, perhaps, is another misperception. Many mystics in the church were activists and reformers. Mystics who retired to meet God often returned to the world to attack spiritual, social, and political problems. Paul, Augustine, Bernard, Luther, Teresa of Avila, and Sundar Singh were mystics who gloried in the presence of God and then penetrated the world to impact it for God. Tozer's contemporaries called him a Christian mystic, meaning a man with a deep personal relationship with Jesus Christ.

This alone—the radiance of Christ in our daily lives—will always be the proof of a genuine Christian spirituality.

Summing Up

God is more than a conclusion to a line of thinking. He is a Person to be engaged and enjoyed. The respected Reformed scholar John Murray put it simply: "There is an intelligent mysticism in the life of faith."[30]

A spirituality that embraces intellectual truth without personally engaging Christ in relationship is not Christian enough! It's like a plant in a closet, cut off from the light so that it withers and dies.

Do you long to experience in your heart what you know in your head?

A person who lacks heart connectedness to the Lord, biblically speaking, does not *know* God in the fullest sense. Faith that remains lodged in the brain cannot satisfy our spiritual and emotional needs in the nitty-gritty of life. In his excellent book, *Desiring God* (1988), John Piper insists that Christians must long for, see, and feel the breathtaking beauty of God.

Yet a life governed by emotion lacks theological controls and is in danger of drifting into doctrinal error and unfruitful practices. *Reliable beliefs. Godly affections. Obedient action.* All three are essential to the Christian life. Emphasizing one, to the neglect of others, leaves us unbalanced and unfulfilled.

To know God is to cultivate a love relationship with Him (see Philippians 3:10). It leads to transformation of your entire being (see 2 Corinthians 5:17, 1 Thessalonians 5:23).

For the Christian, mystical encounter with God is a blessed reality.

Try It Yourself

1. A Biblical Meditation on Experiencing God.

The Scripture passage I have chosen is Paul's prayer recorded in Ephesians 3:14-19. (Because the focus of this passage is corporate, you may want to try this together with two or three other Christians.) Read this short text of Scripture aloud. Then reflect quietly on the passage for a few minutes. Consider the following questions.

- What does Paul mean by the experience of Christ dwelling in our hearts (verse 17)? How can we make our hearts Christ's home? How does faith enter into this process?

- How are we enabled to understand with believers everywhere the length, breadth, and depth of Christ's love (verse 18)? What kind of knowing or understanding does Paul envision? Try to describe in words the grand scope of God's love for you in the family of God.
- What does it mean for Christians to be "filled with the fullness of life and power that comes from God" (verse 19)? How are the spiritual resources available to believers related to God's infinite nature?
- How do believers experience the love of Christ that is beyond our full knowledge (verse 19)? To what extent can Christians know the greatness of God's love for us?
- Pray, asking God to deepen your experiential knowledge of Christ's love, power, and life-giving energy.

2. Pondering a Theologian's Observation.

The paragraph below is taken from J. I. Packer's book, *Keep in Step With the Spirit*, pages 74-75. It relates to the topic of the chapter you have just read. Prayerfully reflect on the paragraph. Then discuss the questions that follow in light of your reading of this fourth chapter. Seek to apply to your Christian life and experience the issues raised. You may do this individually or preferably in a small group, where interaction with others will be mutually enriching. Write your responses to the questions in a notebook or journal.

> *The experiential reality of perceiving God is unfamiliar territory today. The pace and preoccupation of urbanized, mechanized, collectivized, secularized modern life are such that any sort of inner life . . . is very hard to maintain. . . . And if you attempt it, you will certainly seem eccentric to your peers, for nowadays involvement in a stream of activities is decidedly in, and the older idea of a quiet, contemplative life is just as decidedly out. . . . The concept of a Christian life as sanctified rush and bustle still*

dominates, and as a result the experiential side of Christian holiness remains very much a closed book.

- Dr. Packer speaks of "the experiential reality of perceiving God." In what sense is authentic knowledge of God always experiential? Explain what you mean.
- Have we as Christians today lost a sense of the lived presence of Christ in our hearts? How does this apply to your life? With what results?
- Dr. Packer says that in today's fast-paced, and we might add, technologized world, "any sort of inner life . . . is very hard to maintain." How has the rush of modern life made deepening relationship with Christ difficult or frustrating for you?
- Prayerfully consider what you, your family, small group, or church might do to resist the pressures of today's world that makes deepening relationship with Christ difficult. Formulate a plan for strengthening your relationship with Christ. Write it down and revisit it occasionally to ensure that you're on track.

Suggestions for Further Reading

Edwards, Jonathan. *Religious Affections*, ed. James Houston. Portland: Multnomah Press, 1984.

Gire, Ken. *Intimate Moments with the Savior.* Grand Rapids: Zondervan, 1989.

Nouwen, Henri J. M. *Reaching Out: The Three Movements of the Spiritual Life.* Garden City, N.Y.: Doubleday, 1975.

——— *Lifesigns: Intimacy, Fecundity, and Ecstasy in Christian Perspective.* New York: Doubleday/Image, 1986.

Packer, J. I. *Knowing God.* London: Hodder & Stoughton, 1973.

Tozer, A. W. *The Pursuit of God.* Harrisburg, Penn.: Christian Publications, 1982.

CHAPTER FIVE

Word That Feeds the Soul

"Oh, how I love your law! I meditate on it all day long."
"My eyes stay open through the watches of the night, that I may meditate on your promises."

PSALM 119:97,148 (NIV)

"Why do I meditate?
Because I am a Christian. Therefore, every day in which I do not penetrate more deeply into the knowledge of God's Word in Holy Scripture is a lost day for me. I can only move forward with certainty upon the firm ground of the Word of God."

DIETRICH BONHOEFFER[1]

SANDY, THE YOUTH PASTOR IN A growing suburban church, was also made pastor of evangelism and outreach by the board, which pushed the demand on him to seventy hours a week. Suddenly the ministry that had been his passion turned into a burden. There was little time to be quiet before the Lord or to meditate on Scripture. The people who sought his help began to feel like irritations, and he found himself caught between the need to justify his employment to the board and the growing desire to dodge the many people who needed him.

One morning Sandy faced himself in the mirror and admitted that his attitude was poor, his desire to minister was weak, and he thought about quitting far too often. He realized he'd barely prayed in months. As a result, he sought the help and counsel of the church board. Fortunately they agreed with his concerns and reduced his workload to allow for a more nurturing devotional life.

The first thing Sandy did was to take a full day in solitude at a friend's mountain cabin to feed on the Word of God. Several of the psalms powerfully refocused him on the might and beauty of God, leading him into praise and worship of the Father. That alone restored his right focus, reminding him of the One he was serving, and began to restore his will to minister to God's people.

That evening, as he drove home from the mountains, Sandy knew he *needed* to make Scripture meditation a priority if he was going to walk with God.

A FRESH WAVE

There's a fresh wave of interest in meditation in the Western world. This may be due in part to the current popularity of the Dalai Lama (the spiritual leader of Tibet), the resurgence of Eastern religions in the West, or simply the felt need for greater peace in our busy lives. Today, movie stars, professional athletes, and ordinary people are practicing meditation and chanting

Buddhist or Hindu mantras. Community colleges, corporations, and recreation centers (even YMCAs and YWCAs) offer courses on yoga and Transcendental Meditation (TM).

This has led to some confusion and resistance to the discipline of meditation on the part of conservative Christians.

Does meditation play a role in renewing the spirit of a Christian? If so, how can we pursue an authentically Christian path and avoid wandering off into nonChristian practices?

It is my purpose here to suggest safe and fruitful ways in which Christians may meditate. What we'll explore in this chapter are the secrets of meditation on the Scriptures, on devotional writings that edify, on great hymns of the faith, and on works of art that reflect Christian themes. Along the way I will identify what meditative exercises are properly Christian, leading the soul deeper into a Christlike relationship with the Father, and which ones cross biblical boundaries.

Too Busy for God?

At the most basic level, meditation is a practice that is necessary to refocus the inner man from the push-and-shove outer world to the eternal—to move us from preoccupation with ourselves to thoughts of God and His concerns.

Robert Kohl's book, *A Survivor's Guide to Overseas Living,* identifies common stereotypes held by foreigners about Americans. Among the dozen or so traits cited, I mention three. Foreigners perceive Americans to be immature, hard-working, and always in a hurry.[2] Who doubts that North Americans are a habitually busy people, perpetually on the go? A recent study of American adults concluded that 92 percent feel that their life is like a treadmill; 78 percent said they need to stop and smell the roses. We schedule ourselves to the eyebrows and leave little time for reflection on matters of spiritual significance. The U.S. military, which loves euphemisms, calls this "task saturation."

Why do we drive ourselves so mercilessly?

Some of us keep unduly busy to boost our sagging egos, to "prove" our worth, or to avoid aspects of our selves too painful to confront. A pastor friend whose life was transformed by contemplative retreat experiences concludes that "evangelicals run in overdrive from morning to night with little time for pious reflection." Perhaps you've seen a new bumper sticker that's out. It reads, "Jesus is coming soon. Look busy!"

Thomas Moore, whose generic spirituality I critiqued in chapter 3, does point out a truth we need to face:

> Some people are incapable of being arrested by things because they are always on the move. A common symptom of modern life is that there is no time for thought, or even for letting impressions of a day sink in. . . . The vessel in which soul-making takes place is an inner container scooped out by reflection and wonder. There is no doubt that some people could spare the expense and trouble of psychotherapy simply by giving themselves a few minutes each day for quiet reflection.[3]

Some of us live our lives so chock-full that the Lord can't get our attention long enough to make Himself known. Our psyches are so programmed for action and accomplishment that we're unable to hear God speak. The static in our souls is sufficiently loud that the whisper of the Spirit gets drowned out. Our hurrying disease—or urgency addiction—sucks spiritual life out of us and turns us into hollow performance machines.

Here's a spiritual principle you and I need to consider: When our lives feel mechanical and driven, we are effectively closed to the grace of God. We may busily serve God but, ironically, the God we serve becomes a stranger. Our lives and Christian service echo with a haunting emptiness.

Quieting and Composing the Soul

When we are running in overdrive, quieting of the heart is not just a luxury, it's necessary for life of the soul. The inner man *needs* to breathe in stillness.

Primarily, the outer world with its demands and our own inner world with its cares and ambitions fill us with clutter and noise. In the din, we are less able to hear the still, small voice of God. Picture for a moment a favorite lake or pond. A thunderstorm blows in, wrinkling the surface so that nothing is reflected. In a moment, the storm departs, the water's surface stills, and in the peaceful calm the surrounding landscape and sky are clearly imaged. In a similar way, our full agendas agitate the soul. But in calm and quiet, our souls refocus on the presence, beauty, power, and directives of our omnipresent God. And others see His light more readily in us. Morton Kelsey puts it this way: "As long as my mind is raging with thoughts ideas, plans, and fears, I cannot listen significantly to God or any other dimension of reality."[4]

Also, our culture pushes us to take in an overload of information and make constant decisions. We're forced to operate out of an overstimulated logic, so that our minds actually feel burned-out by the end of the day. Our intuitive, sensing/perceiving, imagining right brain is pushed aside and undernourished. And so our lives can grow away from concerns like reaching the lost, helping the poor, bringing light to prisoners, that lie on the heart of God. Head-centered people *need* to quiet their minds to allow the heart to develop through the discipline of quiet.

Finally, quietness creates a context in which our deepest self comes to the fore, where it may be yielded to the Lord of all. How easy it is for our lives to be governed by a steady ambition to acquire more wealth, more power, more distance from responsibility, even as we sing hymns and choruses about surrender and service to God. Our independence, striving, and controlling *must* be surrendered to God's will. Pride—the drive to run our lives our way—is spiritually deadly.

Fortunately, God is lovingly present to His children. And our response to this grace is to still ourselves long enough to see our true inner selves, in order to relinquish our core drives to Him.

A Theology of Silence

Sadly, my evangelical Christian tradition ascribes little importance to quietness and solitude. Searching for Scripture texts on the subject in the popular *Nave's Topical Bible*, I find no entries under "quietness," "silence," or "solitude."

Henri Nouwen observes, "There was a time when silence was normal and a lot of racket disturbed us. But today, noise is the normal fare, and silence, strange as it may seem, has become the real disturbance."[5] Apart from the nebulous "quiet time," I was never taught the value of silence or solitude in church or seminary training. Perhaps this is why many people (even some Christians) are attracted to the seemingly peaceful experiences offered by Eastern religions.

The discipline of silence enjoys an honored place in Christian spirituality. Thomas à Kempis (d. 1471) writes, "Jesus will stay with you as long as you are humble and quiet in your spirit."[6] According to John of the Cross (d. 1591), "The Father utters one Word. That Word is his Son, and he utters Him forever in everlasting silence. In silence the soul has to hear him."[7] Mother Teresa (d. 1997) claimed that

> we need to find God, and he cannot be found in noise and restlessness. God is the friend of silence. See how nature—trees, flowers, grass—grow in silence; see the stars, the moon and sun, how they move in silence. . . . The more we receive in silent prayer, the more we can give in our active life. We need silence to touch souls.[8]

Bill Hybels somewhere says that our hearts are so preoccupied that often when the Spirit tries to get through to us He gets a busy signal.

Scripture plainly commends silence for restoring our spiritual hearts. The Lord says to His fast-paced people today, "Be silent, and know that I am God! . . . I will be honored throughout the world" (Psalm 46:10). Through the prophet Isaiah the Lord says, "Only in returning to me and waiting for me will you be saved.

In quietness and confidence is your strength" (Isaiah 30:15). Habakkuk declared to wayward Israel, "The LORD is in his holy Temple. Let all the earth be silent before him" (2:20). Glancing over the nations, the prophet Zechariah issues the command, "Be silent before the LORD, all humanity . . ." (2:13). In the New Testament, Peter writes that Christians "should be known for the . . . unfading beauty of a gentle and quiet spirit, which is so precious to God" (1 Peter 3:4).

By quieting our souls, we create an empty space in our busy lives for God. With stilled and composed hearts, we present ourselves to Him. We dismiss from our lives the accumulated garbage so that God can fill us with His pure presence. As we wait before God, we listen to His voice. We turn our attention from the past, with its failures and guilt, and from the future, with its worries and fears. We focus on the present, where Christ resides at the center of the Christian's being. Donald Bloesch wisely reminds us that "Biblical spirituality makes a place for silence, yet silence is to be used not to get beyond the Word but to prepare ourselves to hear the Word."[9]

The God of the Bible is not far removed from us because He's off ruling remote galaxies. *He is close at hand.* And He is constantly communicating to us. Scripture teaches that the Lord is beside us—before, behind, and beneath us, too (Psalm 139:7-10). Closer than our very breath.

Do we stop long enough to quiet ourselves to grasp the slightest notion of what this means?

Our great need is to dispose ourselves properly to receive Him. Our theology may be impeccable, but if our souls are anxious and distracted, our life-connection with God will suffer. The more we're led into quietness, the more attuned we become to God's healing and renewing Word.

John Calvin (d. 1564), the great Reformer, put it this way: "We [must] be disposed in mind and heart as befits those who enter conversation with God. We are to rid ourselves of all alien and outside cares, by which the mind, itself a wanderer, is borne about hither and thither, drawn away from heaven, and pressed down to earth."[10]

Achieving this kind of composure is more easily said than done. Too often the heart is a geyser of unsettling thoughts and emotions. When we try to focus on God, we're distracted by a "to do" list of tasks to be done and people to see. Then there is the background rumble of those troubling emotions—anxiety, worry, and fear—stirred up by thoughts that are not fixed on God. *"Why was I so crazy to let her talk me into . . ." "I wonder if the boss knows I didn't get the support figures out to the field in time, and the contract went down because of me. I could kick myself."*

Morton Kelsey correctly says, "As long as one is like a Ping-Pong ball, bounced back and forth by every emotion and outer relationship, it is hardly possible to enter the meditative process."[11] The late Henri Nouwen, a deeply spiritual man, struggled with this obstacle to relationship:

> It is so hard to be silent, silent with my mouth, but even more, silent with my heart. There is so much talking going on within me. It seems that I am always involved in inner debates with myself, my friends, my enemies, my supporters, my opponents, my colleagues, and my rivals. But this inner debate reveals how far my heart is from you.[12]

Exercises for Stilling the Soul

God counts on us to calm our hearts in preparation for meditation and prayer. How we do this will vary according to our temperament and emotional state. For some, listening to classical music or a quiet walk in nature sufficiently recollects the soul. Others require more disciplined regimens. Jesus taught that we must actively "seek" his kingdom (Matthew 6:33). Cultivating a healthy spiritual and emotional life is not easy. It requires serious intention and sometimes just plain, hard work.

Exercises that focus your breathing help to quiet the restless heart. Some conservative critics of meditation become uncomfortable when we talk about the need to quiet and focus the soul by attention to our breathing. Once again, they insist the only habit we need to cultivate is focusing our mind on the words of Scripture. But focusing on our physical being has the wonderful benefit of helping our conscious mind perceive the truth about what's going on in our soul—the tension, irritation, or worry we may be carrying while our mind is preoccupied with other details. In effect, we get in touch with our soul's state, and the soul is what we want to bring into the light, where contact with God can comfort, correct, encourage, and redirect it in more godly responses.

The Bible does not overlook this important connection between the state of the soul (evidenced in our physical body) and our relationship to God.

The Hebrew word *rûaḥ* signifies God's Spirit (see Genesis 1:2, Psalm 51:11, Isaiah 48:16) as well as the human breath. Note that when Jesus breathed on His disciples, they received the Holy Spirit (see John 20:22). Jonathan Edwards cites the connection between human breath and the Holy Spirit: "Our breath to support life [is] a representation of our dependence on the Spirit of God for spiritual life."[13]

If your soul needs quieting, try this simple exercise:

Sit comfortably, and just breathe normally. As you breathe, focus attention on the air as it enters and leaves your nostrils. Should your mind wander, gently bring the focus back to awareness of your breath. Continue this for several minutes.

No, the purpose of the exercise is not to breathe in "energy fields" or "forces," as in Eastern religions. Rather it is to quiet the soul and dispose you to an awareness of God, Who moves upon and within the heart. Its benefits are heightened emotional composure and, more importantly, greater receptiveness to God.

In this quieted state, does God call your attention to a concern you've failed to act upon—say, the need to visit an elderly, ailing relative? Does He help you reorder your priorities so you stop rationalizing your inaction? Does He call your attention to angry slanders, jealousy, or the blame you harbor toward another? Does He convict you to forgive and surrender the other person to His dealings, or give you wise and gracious words to resolve your conflict?

Through the centuries, many Christian writers have recommended deep and quiet breathing as an aid to effective meditation. In our day, Kelsey observes, "This is a process of slowing the ego down, of letting self-centeredness fade out so that the larger self can take over and be moved by God's grace."[14]

A second quieting exercise many find helpful goes like this: Again breathe normally. As you exhale, imagine with God's help that you are breathing spiritual and emotional impurities out of your life. These might include worry (see Luke 12:22,25-26), fear (see 1 John 4:18), or anger (see Psalm 37:8, Colossians 3:8). Focus for a few moments on one impurity, then on another. This act of the will aids conscious release of sinful impulses—a silencing of the false-self that Scripture describes as the "old man" (KJV) or the "evil nature" (see Romans 6:6, Ephesians 4:22, Colossians 3:9).

Focus on your inhalations. Imagine, with God's help, that you are breathing in positive graces commended by Scripture. These include love (see 1 John 4:10-11,19), peace (see Isaiah 26:3, John 14:27), goodness (see Galatians 5:22, 2 Peter 1:5), gentleness (see Galatians 5:23, 1 Peter 3:4), and so on. This act of the will amounts to a conscious appropriation of biblical virtues—an enhancing of the true self that Scripture calls the "new man" (KJV) or the "new nature" (see Ephesians 4:24, Colossians 3:10). Physically and emotionally, these exercises promote relaxation. Spiritually, they facilitate dismissal of the sinful self and enhancement of the new nature in Christ. Such exercises acknowledge our created humanity—that God made us as souls in physical bodies.

The Strength of Godly Wisdom

After discovering these exercises for myself some years ago, I met in India Dr. Sam Kamileson, who at the time was a vice president with World Vision International, responsible for arranging pastors' conferences throughout Asia. I asked Dr. Kamileson, a respected Indian Christian leader familiar with Eastern and Western worlds, for his evaluation of these exercises. Without blinking an eye,

Dr. Kamileson answered that such exercises represent "an excellent preparation for prayer." Peter Toon, the British evangelical pastor and theologian, also approves of such quieting disciplines.

> Preparatory relaxation (to meditation) can include the use of breathing exercises and bodily postures and will vary according to varying needs and personalities. The purpose is to create in me an atmosphere of calm and silence; in particular, it is to establish harmony between body and soul (and spirit) so that nothing from my side will prevent the movement of God's Spirit towards me.[15]

What Do We Mean by Meditation?

To meditate as a Christian is to cultivate the soil of the soul, which the traffic of the world compacts and hardens. It is the replanting of the Word's seed, the uprooting of sin's weeds, the nurturing of truth into fruitful activity. It is cooperating with God Himself as He moves among us, His trees of righteousness planted by the river of the Spirit's living water.

A quieted heart is our best preparation for all this work of God, which begins as we meditate on the Word of God. Someone has said that meditation is "giving *attention* with *intention.*" Meditation refocuses us from ourselves and from the world so that we reflect on God's Word, His nature, His abilities, and His works. As we come before the Scriptures, we believe that God has something very personal to say. So we prayerfully ponder, muse, and "chew" the words of Scripture and other Christian writings. The purpose of meditation is not to prepare a Bible study or sermon; there's a time and place for that. The goal is simply to permit the Holy Spirit to activate the life-giving Word of God so that something more of our lives is transformed to bring us, every day, a little closer to the image of Christ.

Meditation, when it is effective, engages the whole heart: intellect, intuition, will, affections, and moral sense. There are two principal Hebrew words for meditation. One, the verb *hāgâ,* means to "utter, groan, meditate, ponder." In the natural world it refers to sounds such as the repetitive mourning call of a dove or the growl of a lion. The second verb, *śîhaḥ,* means to "muse, rehearse (in the mind), contemplate." Meditation, therefore, involves deep, repetitive reflection on eternal truth.

Though meditation is commanded by Scripture, it has become a neglected discipline in the spiritual formation of conservative Christians over the last two hundred years. Of late we've been frightened off by Buddhist, Hindu, or New Age forms of meditation. J. I. Packer says that "meditation is a lost art today. Christian people suffer grievously from their ignorance of this practice."[16]

As the director of the underground seminary at Finkewalde in Germany during World War II, Dietrich Bonhoeffer (d. 1945) required seminarians to devote thirty minutes each morning to silent meditation on Scripture. Many future pastors in the seminary didn't know what to do with the time. Some worked on sermons, others daydreamed, and some fell asleep. With so little attention to this art, especially on the part of spiritual leaders, it's no wonder that rank and file Christians need guidance in the practice of Christian meditation.

Despite our recent neglect, we dare not underestimate the value of regular Christian meditation. This important discipline serves as the integrating point of our day and, indeed, our whole life.

Meditating on God's Word

The God who created and knows us calls us to meditate on His Word.

As Israel was about to cross the Jordan River into the Promised Land, God said to Joshua: "Study this Book of the Law continually. Meditate on it day and night so you may be sure to obey all that is written in it. Only then will you succeed" (Joshua 1:8). The opening psalm in Israel's hymn book attributes the blessedness of the righteous to the fact that "day and night they think about his [God's] law" (Psalm 1:2).

Psalm 119 repeatedly testifies to the value of prayerful meditation on God's Word: "I meditate on your age-old laws; O LORD, they comfort me" (verse 52); "I will quietly keep my mind on your decrees" (verse 95); "I stay awake through the night, thinking about your promise" (verse 148; compare verses 23,48,97,99). New Testament Scriptures, such as Philippians 4:8 and Revelation 1:3, also encourage meditation on God's unshakable Word.

Christian Testimonies to Biblical Meditation

For centuries the church has treasured meditation on Scripture. Late in the fourth century, Evagrius of Pontus (d. 399) summarized the Christian life as resisting temptation and growing in contemplation or meditation. In his famous treatise, *On Loving God*, Bernard of Clairvaux (d. 1153) teaches that meditation allows the Word to descend from the mind to the heart in order to renew the entire person.

Richard Baxter (d. 1691) believed that meditation should engage all the soul's powers, not just the mind. He wrote, "The understanding is not the whole soul, and therefore cannot do the whole work."[17] Reason's servant-task is to "open the door between the head and the heart."[18] Meditation on God's Word excites affections of love, hope, courage, and joy. As part of the meditation process, Baxter commends soliloquy—that is, dialoging with one's own heart (Psalm 42:5,11), and prayer—speaking to God about our spiritual concerns (Psalm 42:9).

Dietrich Bonhoeffer, the German pastor martyred by the Nazis during World War II, asked himself, *What do we want from meditation?* His answer? "We want . . . to rise up from our meditation in a different state from when we sat down. We want to meet Christ in His Word. We turn to the text in our desire to hear what it is that He wants to give us and teach us today through His Word. Meet Him first in the day before you meet other people."[19]

Lectio Divina

The method of biblical meditation known as *lectio divina* ("sacred reading") has been practiced by Christians since the fourth century. In recent decades, growing numbers of Protestant Christians have taken up *lectio* to their spiritual profit. This exercise, otherwise known as "reading with the heart" (Richard Foster), represents a wholistic approach to biblical meditation.

Lectio divina proceeds in four stages. In the language of the centuries they are *lectio* (reading), *meditatio* (discursive meditation), *oratio* (affective prayer), and *contemplatio* (contemplation). As preparation for *lectio*, yield all your cares and concerns to the Lord. Invite the Holy Spirit, who inspired the Word, to illumine its message to your heart.

Here are some steps to guide you:

First, select a Scripture passage. You might begin with a psalm, a biblical prayer, or a discourse of Jesus—or perhaps one of Jesus' rich parables. Take the attitude that God has given this Scripture for your spiritual nourishment. With a listening heart, read aloud the biblical text slowly and deliberately. When you alight upon a word, a phrase, or a sentence that speaks to your heart, pause in your reading.

Second, meditate—or mull over—the word or words that captured your attention. Listen to, ponder, and savor the love message from God until it settles in your soul. Through reverent reflection, allow the sacred text to become your spiritual meat and drink. Permit it to nurture, challenge, or test something in you.

It's helpful to read the Word with a view to relationship. Search for relational images that connect you with each of the members of the Godhead. Place yourself in the Scripture so that it speaks to your life. Permit the biblical words, which are "full of living power" (Hebrews 4:12), to probe your attitudes, emotions, and aspirations. Truths received in faith become sweetness to the soul; other truths resisted will be more bitter. In the meditative stillness, listen to the voice of God as He leads you on the path of spiritual growth. This meditation stage of *lectio* assumes that God's revelation is personal as well as propositional. The Word imparts information but pausing to take time with it brings the reader face-to-face with the living Lord.

Third, return the Scripture you have just read to the Father by praising Him for its work in you. Talk to the Lord about your reading. Your petition might take the form of calm reasoning or an impassioned plea. Thank the Father for the grace that works through His Spirit and the Word. Ask Him to make experiential other biblical truths that have not yet found residence in your heart. Petition the Lord for the grace to obey His nourishing revelation.

The *final stage* of the *lectio* involves resting in the Lord's presence. This is the act of *simply being there with God*, and it acknowledges that He is the agent of spiritual growth. Resting in God's real presence has been called *the prayer of simple devotion*.

Simply being present to God in loving communion serves as the exclamation point to the meditative moment.

The Formative Reading of Scripture

Robert Mulholland and Peter Toon offer helpful adaptations of *lectio divina* for today's world. Toon, an Anglican evangelical, calls this method, "formative reading" of Scripture. Informational reading, as we've said elsewhere, seeks to gather factual knowledge. It uses exegesis, lexical study, and a scientific method of interpretation. Informational reading is necessary, but not sufficient, for cultivating Christian character.

Formative reading seeks to shape the reader spiritually by the inspired text of Scripture. According to this method, the reader places himself before the Word to hear what God has to say and to respond obediently. He approaches the sacred text with a view to Christ directing his thoughts, enlarging his heart, and leading him to greater spiritual maturity.

Toon writes that the "aim of formative reading is to seek Christ in the inspired and sacred text in order to discover the love of God, to savor that love, and to be united in faith and love with the Bridegroom of our souls."[20]

Formative reading is similar to *lectio*, with subtle differences:

Begin with a biblical text that is familiar from previous study. View the text as a love letter from God. Read the passage aloud several times, slowly and prayerfully. Savor the text and reflect on the spiritual significance of the biblical words. Carefully attend to what God, through the Spirit, may be saying to you.

Then ask God, "How do You want me to respond to what You're saying?"

Allow your reading to lead naturally into prayers of praise, petition, and intercession as you lift up the text to God. You may wish to record your insights in a notebook or journal. Toon notes that "Psychologically, [formative reading] provides a delightful respite from the dry labor of discursive meditation."[21] Believers who practice formative reading of Scripture testify that through it the Word becomes truly nourishing and life-giving.

Of course, meditating on God's Word every day is the best idea. But success in cultivating this habit is what's most important at the outset. My suggestion is that you choose one day in the week, to start off with, when you spend an extended time in meditation. The Lord's Day is certainly a good choice because it stands at both the close of an old week and the opening of a new one. My firm belief is that you will quickly come to enjoy and benefit from this experience—and you will soon make a space for it on weekdays, too!

Meditating on Secondary Christian Writings

God also graciously speaks to His children through Christian books, hymns, and religious art. Gifted Christian writers, poets, and artists have gleaned gems of truth that we need to know, from Scripture and from living out their commitment to God under challenging circumstances.

Christian Devotional Literature

You will benefit greatly, I promise you, by spending time with a classic work on the spiritual life. I wholeheartedly recommend that you delve into works by such faithful Christian leaders and writers as Augustine, Thomas à Kempis, Teresa of Avila, William Law, Jonathan Edwards, Amy Carmichael, A. W. Tozer, Henri Nouwen, or Richard Foster.

This is the approach I recommend: Don't read as a "scholar," searching for information; instead come as a disciple who seeks insight from a learned mentor. It can help to know something about the author, his or her times, and the circumstances that prompted the writing. Prayerfully invite the Spirit to speak to you during your reading.

Similar to the meditative reading of Scripture, select a manageable portion of the book or read until an insight leaps out at you. Be relaxed and unhurried in your reading. When a passage does touch your heart, pause and prayerfully reflect on what God is saying to you.

Ask yourself questions such as: Does this passage give me new insight into the nature of God? Does it explain something of the spiritual life I didn't really understand—like trusting God in difficult times, or how to forgive and let go of offenses, or how to know I am living out God's purpose for my life? How do I need to alter my life to act on the insight I've gained?

Rest quietly in the truths you have pondered, alert to the gentle movements of the Spirit. Then dialogue with the Lord about what you have read. He welcomes your responses, for He is behind your discoveries.

I also highly recommend writing down your new insights and commitments in a notebook or spiritual journal. Journaling is an extension of meditation and spiritual reading—a practice that can assist in turning insight into real transformation in your life.

Great Hymns of the Church

Christian music lifts the heart to God. Even if you are not musically gifted, you can grow spiritually by meditating on hymns composed by devout saints.

Scripture recognizes the spiritual value of Christ-honoring music. "Let us come before him with thanksgiving. Let us sing him psalms of praise" (Psalm 95:2). Again, "sing psalms and hymns and spiritual songs among yourselves, making music to the Lord in your hearts" (Ephesians 5:19).

Get hold of a good hymn book of the faith. Old and worn hymnals contain some surprising treasures! From the title or topical indexes, select a hymn for meditation. Some hymns contain solid doctrinal material; most contain devotional insights that will edify and renew your soul. Carefully read, ponder, pray over, and apply the words of the hymn to your life. Follow the method of *lectio* or formative reading in your meditation on the hymn. Here are two selections from great hymns of the faith that you might wish to meditate upon.

I love the hymn *There's a Wideness in God's Mercy* written in 1854 by Frederick W. Faber, an Anglican clergyman who converted to Catholicism. Its lyrics move me, not only to think on God's boundless saving mercy through Christ, but to exercise mercy toward people, for the sake of Christ, who wrong me.

There's a wideness in God's mercy,
  Like the wideness of the sea;
There's a kindness in God's justice,
  Which is more than liberty.
There is no place where earth's sorrows
  Are more felt than up in heaven;
There is no place where earth's failings
  Have such kindly judgment given.[22]

Other hymns remind us of God's gracious provision of our deepest spiritual needs. Consider the hymn *My Shepherd Will Supply My Need*, a 1719 musical paraphrase of Psalm 23 by Isaac Watts:

My shepherd will supply my need;
  Jehovah is His name:
In pastures fresh He makes me feed,
  Beside the living stream.
He brings my wandering spirit back,
  When I forsake His ways;

And leads me, for His mercy's sake,
In paths of truth and grace.[23]

Meditating on Visual Art

Our Enlightenment-based preference for reason often neglects the visual arts as fruitful sources of Christian meditation. If doctrine engages our rational and verbal left brain, art appeals to our intuitive and nonverbal right brain. How suitable is religious art for purposes of Christian meditation?

Religious Art

Some people oppose meditating on pieces of art, believing that the second commandment forbids such a practice: "Do not make idols of any kind, whether in the shape of birds or animals or fish. You must never worship or bow down to them, for I, the Lord your God, am a jealous God" (Exodus 20:4-5). This command, however, forbids making and worshiping three-dimensional representations of the invisible God. The spirit of iconoclasm (the rejection of images) claims that using art—*any art*—for spiritual purposes detracts from the authority of the Bible. Anti-art people today call on the authority of certain forebears, for instance, Clement of Alexandria (d. 215), who claimed that painted images divert the mind from the invisible God to visible objects. Tertullian (d. 230) even condemned art as the work of the Devil. It's possible these church fathers were really reacting to the pull of pagan art and statuary, which surrounded new believers with misguiding images—much the way television and other media pour ungodly influences over our lives today. Much later, Protestants such as Zwingli (d. 1531) banished, visual arts (paintings, murals, sculptures) from Reformation churches. Some Puritan divines did the same thing.

Others believe that meditation on Christian art is a spiritually edifying practice. They remind us that persecuted Christians painted Old Testament scenes and heroes as well as Christian symbols, such as the fish, anchor, dove, and palm branch on catacomb walls.

The great church historian Eusebius (d. 339), in a sermon

dedicating a fourth-century church in Tyre, called the painters and artisans of the building a "new Bezalel . . . or a Solomon"—a reference to architects of the great temple in Jerusalem. John Calvin (d. 1564) saw spiritual value in faithful art forms. "Sculpture and painting are gifts of God, . . . which the Lord has conferred upon us for his glory and our good."[24] Stained glass windows depicting biblical characters and scenes have been a tradition in Christian churches for centuries.

Meditating on Christian art is supported by the doctrine of creation, where God judged the physical order "very good," and from the doctrine of the Incarnation, where Christ entered the material world in human flesh.

Moreover, the rich ornamentation of the tabernacle and the temple testify to God's respect for painting and sculpture. Exodus 25–28 and 35–40 describe the artistry reflected in the ark of the covenant, the mercy seat, the table holding the bread of the Presence, the altars, and the lampstands. The tabernacle was fashioned after the pattern God gave on Mount Sinai (see Exodus 25:9,40; 26:30). Moses said of the tabernacle's artists, "The LORD has chosen Bezalel son of Uri. . . . The LORD has filled Bezalel with the Spirit of God, giving him great wisdom, intelligence, and skill in all kinds of crafts. He is able to create beautiful objects from gold, silver, and bronze. He is skilled in cutting and setting gemstones and in carving wood" (Exodus 35:30-33).

The same was true of the Jerusalem temple, but on an even grander scale (see 1 Kings 5–7, 2 Chronicles 3–4). God outdid Himself in artistic direction! We can only imagine the magnificence of the cedar paneling, the gold-plated cherubim fifteen feet tall, the many engravings of palm trees, pomegranates, gourds, flowers, lions, and bulls, and the richly adorned curtain. "Every part of this plan," David told Solomon, "was given to me in writing from the hand of the LORD" (1 Chronicles 28:19).

Art is a powerful form of symbolic communication. Through visible images, light and darkness, color and texture, paintings portray the agony and ecstasy of human experience. As a respected Christian art interpreter puts it, "A work of art is a lens or window or lattice through which we see ourselves and our world."[25] Concepts and propositions help define and quantify our experiences, but truth communicated by story, symbolism, and imagery enriches our grasp of reality. Madeleine L'Engle somewhere said that if you're looking for facts, go to an encyclopedia, but if you're looking for truth and meaning, reflect on art, music, and sculpture.

Here's the point: Thoughtful reflection on responsible art stimulates deeper perception of truth and value. Well-crafted art stirs our emotions and evokes our heartfelt response. Art produced by nonChristians often reflects the futility of life without God; what is foolish or decadent is of little value for Christian meditation (see Exodus 32:1-20, Romans 1:21-23). But art creatively crafted by Christians unfolds fresh dimensions of God's goodness. Christians, therefore, profitably meditate on the great works of painters such as da Vinci *(The Last Supper),* Michelangelo *(David),* and Raphael *(The Transfiguration).*

As we contemplate artistic representations of the human condition and God's provision, our shallow souls become more deeply sculpted in truth.

Make no mistake, I'm not suggesting some esoteric exercise for the "refinement" of your sensibilities. You may encounter God's real power here.

Francis of Assisi (d. 1226) was meditating on an image of the crucified Christ when he was called to start a spiritual movement that shook all of Europe and lasts to this day.

Henri Nouwen began meditating on Rembrandt's eight-by-six-foot painting *The Return of the Prodigal Son* (c. 1666) at the Hermitage in St. Petersburg, Russia. In the painting, you see the prodigal son kneeling with shaven head, his face pressed against the father's chest in a spirit of contrition. The father's red tunic arches over the son, suggesting a place of safe haven. In the son's ragged clothes and scarred feet, we are confronted by the pain and degradation of our separation from God. Peering over the father's shoulder, coldly, is the resentful elder brother.

And then your eye falls on the father's hands, resting on

the young man's shoulders: The left hand is large and muscular, suggesting the strength of authority to set the young man right again; the right hand is smaller and more tender, suggesting the maternal comforts offered by God to every one of us "prodigals" who "come home."

Nouwen's extended meditation upon Rembrandt's painting enriched his life emotionally and spiritually, and inspired the creation of a novel. He was deeply moved at the thought of Christ leaving heaven's glory for a cruel death . . . and His rising again to a joyous reunion with the Father. Meditating on the painting healed his own wounded spirit and restored his identity as a beloved child of the Father. Nouwen saw himself in the painting, not only as the repentant prodigal but also as the self-righteous and resentful elder son. He grasped that the compassionate Father longs to heal and restore both sons. Meditation on the painting also led to renewed relationship with Henri's earthly father. Nouwen believed that Rembrandt's painting communicated to him visually as much as any sermon conveyed in words.

Meditate on Icons?

A recent article in my daily newspaper reported that religious images are selling like hotcakes.[26] Crucifixes, angel-figures made of pewter, mouse pads depicting patron saints, and framed icons are the latest rage.

An icon (from the Greek *eikōn*, meaning "form, image, statue") is a painted or sculpted representation of Christ or a saint and is used in worship or devotion. In Eastern Orthodoxy the veneration of icons is an essential part of the spiritual path. We know that Christians made paintings of biblical scenes in the catacombs and etched figures and inscriptions on the stone coffins of their dead (called *sarcophagi*). The remains of a third-century church contain frescoes of biblical scenes in the sanctuary and adjacent baptistry. Many churches from the fourth century on contain visual representations of biblical persons, Old Testament events, and scenes from the life of Christ.

Debate over the use of icons has gone on, sometimes raging, since the eighth- and ninth-century church. This argument, especially in its first explosion, has been called the iconoclastic controversy.

The dispute began when certain Eastern emperors (partly for political reasons) ordered the destruction of religious pictures and images in churches. The iconoclasts (destroyers of images), as they were called, appealed to the second commandment (see Exodus 20:4-5) and to John 4:24. They claimed that fashioning icons of Jesus, Mary, and the saints was idolatry. Opponents of iconoclasm claimed that the Incarnation justifies the use of icons for worship and devotion. After all, the eternal Word assumed human form (John 1:14) and imaged the Father (John 1:18). They cited God's directives for artistry in tabernacle and temple, which we have reviewed above.

The great theologian of the Eastern church, John of Damascus (d. 749), judged that the worship and veneration of icons were both legitimate. The Seventh Ecumenical Council in Nicea (787) condemned the abolition of icons in churches. Afterward icons became an important part of Christian worship in the East.

For the Eastern church, icons have theological, not merely artistic, value. The icon is said to be a portal to the Divine, facilitating worshipers' access to the heavenly world. This is seen in Greek Orthodox churches, where an icon-covered screen, called the *iconostasis*, separates the altar (heaven) from the nave (earth). For many professing Christians, icons are holy objects worthy of veneration. The faithful bow down and kiss icons; they light candles before icons of saints and petition the latter to intercede with God on their behalf. By the sacramental power of icons, it is believed that prayers are answered and miracles occur. The Protestant Reformers rejected icons. They asserted that Christians meet God through the Word that points to Christ, not through pictures on canvas or statues sculpted in stone.

Let's be clear: Scripture plainly prohibits the *worship* of icons (Exodus 20:3-4). In addition, I find little basis for the veneration of icons because the practice encourages ritualism and superstition. Icons can become a kind of fetish—a material object that supposedly releases to us magical powers. Religious art and icons do, however, possess historical and artistic value. Art and icons may tell a story, stir the emotions, and aid our memory of biblical figures and events. Through paintings, mosaics, sculptures, and the like, Christian artists may portray created—but not uncreated—reality for the glory of God.

WHAT ABOUT THE USE OF IMAGINATION IN MEDITATION?

Though conservatives might accept the types of meditation described so far, many become leery at the idea of using the imagination in meditation. The argument is that the imagination is "fallen" and "self-centered." And the fear is that the imagination is also open to satanic influences, so the Christian may set out to meditate with all good intentions, only to wind up in darkness and deception. These are no small concerns, so we need to address the right use of imagination in meditation.

Imagination is the God-created capacity to form mental images of what is real but not immediately present. The Spiritual Exercises of St. Ignatius (d. 1556) employ the imagination and have been widely used for centuries as an aid to biblical meditation. At the heart of the Ignatian method is *the use of sensory imagination to engage biblical events* at a deeper and more personal level.

Those who oppose using the imagination in meditation claim that it is easily distorted by the meditator or, as I said, subject to deceptive influence by the Devil. These opponents often confuse this type of Christian meditation with a method used in the New Age movement, which uses the imagination to "create" or "influence" reality and expand consciousness. Such practices clearly are unacceptable to Christians.

Evangelicals such as Eugene Peterson and Alister McGrath remind us that Christians used the imagination in meditation for centuries. But the practice fell out of favor under the pressure of Enlightenment rationalism.

Sanctified use of the imagination makes the Scriptures become more real and, therefore, more spiritually transforming. Our creative imaginations are needed to interpret the rich symbolism embedded in the fabric of the Bible. For example, Scripture portrays God as a rock (see Deuteronomy 32:4, Psalm 62:2), a fortress (see Psalm 46:11), a shield (see Psalm 144:2), and a lion (see Hosea 5:14). It depicts Christ as a shepherd (see 1 Peter 5:4), a vine (see John 15:1), a branch (see Zechariah 3:8), and a cornerstone (see 1 Peter 2:6). It represents the Holy Spirit as a stream of living water (see John 7:38-39), a fire (see Acts 2:3), and a dove (see Matthew 3:16). The church is imaged as a body (see 1 Corinthians 12:12-27), a building (see 1 Corinthians 3:9), a bride (see Revelation 19:7; 21:2,9), as well as a family (see Galatians 6:10), a flock (see Psalm 95:7), and a field (see 1 Corinthians 3:9). Jesus' teaching is richly laced with symbolism and imagery, which require the Spirit-led imagination for proper interpretation.

God declares the human being—including the faculty of imagination—to be "very good" (Genesis 1:31). The creative arts, architecture, and city planning—not to mention preaching and teaching—would be impossible without this good gift of imagination. Henry Ward Beecher (d. 1887) says, "The soul without imagination is what an observatory would be without a telescope."[27] A visionary Christian leader, for example, is a person who imagines creative possibilities others have not envisaged. The crucial questions then are, To what use will the imagination be put? Will the imagination be yielded to God and devoted to kingdom purposes? Or will it be put in the service of evil powers?

The universal appeal of writers such as J. R. R. Tolkin and C. S. Lewis is due to their creative use of the imagination. C. S. Lewis believed that reason is the organ of truth, whereas imagination is the organ of meaning. Through the use of imagination, our understanding of spiritual reality is enlarged. Lewis employed his imagination in allegorical fiction such as *The Pilgrim's Regress*, in mythical-poetic writings such as *Screwtape Letters*, in fairy tales such as *Chronicles of Narnia*, and in science fiction works such as his space trilogy (*Out of the Silent Planet*, *Perelandra*, and *That Hideous Strength*). Lewis insisted that we need both good reasoning and good imagination.

The late apologist Francis Schaeffer (d. 1984) said, "Christians . . . ought not be threatened by fantasy and imagination." He added, "The Christian is one whose imagination should fly beyond the stars."[28]

By using the imagination, Christians may enter into biblical scenes that occurred in ancient times and distant places. Imagine yourself a leading character in a biblical scene, such as Jacob wrestling with an angel (see Genesis 32:24-31), Elijah's contest with the false prophets of Baal (see 1 Kings 18), Isaiah's vision in the temple (see Isaiah 6), Jesus washing the disciples' feet (see John 13:1-17), or Paul's trials and afflictions (see 2 Corinthians 11:23-28). Using the sanctified imagination, we can walk the godly path with Abraham, Moses, Daniel, Paul, or John.

How do we proceed? Prayerfully invite the Spirit's leading in the exercise. Read the biblical passage several times with a view to understanding the meaning and message of the text. Enter into the story, reconstructing in your mind as many details as possible. See the sights and colors, hear the sounds, smell the fragrances, so as to make the scene come alive to your senses. Imagine yourself to be a character in the story. How do you think, feel, or respond to the events recorded in the biblical text? How have you experienced God or Jesus in a new way? What does the imaginative meditation tell you about your and others' needs? What step of obedience do you need to take?

The purpose of imaginative meditation on Scripture is not to create reality, which is impossible. It is to open new windows of the soul to revealed truth. The sanctified imagination, working on the words and symbols of Scripture, leads believers to deeper and more relevant dimensions of spiritual understanding. God expects us to use every created capacity—our reason, intuition, imagination, and affections.

The imagination, like the intellect, is trustworthy *when framed by Scripture and yielded to the Spirit.* It can be helpful to check the results of your meditation with spiritually minded friends. We can develop our God-given imaginations by creative, right-brain exercises, such as painting, writing fictional stories, role-playing biblical scenes, or keeping a spiritual journal.

I close this section with an observation from Oswald Chambers (d. 1917), the esteemed British Bible teacher. Chambers quoted Isaiah 26:3—"Thou wilt keep him in perfect peace whose imagination is stayed on Thee"—and commented,

> Is your imagination stayed on God or is it starved? The starvation of the imagination is one of the most fruitful sources of exhaustion and sapping in a worker's life. If you have never used your imagination to put yourself before God, begin to do it now. . . . Imagination is the greatest gift God has given us and it ought to be devoted entirely to Him.[29]

Should Christians Practice Transcendental Meditation?

As we've noted, some Christians claim to have found benefit in nonChristian forms of meditation, especially Transcendental Meditation. What do we say to these claims?

Transcendental Meditation (TM) is a leading form of yoga in the West. From the Sanskrit word meaning "union," yoga is a five-thousand-year-old system of Hindu philosophy and practice that seeks to bring people into union with one's "higher Self" (*atman*), which is the "God Self" (*Brahman*). In 1957, a Hindu monk named Maharishi Mahesh Yogi emerged from seclusion in the Himalayas and began to teach self-realization through Transcendental Meditation. Today millions of people in more than one hundred countries regularly practice the form of meditation found in the Hindu holy books.

Advocates claim that TM is a nonreligious practice suitable for people of all faiths. But the initiation ceremony to obtain one's mantra (a Hindu holy word, often the name of a deity) requires bowing to twenty-six Hindu gods or gurus. The initiate repeats the following words:

> Guru in the glory of Brahman, Guru in
> the glory of Vishnu,
> Guru in the glory of the great Lord Shiva,
> Guru in the glory of the personified
> transcendental fulness of Brahman,
> to Him, to Shri Guru Dev adorned with glory,
> I bow down.

Courts in the United States have ruled that TM is not a secular discipline; it is Hindu religion.[30]

Seated with eyes closed, the meditator repeats a mantra, either silently as a meditation or audibly as a chant. The TM practitioner can meditate on anything because, according to its pantheistic worldview, everything is God! If the practitioner chants the mantra, the vibrations of its sounds are said to return the soul to its Source, that is, Brahman. The goal during meditation is not thought, but simple awareness or connection to the "God Self." In the deep condition of relaxation, the person may go into a trance and lose all sense of separateness from other persons and even the world itself.

Extensive benefits are claimed for TM. The mind is said to achieve a higher level of intelligence and increased creativity. The body may enjoy reduced anxiety, decreased stress, and improved general health. In terms of behavior, the meditator is said to experience heightened self-control, improved interpersonal relations, and greater happiness. Globally, TM allegedly creates a more harmonious environment, which improves the quality of life for the human family.

The wider goal of TM is to rid the world of suffering and bring heavenly enlightenment to earth in a society of happiness and peace. The Maharishi promises that "Heaven will descend on Earth with peace in every home of our world family." Be aware that in this "Heaven" the transcendental meditator loses personal identity by being dissolved into Brahman, much as a dewdrop dissolves in the ocean.

Some Christians insist they find the breathing and relaxation techniques of TM a helpful way to reduce stress. It must be understood that those who practice TM subscribe to a pantheistic, Hindu worldview. In the system of TM, Brahman is universal energy; man's problem is the failure to recognize his inner divinity; the Maharishi is the supreme teacher; and salvation is absorption into Divinity. R. C. Zaehner, the Oxford professor of Eastern religions, claims that because there is no "Other" to worship or commune with, TM is an exercise in "self-deification."[31] Hindus and transcendental meditators actually worship themselves!

As Christians, we cannot allow ourselves to be lured, even by physiological benefits, away from the path that forms us in the image of Christ—the path of humble submission to God.

Be aware that the practice of TM may involve traffic with dark, spiritual powers. People should seek stress reduction and mental alertness by other means consistent with the Christian worldview. The object of the Christian's meditation must always be the true and living God, His revealed Word, and His saving work through Christ.

Summing Up

I sometimes say of my preChristian past that I was running from God so fast that all He could see was my backside. Theologically, of course, this is incorrect. But at a practical level, many of us are moving so fast that we can't hear God speak or effectively touch His heart.

Every one of us must make a strategic decision to break the cycle of perpetual busyness and learn how to quiet our souls before the Lord. We need to move from being externally driven performance machines to internally motivated intimates of God. It's worth repeating: Our loving God never ceases to communicate with His children; and our great need is to become attuned to the subtle whisper and workings of His Spirit.

Quietness provides an environment in which we may

discover the God who is closer to us than life itself. When our noisy, distracted souls are stilled, we give the Lord in all His magnificence permission to meet us.

Sacred Scripture is our primary meeting place with God. Through the written Word, God reveals to us His will, His ways, and best of all, Himself! But we must read the Word as more than a book that yields information because it is a love letter and a promise of real and powerful transformation.

Our goal in meditation is not self-realization or self-deification. It is nothing less than to further our growth in the spiritual likeness of God's Son.

Try It Yourself

1. An exercise in *lectio divina.*

In this exercise you will meditate on a portion of God's Word. You may choose any text of Scripture you like. As an example, I will use a short text from John 7.

> On the last day, the climax of the festival, Jesus stood and shouted to the crowds, "If you are thirsty, come to me! If you believe in me, come and drink! For the Scriptures declare that rivers of living water will flow out from within." (John 7:37-38)

The setting is the Feast of Tabernacles, celebrating God's goodness to Israel during the wilderness wanderings. As you begin reading, observe that on the seventh and final day of the feast, Jesus entered the temple to worship. The Lord did a most unusual thing there. He stood up among the crowd and began to speak, saying, *"If you are thirsty . . ."* As you ponder these words of Jesus, what do they say to you? Perhaps Christ has not been a vital reality in your life for some time. Has the spiritual dryness you experience created a hunger and thirst for God? Talk to the

Lord about your spiritual longings. As you continue reading, Jesus' words, *"Come to me!"* may grab your attention. How does this personal invitation speak to your life? You might tell the Lord how thankful you are that He invites you to come to Him for refreshment. Pause and sense the reality of God's open invitation.

You continue reading and discover that Jesus said, *"If you believe in me, come and drink!"* Pondering these words, can you say that you believe in Jesus with your whole heart? If you truly trust Him, then you meet Jesus' condition for spiritual refreshment.

Talk to the Lord in prayer about this. You might tell Him that you eagerly accept His invitation to partake of the spiritual drink He offers. Rest in the assurance that the living Christ longs to satisfy your spiritual thirst. Return again to the text and read the next words Jesus spoke: *"For the Scriptures declare that rivers of living water will flow out from within."* Meditate on the power of this sure promise of the loving Lord. You might reflect on the fact that, as a true child of God, the all-sufficient Comforter lives within you. Yes, the refreshing water of the Spirit will satisfy your parched soul. Pause, extend open hands, and receive the spiritual refreshment Christ graciously offers.

Choose another biblical text and meditate upon it, using a method suggested in this chapter.

2. Using your imagination in biblical meditation.

Let's do an exercise in biblical meditation using our God-given imaginations. Choose a biblical symbol, imagery, or word picture. Reflect on its spiritual meaning. Relate yourself to that symbol or word picture. In a couple of paragraphs describe how this symbol informs your life spiritually.

As an example, consider the symbolism of the eagle presented in Isaiah 40. Isaiah was a God-fearing prophet wearied by the sins of the people and the grave military threat posed by the world powers, Assyria and Babylon. Seven hundred years before Christ, Isaiah was walking the hills near Jerusalem when he observed an eagle soaring on the thermals. The sight of that graceful and powerful bird afforded him a great sense of comfort. Yahweh is a God who forgives, restores, and strengthens His people in all their trials. Hear the prophet say,

> He gives power to those who are tired and worn out; he offers strength to the weak. Even youths will become exhausted, and young men will give up. But those who wait on the LORD will find new strength. They will fly high on wings like eagles. They will walk and not faint. (Isaiah 40:29-31)

Imagine that you are Isaiah observing the eagle in its soaring flight. What does the eagle's comely form—its pure white head, large wingspan, and graceful movements—suggest to you? The attractiveness of the eagle may remind you of the beauty that has come into your life since you became a Christian. What about the eagle's flight? What does the effortless soaring of the eagle, as it rises high above the earth on thermal currents, represent for you? The broad sweep of the eagle's course may suggest your freedom as a believer to explore dimensions of spiritual reality hitherto unknown. The burdensome weight of sin has been lifted, and your spirit has been set free to soar like an eagle.

What does the eagle's sharp eye—which can detect a small object like a field mouse a mile away—suggest to you? It may symbolize a new spiritual perception. In Christ, you now see realities that your Christless eyes never saw before. What about the eagle's large nest, ensconced in a high tree or crag on a remote cliff? The nest appears precariously perched on a high outcropping. But, in fact, it's secure from all predators. This may indicate to you that in the Lord you are safe amidst life's many dangers. Finally, what does the great strength of this bird of prey portray to you? Its sturdy wings and powerful claws may suggest the spiritual and moral strength that God alone gives. As you trust the Lord, He infuses your life with supernatural power.

Choose another biblical symbol or word picture. Use your imagination to flesh out its spiritual meaning for your personal life and the life of your community.

Suggestions for Further Reading

Hall, Thelma. *Too Deep for Words: Rediscovering Lectio Divina.* New York: Paulist, 1988.

Janzen, Janet Lindeblad. *Songs for Spiritual Renewal.* San Francisco: HarperSanFrancisco, 1995.

McGrath, Alister. *Beyond the Quiet Time.* Grand Rapids: Baker, 1995.

Mulholland, Jr., Robert M. *Shaped by the Word: The Power of Scripture in Spiritual Formation.* Nashville: Upper Room, 1985.

Nouwen, Henri J. M. *The Return of the Prodigal Son.* New York: Doubleday/Image, 1992.

Toon, Peter. *Meditating As a Christian.* London: Collins, 1991.

CHAPTER SIX

The Power of Contemplation

"The one thing I ask of the LORD—the thing I seek most—is to live in the house of the LORD all the days of my life, delighting in the LORD'S perfections and meditating in his Temple."

PSALM 27:4

"The life of contemplation . . . is the life of the Holy Spirit in our inmost souls. The whole duty of contemplation is to abandon what is base and trivial in {your} own life, and do all {you} can to conform . . . to the secret and obscure promptings of the Spirit of God. This requires a constant discipline of humility, obedience, self-distrust, prudence and above all of faith."

THOMAS MERTON[1]

In the last chapter we saw how to grow in the experience of God's presence by meditating on sacred Scripture and on great devotional writings, hymns, and works of art. There is another way to open your soul to the invisible reality of God. That is the long-honored Judeo-Christian practice of looking to the Lord Himself.

In Christian history this is known as *contemplation*—what Brother Lawrence called "the practice of the presence of God."

Christians today often have qualms about the discipline of contemplation. "Isn't it just 'navel gazing'?" "Aren't you talking about escapism?" Not so. Contemplating on the triune God is a healthy biblical practice that makes the soul robust in its connection to God.

David the warrior-king writes, "I lie awake thinking of you, [Lord], meditating on you through the night" (Psalm 63:6). People fix their hearts and center all their energies around a mental image—and idol—of the career, home, or luxury car they want. A woman may hold in her heart a picture that represents the settled, peaceable life she longs for, for her family. A man may envision the dream home he wishes for, to affirm his "success." Similarly, any Christian can anchor his or her existence in a vision of our wonderful God who, age to age, does not change.

Living contemplatively is not a luxury. It is the habit of living in the presence of God, and it provides the solid foundation for the whole of Christian life and service.

Looking into the Face of Holiness and Love

Our God is a God of *wonders*—and in Him lie great depths of holiness and love. Truly He is a God deserving of our reverence and love.

As we've discussed, cultivating any relationship requires openness, availability, attentiveness—and *time* spent understanding each other at deeper levels, *looking into* each other's hearts.

Sadly, surveys show that a typical married couple spends only twenty minutes a day in meaningful conversation. The average Christian spends barely five minutes a day with God in prayer; the typical pastor, only seven. Is it possible for a real relationship to flourish, given such a puny amount of time and contact? I don't think so, do you?

Contemplation is the practice of focusing our inmost being by fixing the eyes of the inner man on God Himself. It's a long-standing practice in our ancient Hebrew-Christian tradition. Why do we not teach the art of contemplation today?

A perceptive seminary student recently said to me: "Most evangelical Protestants at the end of the twentieth century are woefully out of touch with the contemplative side of their Christian walk. Not many yearn for this kind of prayer and devotional life." Another admitted, "Most of my prayers aren't focused on God but on myself, addressing personal needs."

THE PRAYER OF THE HEART

Christians need a new vision of what our Christian forebears called practicing the presence of God, or contemplative prayer.

As an entry point into contemplative living, modern Christians might practice what saints of old called the prayer of the heart or the prayer of simplicity. This is a prayer of *the heart* because it is expressed through the deepest longings of our inner being. It is a prayer of *simplicity* because of its brevity. Some suggest that it is also a *centering* prayer because it gathers the dispersed and fragmented heart into God. A divided heart—one pulled this way and that by competing desires, drives, and demands, as if by an unruly team of horses—is an obstacle to experiencing God's presence and peace.

The purpose of the prayer of the heart is to open believers to the reality of God so that He may speak to core issues of our lives.

At its simplest, the prayer of the heart involves lovingly reciting a biblical word or phrase. This could be an attribute of God or the fruit of His presence, such as *love* or *peace.* It could also be a name of God in English *(Lord)*, Hebrew *(Shaddai),* or Aramaic *(Abba),* or the name *Jesus.* By the powerful name of Jesus, demons are cast out and people are healed. Francis of Assisi (d. 1226) practiced the prayer of the heart by repeating the favorite phrase, "My God and my all," and Thomas Aquinas (d. 1274), by the prayer, "I adore You, hidden God."

A means of cultivating the prayer of the heart is the Jesus Prayer. This prayer is adapted from petitions made to the Lord by a Gentile woman (Matthew 15:22), Bartimaeus (Mark 10:47-48), a tax collector (Luke 18:13), and a beggar (Luke 18:38-39). The Jesus Prayer is simple indeed: *"Lord Jesus Christ, Son of God, have mercy upon me, a sinner."* It has been prayed by Christians from earliest centuries because it contains core convictions of the gospel—Christ's incarnation, deity, and saving action. The prayer is often shortened to *"Lord Jesus, have mercy."*

What does this kind of prayer accomplish?

John Calvin (d. 1564) urges believers to bring lofty ideas in the mind, such as the love and grace of God, into the heart as lived experience. The prayerful repetition of a biblical word or phrase helps this to happen. Henri Nouwen reminds us that "a word or sentence repeated frequently can help us to concentrate, to move to the center, to create an inner stillness and thus to listen to the voice of God."[2]

Many who practice the Jesus Prayer recognize its powerful ability to promote a delightful abandonment to the Lord in faith. We deliberately present ourselves to Christ so that we might be filled with Him. Perhaps you've puzzled over Paul's command to "pray without ceasing" (1 Thessalonians 5:17, KJV). Is Paul suggesting that spoken prayers should flow ceaselessly from our lips? This seems impossible, even for a hermit in a cave. More likely, Paul intended that simple adoration of God should flow from our hearts in an endless stream, and cultivation of the simplest prayer of the heart makes this a growing reality.

Pray Without Confusion

As with other spiritual practices, it's crucial to make distinctions between the *outer appearance* of techniques that Christians and nonChristians may share in common and the *purpose* or *goal* of those techniques.

The prayer of the heart, therefore, must not be confused with Eastern, pantheistic prayers. We've seen that practitioners of TM, for example, chant a meaningless mantra in search of altered states of consciousness. NonChristian techniques such as these never lead to a saving relationship with Christ and can cause practitioners to wrongly believe they are "ascending" above others. Christians meditate in order to know and love the triune God of the Bible.

The prayer of the heart, including the Jesus Prayer, *is* biblically and theologically sound. As practiced by Christians for centuries, this prayer does not bypass Christ because the Son of God Himself is its focus. Nor does it omit the Cross, for Christ's saving work is implicit in the prayer. Because it looks to Christ, it protects believers from evil spirits, rather than exposing them.

Aren't we supposed to avoid "vain repetition" in our prayers? That is true. But the Bible does not prohibit *meaningful* repetition of biblical words and phrases.

Open your Bible and look for words that are repeated in Psalm 136. You notice that the refrain, "*His faithful love endures forever,*" is repeated twenty-six times in this one psalm! Furthermore, devout Jews—and undoubtedly Jesus Himself—reverently repeated the *Shema* of Israel twice daily: "Hear, O Israel! The LORD is our God, the LORD alone" (Deuteronomy 6:4). Moreover, the book of Revelation tells us that angels in heaven repeat eternally the refrain, "Holy, holy, holy, is the Lord God Almighty—the one who always was, who is, and who is still to come" (Revelation 4:8).

What Scripture forbids is not repetition in prayer, but "vain" or meaningless repetition (Matthew 6:7), which applies to such things as the mantras used in other forms of meditation to promote altered states of consciousness. Jesus, more likely, was referring to distraction in prayer and worship, where we are mouthing words while our minds and hearts are elsewhere. And if we're honest, we'll admit that at one time or another we've sung hymns or prayed in a distracted, meaningless frame of mind.

To further our spiritual transformation—to experience a satisfying connection to God—we need to compose our souls and focus single-heartedly on Him. A Christian who is not calmly present to himself cannot be present to God. The psalmist writes, "Be still in the presence of the LORD, and wait patiently for him to act" (Psalm 37:7). Again, "I long for the LORD more than sentries long for the dawn, yes, more than sentries long for the dawn" (Psalm 130:6). In the New Testament, James issues the command, "Draw close to God, and he will draw close to you" (James 4:8). The prayer of the heart, or the prayer of simplicity, helps Christians to be open and present to the God who is always present to us.

PRACTICING THE PRESENCE OF GOD

From the prayer of simplicity, you might transition to the Christian discipline of practicing the presence of God (Brother Lawrence), or contemplative prayer (Thomas Merton). My dictionary defines contemplation as "looking at or viewing an object with continued attention." In this sense, we may contemplate a beautiful flower, a snow-capped mountain, or the altogether lovely God. Of course, no one has seen God with physical eyes (John 1:18).

This leads to the core question that troubles critics of contemplative prayer and new beginners alike: It's one thing to envision the pictures of God given in Scripture, but how can you claim to "see" our invisible God?

Believers may indeed behold God by faith that opens the eyes of the soul, which is to say our spiritual perception. David writes, "One thing I ask of the LORD, this is what I seek: that I may dwell in the house of the LORD all the days of my life, to gaze upon the beauty of the LORD and to seek him in his temple"

(Psalm 27:4, NIV). Scripture often refers to "seeing" the face of God in a spiritual sense, this side of glory (see Psalm 11:7, 63:2, Matthew 5:8, Hebrews 12:14).

Contemplative prayer focuses you on God with your spirit, the discerning eye of the heart.

WHAT ARE WE TALKING ABOUT?

How do you practice this ancient, but neglected, form of prayer? Here are a few simple basics. It isn't difficult really, and it's amazing how natural it becomes.

First, quiet your heart by gently turning aside from the distractions of your life. Begin by focusing your thoughts on an attribute of God, such as His *power*, *goodness*, or *mercy*. Many testify to the fact that focusing on such attributes of the divine nature is radically transforming, as it may occur for the very first time how God has shown Himself powerful, good, or merciful in their lives. Invariably, such an interior realization moves a person to heartfelt worship.

Then rest in the Lord, believing that as you draw near to God, He will draw near to you (James 4:8). Agree with the psalmist, who writes, "My heart has heard you say, 'Come and talk with me.' And my heart responds, 'LORD, I am coming'" (Psalm 27:8). In the sacred place of prayer sit, as it were, at the Lord's feet. Yield your entire being to Him who owns you body, soul, and spirit (Romans 12:2).

At this point, you might pray from the heart, "Lord, You are my Father, and by grace I am Your adopted child. You are the divine Lover, and by Your favor I am the beloved. I surrender all to You so that You might show Yourself as You see fit."

Look to the Lord in faith with singular attentiveness. Listen for His voice. Sense His presence. Rest in His love. Marvel at His purity, holiness, and how altogether right it is for Him to enact His judgments throughout the earth. Then lift your heart in love and adoration to God in whom you delight.

Here is the delightful surprise: Many have brushed aside the practice of contemplation because they believe they're "too busy" for such a luxury. But once they've practiced this ancient and soul-renewing type of prayer form, they find it so inwardly satisfying that they are loathe to live without it!

Is It Prayer If I'm Not Speaking to God?

Some are troubled by this question, but longing, joy, and even contrition do not always need to be communicated in words.

A man may communicate something powerful and heart-connecting to his wife by looking deeply into her eyes while his heart is full of love and contentment. In the same way, we can savor God's presence and give our hearts to Him without offering a litany of requests. There is a story of an old peasant who went every noon to the village church to pray. One day the priest asked him, "Sir, is something troubling you?" "Oh no, father," the old man replied. "I just look at God, and God looks at me." John Calvin agrees, for he writes that "the best prayers are sometimes unspoken."[3]

Contemplation is the perfect counterpart to the biblical meditation that works the words and truths of God into our souls.

As Richard of St. Victor (d. 1173) puts it, "Meditation investigates, contemplation wonders."[4] Both disciplines should be staples in the Christian's spiritual diet. Meditation without contemplation can become dry and ponderous. Contemplation without meditation may lack the surety of biblical rootedness. "Meditation is the act of turning our attention from the things of the world to the things of God, but contemplation involves turning our attention from the things of God to attend to God himself."[5] Growing Christians might follow the order of biblical meditation, verbal prayer, and practicing the presence of God. This is the order of the classical *lectio divina*, which we considered in the previous chapter.

Testimonies from Our Christian Heritage

Practicing the presence of God has been a staple of Christian devotion through the centuries. Augustine (d. 430) describes the prayer of contemplation as a loving gaze of the human spirit directed toward God. The great church father observed that God called some biblical figures, such as Rachel, Mary, and John, to a serious life of contemplation.

Recalling the story of Mary and Martha in Luke 10, John Cassian (d. 435) wrote,

> The Lord establishes as the prime good contemplation, that is, the gaze turned in the direction of the things of God. Hence we say that the other virtues, however useful and good . . . must nevertheless be put on a secondary level, since they are all practiced for the sake of this one. . . . The Lord locates the primary good not in activity, however praiseworthy, however abundantly fruitful, but in the truly simple and unified contemplation of Himself.[6]

Another great theologian of the church, Anselm of Canterbury (d. 1109), said this about the prayer of contemplation:

> Abandon yourself for a little to God and rest for a little in Him. Enter into the little chamber of your soul, shut out everything save God and what can be of help in your quest for Him and having locked the door seek Him out (Matt. 6:6). Speak now, my whole heart, speak now to God: 'I seek Your countenance, O Lord, Your countenance I seek' (Psa. 36:8).
>
> Come then, Lord my god, teach my heart where and how to seek You, where and how to find you.[7]

The great Puritan divine, John Owen (d. 1683), agrees. "One of the greatest privileges and advancement of believers, both in this world and unto eternity, consists in the beholding of the glory of Christ."[8] This is precisely the prayer of the heart, or contemplative prayer.

Though some evangelicals today resist contemplation as "coming from another tradition," earlier Reformed believers defended and practiced it regularly.

Richard Baxter (d. 1691), author of *The Reformed Pastor,* believed that the Reformers overreacted to Rome by vilifying certain spiritually edifying disciplines. Baxter wrote, "We are fled so far from superstitious solitude, that we have cast off the solitude of contemplative devotion."[9] Setting your heart upon God in contemplation is a noble activity, for it "opens the door between the head and the heart"[10] and "presents to the affections those things which are most important."[11] Baxter imagined that at the final judgment "the question will not be, How much have you known, or professed, or talked? but How much have you loved, and Where was your heart?"[12] Knowing the Word is a means to the end of knowing God Himself. And Baxter wrote, "If God's Word be so full of consolation, what overflowing springs should we find in God Himself?"[13]

Lawrence of the Resurrection (d. 1691) was a lay brother who served as a kitchen servant in a Carmelite monastery. Brother Lawrence humbly confessed Christ as his Savior from sin: "Without anxiety, we should expect pardon for our sins by Jesus' blood."[14] His consuming passion was to abide in the presence of the loving God. He wrote, "I just make my business this: To persevere in His holy presence. I stay there by a simple attention and by an absorbing passionate regard for God, which I want to call an *actual presence of God.*"[15] He added, "Often I find myself attached to God with greater delight than a baby at its mother's breast, so that—if I dared use the expression—I would call this closeness to God, suckling at the bosom of God, because of the inexpressible sweetness I taste and experience there."[16] Although God blessed Brother Lawrence with joyous spiritual consolations, he steadfastly believed that "The soul that enjoys God, desires in that experience nothing but Him."[17]

Likewise, the highly respected Norwegian evangelical leader and authority on prayer, Ole Hallesby (d. 1961), recognized the importance of practicing the presence:

> Prayer is really an attitude of our hearts to God. As such it finds expression, at times in words and at times without words, precisely as when two people love each other.

> In the soul's fellowship with God in prayer, there are things which can and should be formulated in words. . . . But there are also things for which we can find no words. Likely it is this to which the apostle makes reference when he speaks in Romans 8:26 of the "groanings which cannot be uttered."[18]

For centuries, then, Christians practiced a full range of prayer that we have lost today. Mental prayer (via the mind), verbal prayer (through the lips), and contemplative prayer (from the heart) were once integrated through the practice of *lectio divina.* And so the whole of man's fallen, scattered being were brought into unity under God. In modern times the mental, verbal, and affective parts of prayer have separated from one another. Given our preference for intellectual activity and action, we've neglected prayer of the heart and contemplative prayer.

Our forebears the Puritans in many respects enjoyed a vital spiritual life. Yet some scholars suggest that Puritan spirituality died out as a cultural force because the contemplative dimension remained undeveloped in the movement.[19] This should serve as a warning to us today.

Biblical Basis

Practicing the presence of God finds clear support of Scripture.

Consider the following verses from Psalm 63: "O God, you are my God; I earnestly search for you. My soul thirsts for you; my whole body longs for you in this parched and weary land where there is no water. I have seen you in your sanctuary and gazed upon your power and glory" (verses 1-2).

You may recall a significant event in the life of the prophet Elijah, recorded in 1 Kings 19. In spite of the great victory over the 850 false prophets on Mount Carmel, Israel continued in their rebellious ways. This hardness of heart caused Elijah to sink into self-pity and despair. The man of God fled the country of Carmel into the Sinai desert. There he spent the night in a cave to await the divine presence. God sent a severe storm into the area. But the Lord was not in the wind, the earthquake, or the fire. Rather, God showed Himself to Elijah through "a sound of sheer silence" (verse 12, NRSV). The Hebrew literally means "through the sound of a gentle whisper." Elijah detected the Lord's voice, came into His presence, and responded obediently to Him.

Have you ever wondered what it means to "wait on the Lord"? I suggest that it is akin to practicing the presence of God. Isaiah declares, "Those who wait on the LORD will find new strength. They will fly high on wings like eagles. They will run and not grow weary. They will walk and not faint" (Isaiah 40:31). Consider, too, the prophet Jeremiah: "The LORD is wonderfully good to those who wait for him and seek him. So it is good to wait quietly for salvation from the LORD" (Lamentations 3:25-26). The biblical language of the believing heart or mind fixed on the Lord suggests the same idea. "You will keep in perfect peace all who trust in you, whose thoughts are fixed on you!" (Isaiah 26:3).

Observe how often in the Gospels Jesus withdrew to a quiet place for undisturbed communion with the Father (Mark 1:35-39, 14:32). Jesus had an active ministry training the disciples, preaching to crowds, healing the sick, and exorcising demons. Yet the Lord sensed the need to deepen relationship with the Father by spending hours alone with Him. On the eve of His crucifixion, Jesus led His disciples into a garden, saying, "Stay here and watch with me" (Matthew 26:38). When the Lord finished praying alone and found His friends sleeping, He said, "Couldn't you stay awake and watch with me even one hour? Keep alert and pray" (verses 40-41). What is this, but the prayer of loving attention?

The apostle Paul was familiar with the habit of practicing the presence. He writes to the Colossian Christians: "Don't shuffle along, eyes to the ground, absorbed with the things right in front of you. Look up, and be alert to what is going on around Christ—that's where the action is" (Colossians 3:1-2, MSG).

It's reported that a priest once asked Mother Teresa for her advice as to how he might be more effective in his calling to Christian ministry. She responded, "Spend one hour a day in adoration of your Lord, and never do anything you know to be wrong, and you will be all right." What is this devotion to the Lord that she commends, but lovingly practicing the presence of God?

Benefits of Contemplative Prayer

What good do we derive from the habit of contemplating God? By practicing the presence, Christians touch the heart of God and are restored and empowered spiritually (Romans 12:2).[20]

I have discovered, from uneven experience, that I love most dearly the person with whom I spend the most time and to whom I most open my heart. It's impossible to love a person I do not know. By balancing verbal prayer with contemplative prayer, God becomes more real to me, and my love for Him more consuming. In verbal prayer, I tell God that He is loved, but through contemplative prayer, God tells me that I am loved with a love that is undying.

The purpose of contemplation is not primarily to form ideas about God. No, it's to enter into God's presence and be touched by the One who lives at the center of our being. Practicing the presence deepens experiential knowledge of God. It enlarges love at a more profound and renewing level than mental reflection alone. A. W. Tozer (d. 1963) comments that verbal prayer, Bible study, and Christian service "are all good and should be engaged in by every Christian. But at the bottom of all these things, giving meaning to them will be the inward habit of beholding God. . . . When the habit of inwardly gazing Godward becomes fixed within us, we shall be ushered onto a new level of spiritual life more in keeping with the promises of God and the mood of the New Testament."[21]

A second benefit of contemplative prayer is the discovery of your true identity as a child of God. As we practice the presence, the Spirit—through an inner anointing—helps us let go of the old "false self" with its insecurities, fears, and hostilities. The Spirit empowers the "new self" in Christ, with its gift of being loved and valued by God. In this way, contemplation of God enhances both spiritual growth and emotional well-being. Augustine recognized these two benefits of contemplative prayer: "May I know You, may I know myself. That is my prayer."[22]

An evangelical pastor friend, who leads a contemplative prayer group, excitedly reports positive spiritual changes in the lives of its members. He comments,

> With great joy I watch God's people change inwardly. They go beyond intellectual comprehension of truths to engaging Christ in existential embrace. As a result of this contemplative experience, members of the group reflect greater spiritual depth as well as enhanced grace and love. Their growing passion for Jesus Christ is a thing of beauty.

Verbal prayer changes circumstances in the external world; contemplative prayer changes the inner world of the Christian who so prays.

Parodies of Practicing the Presence

Unfortunately, there are practices that can imitate Christian contemplation, and those we want to avoid.

Some pseudo-contemplatives operate within a pantheistic worldview. They claim that the human soul is part of the one, all-encompassing Reality. Contemplating the Soul of the universe amounts to practicing the presence of Myself.[23] Others falsely claim that everyone who practices contemplative prayer, even without faith in Christ, engages God in a saving way. They say it makes no difference whether contemplative prayer be performed in a Christian, Buddhist, or Hindu context. Jesus, Buddha, and Krishna are said to be equally suitable objects of contemplation. This belief is a deception.

A Christian contemplative lifestyle forms in us a healthy, right relationship with the living God of the Bible. We will not pass into a blissful nothingness when we die; instead we'll contemplate Christ in His glory through the endless ages of eternity (see Revelation 11:16-17, 19:4-5). We need not be afraid to enter into that satisfying experience here and now.

With joy we contemplate the grace
of our High Priest above;
his heart is made of tenderness;
it overflows with love. (Isaac Watts)[24]

Contemplative Simplicity in Worship

A. W. Tozer (d. 1963) said worship is the missing jewel in the evangelical crown. Our attempts at worship often seem better suited to entertainment than ushering worshipers into God's awesome and holy presence. A newspaper article tells of the growing number of evangelicals who have converted to Eastern Orthodoxy.[25] It mentions Franky Schaeffer, son of the late Francis Schaeffer, as a prominent convert. Schaeffer speaks of the "Disney-fication" of Sunday morning evangelical worship with its man-centered approach, raucous bands, and "one-line mantras." Evangelical converts to Orthodoxy claim to have been drawn to this ancient branch of Christianity (in spite of theological problems) because of its richly aesthetic and contemplative form of worship.

In many ways, evangelicals are just discovering contemplative prayer and worship and are overflowing with contentment as they encounter our majestic God in their souls. Here are a few models of contemplative prayer and worship.

The Taizé Model

The Taizé community in France, founded by Brother Roger (a Reformed pastor), features an uplifting, contemplative style of worship. Some evangelical churches provide periodic Taizé services that attract Christians seeking satisfaction through a personal encounter with the Lord.

An American pastor who visited the Taizé community testifies to a life-changing experience. He relates that entering the Taizé chapel,

> I was filled with awe.
>
> In the candlelit sanctuary, the brothers of Taizé, in shimmering white albs, were chanting to lilting organ and flute music. . . . The white walls were punctuated by beautiful stained glass windows. The candlelight mingled with the red carpeted floor and the white robes. There was a simplicity to that worship space that drew me to God.

Upon returning to his own church, he wrote,

> As a pastor, I began to look at services of worship that I had prepared and led. I found that they had too many words, too many explanations, and too few images. The worship services blurred the view of God because they were cluttered, complicated, and noisy.

He was convinced that "contemplative simplicity in worship would invite people to dwell in the arms of God":

> I search for words and images that hint at the wonder of God. . . . As I plan worship services, I now try to . . . evoke that yearning to praise and worship, nurture that restlessness for God.
>
> I look for music with words and tunes that sink easily into the heart. . . . Favorite old hymns and newly repeated verses can find a resting place deep inside and help us to live each day in the spirit of unceasing prayer.
>
> I am not an architect, but my experience at Taizé taught me that there can be a contemplative simplicity to worship environments that beckons me into the presence of God. When I am in such a space, I feel

> my heart lifted and my eyes focused. I sense a pervasive restfulness and a tender openness. . . The quiet colors of stone and wood, the pencil-thin beams of light, the pure lines of the communion table, the texture of woven paraments all contribute to a pervasive sense of the sacred. I am invited into a hospitable space where clarity, quietness, and simplicity reign.

He concludes that "the simplicity of words and the attention given to sacred space, shape, and sound sensitizes and energizes the worshipers to seek a contemplative simplicity in their weekday world."[26]

Liturgy Revisited

The delicacy and power of the worship experiences in renewal communities that I know is impressive. With extraordinary sensitivity, leaders conduct worshipers into God's presence to behold His beauty and glory. The bulk of my Christian experience has been in nonliturgical settings. But in recent years I have gained a greater appreciation for the life-transforming power of faithful liturgy, which connects worshipers with core convictions of the gospel celebrated by Christians for two millennia.

The word *liturgy* comes from the Greek word *leitourgia,* meaning "service" or "ministry" (see Luke 1:23; 2 Corinthians 9:12; Philippians 2:17,30). It in turn comes from two other Greek words, *laos* ("people") and *ergon* ("work"). Liturgy, therefore, is the labor of the laity or the soul-work of the people. It is the spiritual work that Christians perform in their seasons of public worship.

The Jewish temple practice of singing psalms in short, musical patterns, antiphonally (two groups singing alternate verses), found its way into services of early Christian worship (see Ephesians 5:19, Colossians 3:16). The New Testament itself contains numerous evidences of liturgical responses (see 1 Corinthians 11:24-25, 1 Timothy 3:16, 3 John 15), prayer formulas ("*Maranatha,*" see 1 Corinthians 16:22, Revelation 22:20), and hymn fragments (see Philippians 2:5-11;

Colossians 1:20; Revelation 4:11, 7:12). Worship in New Testament communities involved set formulas as well as spontaneous expressions (see 1 Corinthians 14:26-33). In the post-apostolic church, the early second–century *Didache* (especially chapters 9–10), the writings of Justin Martyr (d. 165), and the *Apostolic Tradition* (c. 215) of Hippolytus, to mention a few, reflect liturgical forms of Christian worship.

Through a biblically based liturgy involving set forms, Christians celebrate God's saving work through Christ. Liturgy includes reading Scripture and sharing in biblical responses, such as the *Magnificat* (see Luke 1:46-55), *Benedictus* (1:68-79), and *Nunc Dimittus* (2:29-32). It includes singing psalms, reciting Christian creeds, speaking prayers, and celebrating the sacraments—all of which contemplatively rehearse the faith of the church. When worship services fail to invite participation by the people, boredom lies at the door. Because liturgy maximizes personal involvement in worship, it enhances satisfaction in God.

Reformers such as Luther, Calvin, and Knox used liturgy in corporate worship. Calvin believed that liturgy limits levity and giddiness in worship. It keeps before the hearts of worshipers the seriousness of the gospel. Some later theologians, such as John Owen, alleged that liturgies stifle the work of the Spirit. I believe, with the Reformers, that faithful liturgy is a tool the Spirit uses to move Christians deeper into the Christian reality. When internalized by faith, biblical and creedal responses in the liturgy restore and reshape the Christian's soul.

An outstanding seminary student who moved from Catholicism to an evangelical denomination offers this candid evaluation: "Treated casually, ritual can become a rut. But the power of aesthetics, biblically based liturgy, and faithful Christian ritual afford Anglicans and Roman Catholics a more profound personal experience of God."

In my experience, some of the free-wheeling worship in our churches is akin to dousing a garden with a high-pressure hose. Much of the water runs off and fails to penetrate the soil. Biblically faithful liturgy, however, is more like a "soaker hose," which slowly but effectively delivers water into the subsoil to nourish plants at their roots. We are well served to reintroduce neglected elements of a biblically based liturgy into our public worship of God.

Worship with Your Senses

The Spirit uses created things to connect worshipers with the living God. These include things that can be *seen* (a magnificent picture of the resurrected Christ), *heard* (the sound of a bell), *touched* (a healing hug), *tasted* (bread and wine), and *smelled* (incense or flowers). The psalmist recognized the importance of the senses when he wrote that idols "cannot . . . see, though they have eyes! They cannot hear with their ears, or smell with their noses" (Psalm 135:16-17). I recall my initial discomfort when worshiping with aspects of my being that had long been neglected. But gradually I discovered the richness of relating to God with all my created faculties and senses. A moment's thought reveals that worshiping God with one's entire being accords with Christ's assumption of our complete (but sinless) humanity at the Incarnation.

Worshiping with the senses means that your eyes perceive spiritual reality, whether looking at a brightly colored banner depicting biblical scenes, a rough-hewn replica of the cross, or an elegant work of religious art.

As the worshiper enters the chapel of the Pecos Abbey, for instance, the eyes immediately focus on a magnificent painting of Christ in His ascension glory. Spotlights shining on this representation of the Savior highlight its splendor. Far from leading astray from spiritual realities, visual displays such as this powerfully draw the heart Godward.

Reacting against late medieval excesses, some Reformers erred by depreciating the material world of symbolism and retreating into the world of ideas. Zwingli (d. 1531), we have seen, stripped the Zürich churches of ornamentation and whitewashed their walls. Later, John Owen (d. 1683) alleged that pictorial displays in churches and pageantry in worship services were a great irreverence. Immodest art is wrong, but faithful representations of biblical realities are fruitful means of lifting the heart heavenward.

Richard Lovelace believes that in its rejection of the visual and the symbolic "the evangelical stream moved away from the sacramental vision of life in the Catholic tradition, in which the created world is not only celebrated as good, but recognized as a constant symbolic message about spiritual reality. Evangelicals moved almost in a Manichaean direction, toward a frame of mind in which the objects of sense and sight could drag us away from what was 'spiritual.'"[27] Every God-created human faculty should be brought into the act of worship. Sensory-rich worship greatly enhances the soul's engagement with the majestic God.

In his classic book, *The Saints' Everlasting Rest*, Richard Baxter wrote that sensible objects on earth enrich worship of God in heaven. Hear Baxter well. "The sense is the natural way to the *Imagination*, and that to the *Understanding*: And he that would have no *sensible* and *natural* pleasures, shall have no *spiritual* pleasure."[28] C. S. Lewis (d. 1961) agreed: "God never meant man to be a purely spiritual creature. . . . He likes matter. He created it."[29]

In our zeal to refute doctrinal error, evangelical spirituality tends to restrict engagement with God to the mind. He invites us to relate to Him with our entire being, including all our faculties and senses (see Deuteronomy 6:5, Mark 12:30).

Worship with Your Body

Another valuable lesson I have learned is that bodily participation enhances our worship experience. We tend to approach spiritual matters abstractly and process the faith by wordy discussions. But performance of a physical act moves believers from the abstract to the concrete more effectively than uttering words alone. Enacting spiritual realities with the body—such as anointing with oil, the washing of feet, or eating and drinking at the Lord's Table—unites the head with gut-level experience.

C. S. Lewis observed that "Certain spiritual gifts are offered us only on condition that we perform certain bodily acts."[30] Robert Johnson comments that for spiritual reality to grip our beings, "it takes a physical act. When it registers physically, it also registers at the deepest levels of the psyche."[31] The old Anglican marriage vow, "With my body I thee worship," applies to our heavenly Father as well as our earthly spouse.

Bodily participation in symbolic actions lies in the very weave of biblical revelation. On the Day of Atonement, the high priest laid hands on the scapegoat, symbolically transferring guilt to the animal before releasing it into the desert (see Leviticus 16:20-22). With a clay jar in hand, Jeremiah led the elders and people to a valley outside Jerusalem. He emptied the contents of the jar on the ground and smashed the jar in pieces as a prophetic sign-act of God's judgment (see Jeremiah 19). In the greatest sign-act of all, Jesus broke a loaf of bread and poured a cup of wine to represent His sacrifice for the sins of the world (see Matthew 26:26-29, 1 Corinthians 11:23-26). Apostles laid hands on missionaries (see Acts 13:3), and elders anointed the sick with oil (see James 5:14).

With stunning clarity, I remember a service of "Forgiveness and Reconciliation" that made creative use of bodily participation. Instruction was given from the Scriptures, spiritual issues that required resolution were identified, and prayer invoking God's blessing was offered. Worshipers approached a large crystal bowl of water and submerged their cupped hands into it, symbolically "holding" the grievance. After prayer was offered for the grace to forgive hurts inflicted by others, the person opened her hands in the water, symbolically surrendering the grievance to God. Many Christians find enormous release by performing such an act. Enacting a ceremony like this with one's body possesses more transforming power than simply uttering the words, "I forgive."

The church throughout history has understood that God communicates spiritual truth through performance of actions—that is, *words made visible*—as well as through spoken declarations.

Is the "Labyrinth Walk" for Christians?

Not all contemplative practices currently offered to Christians aid in their progress in Christlikeness. Some practices may arouse spiritual awareness or evoke strong emotions, but when their emphasis is not on building the surrendered attitude of Jesus in us, we are far better off to avoid them.

Churches around the country are now beginning to promote an event that is supposed to open the soul to God with unusual clarity. It's known as the "Labyrinth Walk."

Spearheading the Labyrinth Walk in our day is Grace Cathedral's non-profit organization Veriditas (meaning "greening power of God"), located in San Francisco.[32] People from many parts of the country and many denominations are being trained in the use of the labyrinth at Grace Cathedral. The labyrinth is a circular pattern about forty feet in diameter with a meandering path about one-third of a mile long. An elaborate numerology and cosmology are associated with the labyrinth, although most people who walk the labyrinth are unaware of this fact. The pattern of the labyrinth is modeled after the design set in the floor of the twelfth-century Chartres Cathedral in France. Promoters claim that the labyrinth was regularly used in the ancient and medieval worlds, but during the Age of Reason, some 350 years ago, it fell out of favor.

Recently a Christian minister in Tennessee spray-painted large concentric rings on his front lawn. He distributed fliers to his neighbors, explaining that the shapes are a replica of the medieval labyrinth used in worship. He invited folks to walk this sacred path with him. Some neighbors were frightened, thinking it was a launching pad for spaceships. Since then, however, hundreds of people from across the state of Tennessee have walked the labyrinth.[33]

A Baptist church in our city invited members and friends to participate in a Labyrinth Walk. That an evangelical church would promote an unfamiliar contemplative exercise such as this caught my attention. For that reason, I accepted the invitation to walk the labyrinth myself.

What is the Labyrinth Walk? Is it a safe and spiritually profitable exercise for growing Christians?

The walker enters the labyrinth and, in a reflective mode, follows the serpentine course to the center of the pattern and then back.

THE LABYRINTH

Behind the Labyrinth Walk is a rather sophisticated theory. The labyrinth is said to be a "sacred archetypal form"[34] that symbolizes the spiritual journey and its goal: to encounter the "Divine Mother, the God within, the Goddess, the Holy in all of creation."[35] Advocates claim that in an age dominated by reason and technology, the labyrinth appeals to the undernourished imaginative, sensing, and feminine principle in us. "The labyrinth does not engage our thinking minds. It invites our intuitive, pattern-seeking, symbolic mind to come forth."[36] Reflectively walking the labyrinth, it is claimed, opens up the consciousness to a new encounter with ourselves and with the Divine.

During the walk, a person may receive an insight into a nagging problem, enjoy a mystical experience, or even observe a miracle. The Labyrinth Walk is promoted as a spiritual tool for people of all faiths and paths. A wide range of organizations—including the Episcopal Church, the Unity Church, Buddhists, and New Agers—promote the exercise. "The labyrinth awaits our discovery, for it will guide us through the troubles of our lives to the grand mysterious patterns that shape the web of creation. It will lead us toward the Source and eventually guide us home."[37]

As explained in the book *Walking a Sacred Path*, the theory behind the labyrinth diverges considerably from orthodox Christian belief. This book contains no reference to biblical authority, human sinfulness, or salvation by faith in Christ alone. It views wholeness in terms of coming alive to one's deepest humanity, or possibly, to the transcendent Mystery.

Christians who "buy into" the symbolism and theory of the labyrinth as described in *Walking a Sacred Path* expose themselves to serious error. Yet it continues to draw many.

The reason for its appeal is most likely that those who walk the labyrinth with an attitude of openness to Christ and a willingness to obey His directives, testify that it offers certain limited benefits. For example, the physical activity of walking the labyrinth path may have a calming effect on the body and soul. It also offers the opportunity for quiet, unrushed meditation on Christ and spiritual things. Additionally, it gives a context for putting one's body into the experience of worship that's similar to sacred dance.

It appears to me that similar benefits might be gained by a reflective walk in God's creation. Because of the unbiblical theory behind the labyrinth, faithful Christians must exercise caution when dealing with the Labyrinth Walk.

Journaling: A Contemplative Spiritual Exercise

For many Christians, keeping a spiritual journal proves to be a rich contemplative experience.

In the spiritual journal you record responses to Scripture meditation, prayer experiences, insights into God's ways, conversations with a spiritual friend, and spiritual struggles and victories. On the pages of the journal you may pour out whatever emotions arise, without fear of embarrassment. If you are not aware of specific ways in which God has been at work in your life, the discipline of writing in a journal may help you become aware.

Journaling has a long history in Christendom. Augustine's *Confessions* weaves his inner, spiritual experience of God into the narrative of his outer journey. The spiritual journals of George Fox, Blaise Pascal, John Wesley, John Woolman, Thomas Merton, and Jim Elliot also have blessed millions of Christian readers. More recently, Henri Nouwen made public his journal material in books such as *Genesee Diary* and *Road to Daybreak*. I encourage you to read some of these inspiring spiritual journals as an aid to personal growth.

Some may be reluctant to keep a journal because of abuses of the practice in certain circles. Ira Progoff is a psychologist and best-selling author of the book *At a Journal Workshop* (1975). His highly structured "Intensive Journal Method" commends free association and dialogue with people, places, and objects. The goal of Progoff's journaling method is to access deeper levels of the human consciousness in order to better understand and empower one's inner Self. Progoff believes that the Jewish and Christian Scriptures are irrelevant for modern people. His interest is wholeness of the human psyche, not salvation of the eternal soul or growth in holiness.

I find ample scriptural support for the discipline of keeping a spiritual journal. The psalmist Asaph writes, "I recall all you have done, O LORD; I remember your wonderful deeds of long ago. They are constantly in my thoughts. I cannot stop thinking about them" (Psalm 77:11-12). David pens these words: "Praise the LORD, I tell myself, and never forget the good things he does for me. He forgives all my sins and heals all my diseases. He ransoms me from death and surrounds me with love and tender mercies. He fills my life with good things" (Psalm 103:2-5).

The book of Psalms can be viewed as a collection of inspired journal entries. Psalm 3 records David's sense of God's protection over his life; Psalm 13, feelings of loneliness and isolation; Psalm 51, agony over personal sin and the joy of forgiveness; Psalm 63, spiritual satisfaction in God; and

Psalm 128, reflections on God's manifold blessings. The apocryphal book of Tobit, while not inspired Scripture, records aspects of Jewish piety during the period between the Testaments. After the archangel Raphael reminds Tobit and his son Tobias of the Lord's goodness to them, he instructs them to "write down all these things that have happened to you" (Tobit 12:20). Christians who keep a spiritual journal heed the command in James 1:23-25 to listen to God, obey His Word, and not forget His wonderful ways with us.

Writing in a spiritual journal can pay rich spiritual dividends for believers and is a valuable vehicle for expanding relationship with God. Journaling is a contemplative exercise that brings the experiences of our inner world into sharper focus. Like the adjusting mechanism of a telescope, a journal sharpens our perspective on the footprints of God in our lives. It also affords opportunity for inner dialogue with God. When, in the pages of my journal, I am totally honest with myself and God, the Spirit makes God real. As I record responses to God's initiative in my life, dialogue with God deepens.

It's helpful to periodically reread our journal entries, which provide a written account of the great things God has done for us. Our journals help us to remember God's goodness and grace in our lives. The journal becomes a permanent record of where we have been, where we are, and where we are going.

Contemplation and Action: A Winning Combination

Getting caught up in the pressure of life hinders connectedness to God, spiritual growth, and personal satisfaction. And it makes us more like the world we are trying to season with salt, light, and grace.

God calls His people to a counter-cultural lifestyle—to a mode of living that reflects God's presence in us. We are not meant to be overwhelmed with commitments, but to be enveloped in the peace of Christ. The great reality of the Christian life is that Christ lives in us by the Spirit, and we live in Him. Our highest priority, therefore, must be to cultivate the presence of the One in whom "we live and move and exist" (Acts 17:28).

Neglecting the contemplative dimension not only lets the fires of inner passion burn down; ultimately it leads to real lethargy and ineffective service.

A. W. Tozer observed that in his day there were many Bible teachers and preachers around: "Too many of these seemed satisfied to teach the fundamentals of the faith year after year, strangely unaware that there is in their ministry no manifest Presence, nor anything unusual in their lives." Tozer concluded, "It is not mere words that nourish the soul, but God himself."[38] God shows Himself to us, not only in silence and solitude but as we follow Him in obedience.

As Christians we achieve balance in contemplative living with prayer and action. Activity for God must be born of reflection; service, of contemplation; and action, of prayer. Outward acts of evangelism, discipling, and social concern, to which we are called, must be fueled by the fire of spiritual consideration. John of the Cross (d. 1591) wisely wrote, "What we have joyously harvested with the sickle of contemplation in solitude, we must thresh on the floor of preaching, and so broadcast."[39] Kingdom service, in turn, stimulates deeper reflection and contemplation, thereby completing the circle of truth.

Augustine urged Christians to pursue both contemplation and action. "No man must be so committed to contemplation as, in his contemplation, to give no thought to his neighbor's needs, nor so absorbed in action as to dispense with the contemplation of God."[40]

Try It Yourself

1. An exercise in contemplation.

Try a personal experience of practicing the presence of God. Find a quiet place and assume a comfortable and relaxed position. Read a portion of Scripture, such as John 14, that speaks of intimate relationship with the Lord. If your soul is restless or anxious, take a few minutes to quiet down by means of exercises suggested in this and the previous chapter. Affirm your faith in Christ and your love for Him. Imagine that you are John, reclining close to Jesus (see John 13:23-25), or Mary as she adoringly focuses her heart on the Lord (see Luke 10:39).

Select a word or phrase that expresses your heart's desire for Christ, such as *Abba*; *Come, Lord Jesus*; *I love you, Lord*; or *Lord, have mercy*. Repeat this gently from your heart for ten minutes or so. Use the chosen word or phrase to express your love for the Lord. If your mind wanders, gently bring its focus back to Him. When you are ready, close by quietly reciting the Lord's Prayer (Matthew 6:9-13). Then rest in the Lord for a while. Practice this prayer of loving attention daily for the next two weeks.

Bear in mind that you and I cannot manipulate God. We may not experience His presence in every hour of prayer. Our responsibility is to show up for prayer faithfully and leave the results to His wisdom.

- Did you sense closeness to the Lord during these moments, perhaps like John or Mary in the Gospels?
- Did your love for Christ come alive or grow deeper as a result of your prayer of loving attention?
- After practicing this prayer for a week or two, do you feel it has made a difference in your life spiritually?
- Do you desire to build this discipline of practicing the presence into your ongoing devotional life?

2. A journaling exercise.

Participate in some form of contemplative experience that emphasizes spiritual renewal, prayer, or relationship with God. This might be a retreat in a house of prayer, a workshop on the spiritual life, a Taizé service, or a RENOVARÉ conference. Ask your pastor, spiritual mentor, or area Christian college or seminary to recommend a suitable venue for this exercise.

At the retreat or workshop, allow time for group worship, personal biblical meditation, waiting on the Lord in silence, a quiet walk in nature, or focused conversation with a spiritual friend. Record in your journal your reflections on this experience. Use your journal to write your responses to the following questions.

- Did you feel more calm, composed, and open to the Lord during this special time?
- How did the Lord show Himself to you, and how did you respond to the wooing of His Spirit?
- What new insight did you discover about your deepening relationship with Christ? Explain what this might mean for your life in the days ahead.
- How did interaction with other believers in the group or gathering enrich your experience with the Lord?

3. An exercise in reflection.

Evangelical theologian Dr. Clark Pinnock writes the following concerning Christian devotion and worship. Prayerfully reflect on this selection with an open heart and mind. Ponder the questions that follow, and record your answers in your diary or journal.

> *The life of many churches needs to be enriched with more signs and symbols. Iconoclasm has impoverished the life of the church and often reduced worship to a cognitive affair. This means that the Spirit is denied certain tools for enrichment. We are impoverished when we have no place for festivals, drama, processions, banners, dance, color, movement, instruments, percussion and incense. There are many notes on the Spirit's keyboard which we often neglect to sound, with the result that God's presence can be hard to access. . . .*
>
> *Let us not impoverish ourselves. Let us not, in reaction to excess, go to the extreme of reducing worship to grim austerity and hyperspirituality. . . . We should not put*

> *aside means of grace that can enrich our lives. We do ourselves harm when we eliminate arts, drama, color, vestments, pageantry, incense, saints, calendars lectionary, sculpture. To do so is to threaten the mystery.*[41]

- Is there adequate biblical basis for worshiping God not only with our mind, but also with our senses, imagination, and body?
- Why have we often been reluctant to worship the Lord in the full-orbed manner Dr. Pinnock recommends?

Search for a Christian context where worship is rich with sights and sounds—where Christians come before God using all their created faculties. Participate in worship experiences in that setting. What are your reactions to worshiping God in this way? What new insights into God's majesty, holiness, and love have you gained? Record in your journal how your life has been spiritually enriched.

SUGGESTIONS FOR FURTHER READING

Artress, Lauren. *Walking a Sacred Path: Rediscovering the Labyrinth as a Sacred Tool.* New York: Riverhead, 1995. [liberal Episcopal]

Brother Lawrence of the Resurrection, *The Practice of the Presence of God,* ed. Donald E. Demaray. New York: Alba House, 1997.

Foster, Richard J. *Prayer: Finding the Heart's True Home.* San Francisco: HarperSanFrancisco, 1992.

Merton, Thomas. *Seeds of Contemplation.* Westport, Conn.: Greenwood, 1979.

Nouwen, Henri J. M. *Spiritual Journals.* New York: Continuum, 1998.

CHAPTER SEVEN

Spiritual Helpers

"Those who plant in tears will harvest with shouts of joy. They weep as they go to plant their seed, but they sing as they return with the harvest."

PSALM 126:5-6

"Spiritual direction . . . spares us the hassle of quick-fix, over-programmed, simplistic solutions. It meets the genuine felt need among Christians who earnestly desire to be guided by the Word of God from immaturity to maturity, from confusion to understanding, from complexity to simplicity. True spiritual direction does not complicate life, it clarifies it."

DOUGLAS WEBSTER[1]

Few things have commanded my spiritual passion and excitement the way missions has. Teaming with other men and women to deliver the gospel to lost and suffering people fulfills something deep inside a Christian.

Even with the vast work that's left to do, I'd say that as evangelicals we're doing a great job strategizing in the area of missions and taking the gospel to the world. I wonder though, are we as effective in guiding Christians to spiritual maturity?

Our forebears clearly understood that coming to Christ puts a person at the head of a path, in the way that, say, getting into medical school sets you on the path to becoming a doctor. After conversion, the soul needs to be guided along the path, through spiritual helping ministries. But when it comes to that, we seem far less adept today at the care and cure of souls.

Richard Foster laments our neglect of the ancient Christian ministry of spiritual direction. "Today the concept is hardly understood, let alone practiced, except in the Roman Catholic monastic system."[2]

Ministries of soul care have caught the attention of the national newspaper *USA Today.* A recent article highlighted the exploding interest across the country in "spiritual companions." People searching for relationship with God and soul satisfaction are visiting centers of spiritual guidance, meeting with spiritual directors, and consulting spiritual mentors on the Internet.[3]

This hunger tells us the Holy Spirit has not been asleep in His oversight of the church. For as the ancients knew, it is God who creates in us the desire for Himself. Encouraging signs abound that ministries of soul-care are being revisited in the church today.

What do we make of ministries of spiritual formation as practiced by the church through the centuries? Should we be more intentional in practicing them today? This chapter explores the role of "spiritual helpers" in the formation of growing disciples.

A spiritual helper, in the broadest sense, is a mature Christian who offers soul-care in the form of spiritual friendship, spiritual guidance, spiritual mentoring, or spiritual direction.

Discipleship Models

Since World War II, parachurch discipleship ministries have labored to grow converts through structured programs of teaching and training. Churches have adapted these discipleship methods to the people under their care. Scores of discipleship programs appear in books, seminars, and audio and videotapes.

Discipleship is an important biblical concept that must not be abandoned. The Greek word for *disciple* (*mathētēs*) occurs some 265 times in the New Testament—exclusively in the Gospels and Acts. (The verb to "make" or "become disciples" occurs four times: Matthew 13:52, 27:57, 28:19, Acts 14:21). Discipleship is the teaching, training, and helping ministry commanded by Christ. Far more than teaching doctrine—though it does do that—an effective discipleship program enables believers to grow in the Spirit, to live out the Savior's values, and to serve the Father's kingdom purposes.

Michael Wilkins paints a similar, broad picture of discipleship. "In many ways, discipleship is the overall goal of the church, including evangelism, nurturing, fellowship, leadership, worship." He adds, "All that we do in the church is somehow related to discipleship and discipling."[4]

Some discipleship concepts are unfortunately narrow in scope, as if the activities of a disciple are limited to such things as witnessing and Bible teaching. These can be programmatic in that they seek to "mass-produce" disciples, as if we should all look and sound like we came from a common mold. So we find discipleship programs with titles such as *Seven Steps to Spiritual Growth* or *Ten Basic Steps Toward Christian Maturity.* This approach suggests that growth will occur automatically if we perform certain activities.

For example, if the "disciple" has a daily quiet time, joins a good church and witnesses for Jesus, it is thought that he or she will become a mature and healthy follower of Christ. But life is more complex than that, and God is also at work in different ways in the life of each individual. Programs hardly account for the many subtle factors that can advance or retard an individual's spiritual growth. Biblical discipling is a personalized ministry, taking into account the person's uniqueness and the call of God on his or her life.

Other discipleship programs promote a "follow-the-leader" approach: "Follow me and I'll show you how to live a successful Christian life." These may involve building the *leader's* life, rather than the life of *Christ,* into the disciple.

When our discipleship plans focus on gaining information (knowing) and acquiring skills (doing), rather than cultivating the inner life (being), crucial issues of the soul are overlooked. For instance, often we urge new believers to join a mission project without first leading them to a mature relationship with Jesus.

Perhaps our limited view of discipleship shows up best in this fact: We often view discipleship training as having a limited duration—as if it were army boot camp—rather than a lifelong process of learning, deepening, and growing more in the character of Christ.

We fool ourselves if we think that after completing a six- or eight-week training program, young Christians have been "discipled." Jesus' mandate in Matthew 28:19-20 is much more comprehensive than most of our programs recognize.

A Spectrum of Soul-Care Ministries

An effective approach to discipleship addresses all the basic issues of Christian faith and life: training in essential Christian doctrines, structuring a quiet time, cultivating Christian fellowship, witnessing. But because each of us has a special calling from God and particular needs, spiritual helpers must be people who know how to lead us more deeply into God's will, ministering to us as God's unique plan unfolds.

Consider, for example, a baseball pitching coach. He instructs all the pitchers under him in the fundamentals of pitching. But he also works with individual throwers to help them develop new pitches and overcome flaws in their delivery.

Christian helping agents build on the core issues of discipleship and do so by practicing personalized soul-care ministries that cultivate Christlikeness. I will refer to these helping ministries as *spiritual friendship, spiritual guidance, spiritual mentoring,* and *spiritual direction.*

Spiritual friendship is the most informal and reciprocal of helping ministries. It involves two or more Christians on a relatively equal basis, who support, encourage, and pray for one another. A Christian woman who befriends and ministers to another woman over a cup of coffee practices spiritual friendship. Aelred of Rievaulx (d. 1167) writes, "What happiness, what confidence, what joy to have a person to whom you dare to speak on terms of equality as to another self. You need have no fear to confess your failings to this person."[5]

Spiritual guidance is another informal helping ministry. Talking with a friend about Christian lifestyle issues; recommending a good book on the spiritual life; counseling another person while enjoying a walk in nature—these are examples of spiritual guidance. The parties involved may differ in spiritual maturity, but not in spiritual authority. The word *guide (hodēgos),* is a biblical term meaning one who leads the way (Romans 2:19, compare Psalm 48:14). It's related to the word *guardian* or *trainer* (*paidagōgas,* 1 Corinthians 4:15). Spiritual guidance sometimes takes place through correspondence. Jerome (d. 420), a great scholar of the early church and translator of the Bible into Latin, wrote many letters of spiritual counsel. In these he warned Christians not to set out on life's journey without a competent spiritual guide.

C. S. Lewis (d. 1963) served as a spiritual guide in three areas of ministry. During thirty years of teaching at Oxford University, Lewis showed concern for the spiritual needs of his students. He also offered spiritual guidance through sermons delivered at colleges, churches, and on the radio. But his greatest contribution to spiritual guidance occurred in his letter writing. Lewis corresponded with thousands of strangers seeking advice and comfort. Many came to faith in Christ, renewed their commitment to the Lord, or entered Christian ministries. Lewis's book *Letters to an American Lady* contains correspondence written to a Roman Catholic widow, whom he never met, on matters of spiritual practice. Lewis also had a "pen-friend" relationship with Joy Davidman Gresham that led to their marriage, beautifully narrated in the film *Shadowlands*. Lewis freely opened his heart and shared his spiritual journey with many spiritual seekers.

Tom is a pastor who sensed the need for training in spiritual formation to equip him for a new phase of ministry. He decided to enroll in the six-week residential program in spiritual formation and direction at the Pecos Abbey. As the start of the program drew near, Tom became unsettled about attending a Benedictine center. He related to me his fears and asked for advice whether he should withdraw or pursue the program. I assured him of the Christ-honoring character of the program and its effectiveness in training and renewing pastors and other caregivers. I encouraged him to carry through with his plans, reminding him to be astute enough while participating in any program to quit if it moved away from biblical principles. Tom decided to go ahead and later told me how life-transforming this experience was. My ministry of encouraging his heart is an example of spiritual guidance.

Spiritual mentoring, the third type, is a more formal arrangement in which a mature Christian offers another believer regular instruction, training, and modeling in spiritual formation and ministry. A Christian man who shows a new convert how to study the Bible and helps him cultivate an effective prayer life functions as a spiritual mentor. So does a pastor who counsels a church intern in spiritual development and assists him in forming a singles' ministry.

Some African-American churches take seriously the ministry of spiritual mentoring. A new member often is placed under the care of a mature spiritual mentor. Martin Luther King, Jr., tells the story of a sensitive woman mentor named Mother Pollard, who came to him one trying day when he was worn out. Dr. King tells about this encounter:

> I immediately hugged her affectionately. "Something is wrong with you," she said. "You didn't talk strong tonight."
>
> Seeking further to disguise my fears, I retorted, "Oh no, Mother Pollard, nothing is wrong. I am feeling as fine as ever."
>
> But her insight was discerning. "Now you can't fool me," she said. "I knows something is wrong. Is it that we ain't doing things to please you? Or is it that the white folks is bothering you?"
>
> Before I could respond, she looked directly into my eyes and said, "I done told you we is with you all the way." Then her face became radiant and she said in words of quiet certainty, "But even if we ain't with you, God's gonna take care of you."
>
> As she spoke these consoling words, everything in me quivered and quickened with the pulsing tremor of raw energy.[6]

Finally, *spiritual direction* refers to the structured ministry in which a gifted and experienced Christian, called a spiritual director, helps another believer grow in relationship with and obedience to Christ. Richard Foster describes spiritual directors as "people gifted in discernment, wisdom, and knowledge. Their task is to help people see the footprints of God in their lives and, now and again, to urge them to move in directions that they might not go otherwise."[7]

Though we do not neglect learning Scripture or actively serving God, spiritual direction focuses particularly on the *being* dimension. The spiritual director is a physician of souls. He or she helps the individual to discern the workings of God in his life, to deepen the individual's relationship with Christ, and to deal constructively with life issues. (In the next chapter I will distinguish spiritual direction from the ministries of pastoral and psychological counseling.)

Spiritual Helpers in History

After the fall of the Roman Empire and the social disintegration that followed, some twenty thousand Christians fled into the deserts of Syria, Palestine, and Egypt. The *abbas* and *ammas* of the desert gave Christ-centered spiritual direction to multitudes of searching Christians. The desert fathers and mothers emphasized spiritual training, taking up Christ's cross, the discerning of spirits, and purity of life. Notable desert fathers include Antony of Egypt (d. 356), Basil (d. 379), and Evagrius (d. 399).

In the fifteenth and sixteenth centuries, monasteries in Europe and the Middle East became important centers of spiritual direction. From them arose many influential spiritual directors and a flood of spiritually edifying writings. *The Imitation of Christ*, commonly attributed to Thomas à Kempis (d. 1471), arose out of a semimonastic movement known as the *Devotio Moderna*. This classic of the faith states, "Ask counsel from a person of sound judgment; ask instruction from one better than you; avoid following your own proud ideas."[8]

Teresa of Avila (d. 1582) was another famous spiritual director of this period. Teresa testified that if she had found a competent spiritual director sooner she would have made greater progress in the spiritual life. Her friend John of the Cross (d. 1591) was one of the great spiritual directors of all time. He wrote, "The person who is alone without a spiritual guide . . . is like a glowing ember that is alone. It will become more frigid rather than hotter."[9] John believed that the needed reform of the church in his day would occur through the ministry of spiritual direction.

Spiritual direction is also a well-founded practice in our Reformed tradition. Puritans and Pietists who practiced spiritual direction include Richard Baxter (d. 1691), the Congregationalist Cotton Mather (d. 1728), and the Anglican William Law (d. 1761). Anglican cleric Jeremy Taylor (d. 1667) wrote, "God hath appointed spiritual persons as guides for souls, whose office it is to direct and to comfort, to give peace, . . . to refresh the weary and to strengthen the weak; and therefore to use their advice is that proper remedy which God hath appointed."[10] From the extensive quotations in their writings, we know the Puritans read the church fathers and mined from them fruitful principles of spiritual formation.

During the Methodist revival, John Wesley (d. 1791) served as an effective spiritual director to class meetings throughout Britain. In our day, interest in spiritual direction is growing. Eugene Peterson graphically portrays spiritual direction as the "unpretentious companionship in venturing step by cautious step into the fiery extravagance of Pentecost and Patmos."[11]

Spiritual friendship, guidance, mentoring, and direction form a spectrum of customized helping ministries within the broader field of biblical discipleship. I represent these ministries in the following figure.

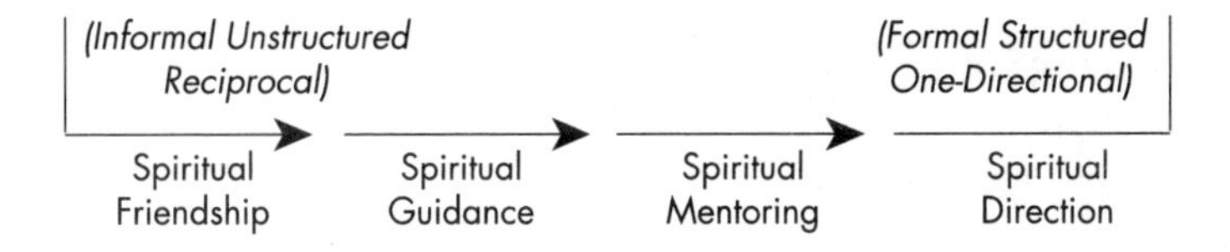

These four soul-care ministries are elastic and overlapping. The spiritual helper may engage in one or more of these ministries, depending on the needs of the disciple and his own giftedness. Spiritual formation can occur in every situation in which we find ourselves: in the home, while hiking in the mountains, or in the pastor's study. The church through the centuries has believed that Christians who are serious about their faith should seek the guidance of a mature and trusted spiritual friend or director.

A Closer Look at Spiritual Direction

Many are starting to use the term *spiritual direction*, and so it's important to look more closely at this practice.

A spiritual director does not exercise total, flat-handed authority because his or her job is to strengthen the soul of the other to make godly choices, so that serving Christ flows out of their inner desire with a sense of "freedom in obedience" to the Lord. A spiritual director demonstrates authority by his or her own example, similar to the way a master painter or a golf pro demonstrates that his skill has taken root in his own life and actions. Too, there is no place for compulsion in spiritual direction. The director is a true companion on the spiritual journey, maintaining a compassionate understanding for the other's struggles while directing them through and beyond it. The director also helps the other sort out religious experiences, aids the discerning of God's will, focuses the prayer life, and encourages the person in Christ-honoring obedience. The spiritual director is prayerfully concerned with the whole of the disciple's life—with every aspiration, joy, frustration, and pain.

Soul-Care Addresses Neglected Aspects of Discipleship

How many of us leave church on Sunday morning with our deeper questions unaddressed? Or with no sense of God's presence and faltering spiritual passion . . . even the pastors among us?

In our day, so little attention is given to nurturing the life of individual Christian souls. Eugene Peterson speaks bluntly: "American pastors are abandoning their posts, left and right, and at an alarming rate. They are not leaving their churches and getting other jobs. . . . They have gone whoring after other gods. What they do with their time under the guise of pastoral ministry hasn't the remotest connection with what the church's pastors have done for most of twenty centuries."[12]

Along with teaching Scripture, we do well to correct the deficit noted by James Houston: "The emotional education of our inner lives does not have much priority in today's church."[13]

Soul-care searches out hindrances to prayer, obstacles to intimacy with Christ, and responsiveness to the Spirit's leading. Spiritual helpers allow the life of Christ in them to flow into other Christians to bless, empower, and release the good seed of faith and love. Some discipleship programs strive to form the Christian from the "outside in." Soul-care, on the other hand, seeks to form the life from the "inside out." Jesus approves of this, for He says, "Make a tree good, and its fruit will be good. Make a tree bad, and its fruit will be bad. . . . A good person produces good words from a good heart, and an evil person produces evil words from an evil heart" (Matthew 12:33,35; compare 23:25-28). Soul-care deals with foundational issues of the heart, recognizing that dysfunction at the core negatively affects everything the disciple does.

Soul-care follows no fixed formula (other than the rule of authoritative Scripture). It respects the God-created uniqueness of the believer. Like a one-of-a-kind snowflake, each disciple is specially gifted, and each has a special calling from God on his life. We must minister to the disciple in his or her God-created uniqueness.

I've heard that Dawson Trotman, founder of The Navigators, used to say, "There is no magic formula [for discipleship]. If you think there is, you've just lost it."

Like the wind, the Spirit moves in each person's life in a way that is only discernible to him who has eyes to see and ears to hear (John 3:8). Soul-care prayerfully listens for the subtle movements of God's Spirit in each heart. For these reasons, all spiritual helping must follow a flexible approach—discerning and accounting for the spiritual needs of the person—within the boundaries provided in Scripture.

Soul-care ministries also recognize that people of varying dispositions relate to God differently. How we guide growing Christians must take into account their personal history and temperament. Mentoring and spiritual direction, therefore, are highly personalized ministries. Our model is Jesus, who called twelve disciples and taught, trained, and nurtured them according to their individual needs.

For example, Jesus ministered to Peter, James, and John, and certainly to Judas, in very different ways, given their differing temperaments, strengths, and weaknesses.

Some evangelical leaders admit that spiritual direction is crucial, but discount it as too demanding and time-consuming. And that is true, no question. It requires knowledge of the ways of God in a life. It requires wisdom and the patience to wait until you perceive the movement of God's Spirit as He opens the heart of the other person, for instance, to see the roots of sin or weakness or to be receptive to new direction. But isn't it true that matters of eternal significance always require our utmost effort? And isn't the health of an immortal soul at least as important as the "health" of a program?

WHY SOUL-CARE IS GREATLY NEEDED TODAY

A doctor of ministries student I mentored wrote a thesis entitled *The Pastor as Coach of the Spiritual Disciplines*. His research uncovered the startling fact that *none* of the many pastors he interviewed were receiving intentional spiritual mentoring themselves, and *none* were providing it for the people under their charge.

Yet I am convinced we evangelicals need to recover the ancient Christian ministry of soul-care for several important reasons.

First, every one of us needs to understand more clearly God's working in our lives, and that requires the gift of objective counsel. We're too close to ourselves to see things as they really are. We need a faithful friend who will help us distinguish the authentic voice of God from confusing voices and sinister spirits.

Bernard of Clairvaux (d. 1153) writes, "He who makes himself his own teacher becomes the pupil of a fool."[14] A lawyer who defends himself in court is irresponsible; a doctor who treats himself or his family for medical problems is unwise. We, too, are foolish if we try to guide ourselves through the maze that is the spiritual journey. The Cistercian abbot Aelred of Rievaulx (d. 1167) noted that the gospel life, with all its twists and turns, is too much for us to handle alone. We need the counsel and support of a Christian friend who will navigate the path with us.

Second, the spiritual path through life is cratered with tragedies waiting to happen. Daily we're worn down by the world and tempted to fall. James Houston comments, "If sin is self-deceiving, then I need a soul friend to give me insights into the ways I am deceived, or insensitive, or hardened by sin within me. I cannot do it alone. Self-examination can take me only so far. I need others to help me understand where sin would deceive and confuse me."[15] As the Teacher in Ecclesiastes says, "If one person falls, the other can reach out and help. But people who are alone when they fall are in real trouble" (Ecclesiastes 4:10).

Third, although the Holy Spirit is our ultimate Guide, God has chosen to use fellow believers as instruments of growth. God could work holiness in our lives by the direct application of His sheer power. But His customary way of working good is through other believers. How true it is that "behind every saint stands another saint."[16] A leading Southern Baptist minister, C. Welton Gaddy, writes candidly about his hospitalization for depression (see chapter 8). From painful experience, he observes, "Every minister needs a minister. The demands for total competency can become heavy. Divine causes can get very sick."[17]

Michael Ramsey (d. 1988), who served as professor of divinity at Cambridge University and later as archbishop of Canterbury, challenges us with this sobering observation: "Amid the spiritual hunger of our times, when many, whose souls are starved by activism, are seeking guidance in the contemplation of God, a terrible judgment rests upon the priest who is unable to give help or guidance because he has ceased to be a man of prayer himself."[18]

Biblical Examples of Spiritual Guides

In the Old Testament, Yahweh Himself was the guide and mentor of His people. The psalmist's words testify, "You will keep on guiding me with your counsel, leading me to a glorious destiny" (Psalm 73:24, compare 48:14). A Jewish spiritual writing between the Testaments says, "The Lord is the guide of wisdom and the corrector of the wise" (Wisdom of Solomon 7:15).

God graciously gave Israel human spiritual guides, as well—prophets, priests, wise men, and holy women—for instruction and growth. An extra-canonical Jewish writing urges the faithful to seek guidance from godly persons: "Who is wise? Attach yourself to such a one. Be ready to listen to every godly discourse. If you are an intelligent person let your foot wear out his doorstep" (Sirach 6:34-36). Again, "Associate with a godly person whom you know to be a keeper of the commandments, who is like-minded with yourself, and who will grieve with you if you fall" (Sirach 37:12).

God called *Moses* to be a guide and mentor for the people of Israel. Picture Israel gathered at the base of Mount Sinai (see Exodus 19–40). Moses went up to God on the mountain (19:3), where the Lord made a covenant with the people of Israel (the Mosaic covenant, 19:3-6). Moses related to the elders and the people all that the Lord had told him (19:7-8). Moses then spoke with the Lord about the people's needs and dreams (19:9,19). Later Moses led the people into God's presence to experience His awesome glory (19:17-19). The Lord then revealed further aspects of His will (19:21-24), which Moses faithfully delivered to the people (19:25).

Moses again entered Yahweh's presence to engage His glory (24:9-10, 33:18-23). Moses spoke to the Lord about the people (34:29,35), and the Lord in turn spoke with Moses. "The LORD would speak to Moses face to face, as a man speaks to a friend" (33:11). Moses communicated to the people all that God had told him, urging the covenant people to obedience. When they failed to heed God's word, Moses rebuked them for their disobedience (32:30). Yet he earnestly interceded before the Lord on their behalf (32:11-13). When the time came to move on, Moses led the people to the Promised Land (32:34). He was a faithful mediator between Yahweh and Israel—a godly guide and mentor of the covenant people.

Moses also mentored individuals, such as Joshua. Recognizing that his young assistant was a man of spiritual destiny, Moses changed his name from Hoshea to Joshua ("the LORD saves," Numbers 13:16). Moses taught Joshua principles of warfare that were invaluable for his later role as commander in the conquest of Canaan (see Exodus 17:9-13). He also taught Joshua courage and leadership. Moses appointed Joshua to the band of twelve that spied out Canaan. After returning from the spy mission, Joshua and Caleb urged the grumbling people to trust the Lord and seize the good land God had given them (see Numbers 14:6-9). At God's command, Moses passed the mantle of leadership to Joshua, with the Spirit's anointing upon him (see Numbers 27:18-23). Moses mentored Joshua well, for near the end of his life Joshua testified, "as for me and my family, we will serve the LORD" (see Joshua 24:15).

Jesus was the mentor *par excellence* for His disciples. The disciples joined Jesus' company, listened to His teaching, observed His manner of life, and found their lives challenged and comforted by the Lord. Jesus poured His life into His disciples, loving them as brothers and sending them forth in kingdom service. We can learn a great deal from Jesus' mentoring relationship with Peter.

When the Lord called Peter to leave his fishing nets and follow, He undoubtedly spoke to a deep need in Peter's soul for purpose and an encounter with God (see Mark 3:13-16). Peter had obvious flaws—he was impulsive, overly confident, and at times weak in faith—but Jesus saw possibilities in Peter and told him so (John 1:42). Jesus instructed Peter in moral and spiritual matters, often by telling a parable or by giving an object lesson (Matthew 16:13-17, 18:21-35, John 21:6-10). On more than one occasion, Jesus chided Peter for his faults (Mark 8:33, 14:37-38). Later the Lord appointed Peter to a place of leadership among the disciples (Matthew 16:18-19) and then patiently bore with Peter's denial (Mark 14:66-72). Gently the risen Lord drew Peter into heart relationship with Himself and restored him to leadership in ministry (John 21:15-17). Finally, the Lord prepared Peter for martyrdom by crucifixion—the outcome of his courageous witness for Jesus (John 21:18-19).

Qualities of a Spiritual Helper

What are the qualities, then, of a spiritual helper?

Foremost, the spiritual helper should be a person of *vital Christian faith*. Only when the helper is closely connected to Jesus can new life be called forth in the other. John of the Cross wrote, "Although the foundation for guiding a soul is knowledge and discretion, the director will not succeed in leading a soul onward . . . if he has not deep experience of God."[19] Recall the Lord's warning that "if one blind person guides another, they will both fall into a ditch" (Matthew 15:14). Mature faith, a close relationship with God, and a rich life of prayer are all necessary.

The spiritual guide, *second*, should possess *knowledge* (see 2 Peter 1:5), including a good understanding of Scripture, theology, the spiritual classics, and the psyche. It's helpful to be able to recognize emotional dysfunctions, to know how to deal with minor problems, and when to refer more serious cases to a better trained counselor or therapist.

Many older spiritual mentors have stressed the importance of sound, practical knowledge. Teresa of Avila said, "Learning is a great thing because learned persons teach and enlighten us who know little. . . . May God deliver us from an empty piety."[20]

Third, the spiritual helper should be a person of *loving concern* (see Philippians 1:7-8, 1 Thessalonians 2:8). The mentor must experience the love of God himself and be able to communicate love to others in the language of the heart. Love is the pure conduit through which God's grace flows into a life. The mentor heeds the words of Jesus, "I command you to love each other in the same way that I love you" (John 15:12).

The spiritual guide should possess *discernment* as a *fourth* trait. The Greek word *diakrisis* ("insight, perception," 1 Corinthians 12:10, Hebrews 5:14, 1 John 4:1) is common in the writings of spiritual direction from the desert fathers onward. God is infinite, each soul is unique, and each journey is special. Hence discernment is a necessary competency for effective spiritual guides. Spiritual discernment is the ability to read hearts and to exegete souls. Jesus exercised discernment when He probed the heart of the woman at the well (John 4:16-20). Through discernment we differentiate the bright work of God from the dark work of evil spirits. Discernment tells us when to push and when to back off, when to rebuke and when to comfort. John Cassian (d. 435) urged spiritual guides to become "skilled changers of currency whose greatest skill and knowledge consist in the fact that they can tell the difference between purest gold and . . . standard gold."[21] Spiritual guides should pray for the gift of discernment (1 Corinthians 12:10) and develop it by prayerful use.

Fifth, the effective spiritual helper has experienced some *suffering and failure* in life. A person who has known only the comforts of salvation, and not brokenness, has difficulty identifying with those undergoing trials (2 Corinthians 1:3-6). But a Christian who has dealt redemptively with doubt, betrayal, and failure is able to minister more effectively to persons struggling with such issues.

My local newspaper featured a report from the *New York Times* entitled "President Recruits Spiritual Helpers."[22] The article related that in the aftermath of his moral failure, President Clinton has asked Tony Campolo and Gordon MacDonald to give him periodic spiritual counsel. The president chose MacDonald after reading his book *Rebuilding Your Broken World* (1988)—a book that relates the story of his own unfortunate moral failure and full restoration.

The key here is that by God's grace the mentor has worked through and overcome his failures. David and Peter of Scripture serve as examples of this. Some large corporations today are wary of hiring executives unless they have at least one failure on their professional record—a policy that highlights the redemptive value of learning from mistakes.

Reginald Somerset Ward (d. 1962), a leading Anglican spiritual director, somewhere identified the following ingredients of successful soul-care: *"One pound of spiritual direction is made up of 8 ounces of prayer, 3 ounces of theology, 3 ounces of common sense, and 2 ounces of psychology."* Take note of the proportion of desirable qualities in the spiritual mentor or director.

The Practice of Spiritual Mentoring or Direction

Let's say that a Christian who is trained in the basics of Christian living comes to you seeking a more intimate and satisfying relationship with Christ. The following guidelines—not to be viewed as rigid rules—may help you minister to this person in his or her unique needs.

Ask relevant questions.

Jesus posed probing questions to people in the course of His ministry. The Lord asked Peter, "Who do you say I am?" (Matthew 16:15). He asked blind Bartimaeus, "What do you want me to do for you?" (Mark 10:51). And he inquired of the Pharisees, "What do you think about the Messiah? Whose son is he?" (Matthew 22:42).

The mentor or director asks questions that help him become better acquainted with the disciple. Questions might include: "How did you meet the Lord?" "What is your picture of God?" And "Who is Christ for you?" The mentor might follow with questions that evaluate the quality of the person's spiritual life: "Where are you on the spiritual journey?" "Where has God been at work in your life of late?" And "What disciplines or experiences have been life-giving to you?"

You might then ask questions that clarify the individual's real needs: "How satisfying is your prayer life?" "What recurring patterns of behavior do you experience that seem to interfere with your experience of God?" And "Where do you seem to be stuck spiritually?" The mentor also asks questions that kindle a hunger for spiritual growth: "If Jesus were to come to you and speak grace into your life, what gifts would you desire of Him?" And "What might Jesus say to you that would nourish your heart and bless you?"

Listen carefully to the one seeking direction.
Encourage the person to tell his or her personal story. The simple act of relating one's story can be a healing experience. Practice the art of "active listening"—listening in a way that enters into the life experience of the other person. A common mistake of mentors or spiritual directors is to talk when they should be listening.

The German martyr Dietrich Bonhoeffer (d. 1945) commented that "Christians, especially ministers, so often think they must always contribute something when they are in the company of others . . . they forget that listening can be a greater service than speaking." He added, "Often a person can be helped merely by having someone who can listen to him seriously. . . . We should listen with the *ears* of God that we may speak the Word of God."[23]

The Spirit will give the trusting mentor insight into the disciple's needs (1 Corinthians 2:10-12).

Help the individual learn how to listen to God as He reveals Himself.
Relationships develop and new life flows when people pay attention to one another. We know something of what it means to pay attention to another human being. But how does a person pay attention to the infinite God?

First, by being *attentive in stillness.* We saw in chapter 5 that quietness before God greatly aids in knowing Him. Both mentor and disciple need to silence distractions and listen to the still, small voice of the Spirit within, so their souls become committed to Him.

Second, we listen to God by prayerfully *meditating on the Scriptures.* The written Word of God is the customary way the Lord speaks to us. "His delight is in the law of the Lord, and on his law he meditates day and night" (see Psalm 1:2, NIV). Encourage the growing Christian in the daily practice of Bible reading and reflection.

Third, we pay attention through the *discipline of prayer*—not prayer in the form of a grocery list of requests, but prayer of the heart, prayer of simplicity, or contemplative prayer. This prayer form that we explored in chapter 6 focuses the heart on God Himself. A verse of Jewish spirituality from the Apocrypha underscores the importance of attentively listening to God: "If you love to listen you will gain knowledge, and if you pay attention you will become wise" (Sirach 6:33).

Bring to light any obstacles to a relationship with Christ. Any hidden moral fault or unhealed emotional wound hinders the soul's progress. Prayerfully seek to diagnose hindrances to relationship with the Lord. If the individual's struggle is with unbelief, encourage wholehearted trust in God amidst the confusion. If pride is the problem, help the person to see that glory belongs to God alone. If the fault is selfishness, point the disciple to the Cross, where his helpless condition is laid bare. If the disciple's sin is sensuality or lust, remind him that its consequences are destructive—a cutting off from God and an inability to pray.

There may be secret sins that need to be brought into God's cleansing and healing light (see Psalm 90:8). Remind the individual of David's words, born out of painful experience: "If I had not confessed the sin in my heart, my Lord would not have listened" (Psalm 66:18). Where the disciple struggles with a stubbornly oppressive thought, invite him to pray sincerely the prayer, "Disinfect my mind, O Lord, of this thought and remove it from me forever."

Rebuke firmly but gently, when necessary.
The spiritual helper's primary calling is to be the conduit through which Christ's love flows into the other person. But sometimes love requires that we rebuke and correct. When someone has fallen into a moral or spiritual trap, confront him compassionately from the Word (see Romans 15:14-15).

In his strong desire to succeed in ministry, Bill, a respected pastor, became compulsive in his church work, driving himself so hard he was dangerously close to a physical and emotional breakdown. Discerning the nature of his compulsion, his spiritual director said to him, "Do you value your work more than your health?" and "Do you value your congregation more than your family?"

As Bill admitted later, these words hit him squarely between the eyes. He knew that he had to make immediate changes in his priorities and lifestyle if he would grow in connection to Christ.

Facilitate the disciple's repentance, where necessary.
Before Christ's life can flow freely, the residue of sin must be excised. The prophet says to wayward Israel, "Your sins have cut you off from God. Because of your sin, he has turned away and will not listen anymore" (Isaiah 59:2).

If someone is trapped in a moral fault, encourage him to feel sorrow for his sin, confess it, and receive Christ's forgiveness. Repressing our sin is unhealthy—spiritually, emotionally, and even physically (see Psalm 32:3-4). How important it is to bring our sins of omission and commission to God for His cleansing touch!

Be a coach of the spiritual disciplines.
New Christians may not know where to begin with private disciplines such as fasting, contemplative prayer, and journaling; or with public disciplines such as confession, celebration, and service. The spiritual mentor guides the disciple in the regular practice of healthy spiritual habits. We form spiritual disciplines, and in time they form us.

Scripture commands us to discipline ourselves intentionally unto godliness (see 1 Timothy 4:7). A novice needs a coach to teach him how to swing a golf club or cast a flyline. Similarly, a young Christian needs someone to coach him in the disciplines of the spiritual life. Always keep in mind that the disciplines are not ends in themselves, but means to deepening friendship with God.

Help the disciple learn how God speaks individually to him or her.
Some Christians find that God speaks very directly to their souls in such things as dreams. This point may be controversial, so please follow me carefully.

Dreaming is a normal human activity that some groups admittedly abuse for religious purposes. The occult, for example, regards dreams as vehicles of psychic communication and a means of inducing altered states of consciousness. But the fact that dreams have been misused does not mean they should be disregarded. Many church fathers used dreams in spiritual direction to determine how God was working in their directees. Origen, Tertullian, Athanasius, Chrysostom, Cyprian, Basil, Gregory of Nazianzus, Gregory of Nyssa, Gregory the Great, and John Cassian are leading examples.

Biblically and theologically we must distinguish between *special revelation dreams* and *general revelation dreams.* The former are dreams recorded in the Bible that contribute to the story of salvation. The Old Testament records special revelation dreams to Jacob (see Genesis 28:10-17), Pharaoh (see Genesis 41:1-15), Joseph (see Genesis 37:5-7), Solomon (see 1 Kings 3:5-15), and so on. The New Testament certifies special revelation dreams to Joseph (see Matthew 1:20-21; 2:13,19) and Pilate's wife (see Matthew 27:19).

I believe that special revelation dreams ceased with the close of the biblical canon, near the end of the first century. General revelation dreams, however, are a natural function of the human psyche and continue today. Psychologically, general revelation dreams represent the emergence of unconscious images when our conscious controls are relaxed during sleep.

Christians throughout history have recognized that general revelation dreams perform certain valuable functions. Two spiritual benefits deserve mention.

First, through a dream God may disclose His will for our lives. Allow me to share a personal example. After college Elsie and I volunteered for a short-term mission opportunity in Nigeria. Four years later, I began a doctoral program in theology with Professor F. F. Bruce at a university in England. At the end of the year we planned to return to missionary service in Africa and to continue research on the side. As the year wound down, Professor Bruce informed me that research in Africa was not feasible. He said that if I wanted to continue the doctoral program

I must remain in England. Our plan suddenly was blocked! Should we remain in England, or should we return to Africa and forget about the doctorate? I had no idea what to do.

The following Saturday, I took a walk in the English countryside to contemplate our options. As the warm sun broke through the thick clouds, I sat down against a stone wall. Tired from a busy week, I dozed off for a few moments and experienced a dream. A male figure stood before me in the dream and said in plain words, "Stay in England and work with international students." The dream ended as abruptly as it began. Nothing like this had happened to me before. But I was certain that it was God who had spoken! I sensed that I needed confirmation of the dream.

Shortly thereafter I contacted the University and Colleges Christian Fellowship in London (formerly the British InterVarsity Fellowship). I asked the director of International Student Ministries if he needed someone to work with internationals in the Manchester-Liverpool area. He answered, "It's strange that you should phone, because only last week we decided to launch a ministry to international students in the North of England. Yes, we're looking for a campus minister. How did you hear about this?" I responded, partly in jest, "A good Friend told me!" Within a week I began an exciting ministry working with international students, and two years later I completed the doctorate. God directed the future of our entire family (their spouses, careers, and ministries) through that dream. Henry Blackaby and Claude King observe that in the Bible, when God spoke, people knew that it was the Lord; they knew what He was saying, and they knew what He expected them to do.[24] I find this to be true in my own experience.

Second, God uses dreams to disclose the state of our souls. Several years ago I became overextended in ministry. While ministering in a mountain resort, Elsie and I browsed through old shops on the town's main street. We enjoyed one shop in particular that sold outdoor gear and sports clothing.

Back home, I dreamed that we paid another visit to this store. Entering the shop, I was struck by the absence of merchandise on the shelves. The well-worn, oak floor was empty of displays. The shelves that usually held neat stacks of clothing were bare. How odd for a retailer at the height of the tourist season! I asked a salesperson what happened to the merchandise. She replied, "Our prices were too high, so we had to clear the goods from the store for repricing."

When I related this vivid dream to a spiritual friend, his interpretation spoke directly to my situation. With my work overload, I had cleared the leisure sector out of my life and was paying too high a price. God told me through this general revelation dream that I must reduce my commitments and achieve better balance.

After serious surgery, J. B. Phillips struggled with a life-threatening illness. During this time he had a vivid dream in which a man clothed in white showed him the glories of heaven. The dream was deeply moving, but Phillips found it impossible to explain adequately, in words, how it ministered extraordinary comfort and encouragement in his time of trial.[25]

Christians who walk in the light of God's presence (see 1 John 1:7) know which dreams come from the Lord and which originate from an evil power. John of the Cross said that messages from God are peaceful; they foster love, humility, and gentleness in the recipient; and they strengthen our resolve to do God's will. No dream from God will contradict His Word. Should the Lord provide a dream to remind us of some sin in our lives, the dream might involve a degree of tension. Dreams inspired by dark powers, on the other hand, are disturbing; they draw us away from God by inducing pride and hardness of heart, and they are lacking in love.

I recommend that Christians keep a record of their dreams and find a gifted believer to help interpret them.

Problem Solving in Soul-Care/Spiritual Direction

Relationships between people don't always develop in an ascending line. Difficulties and failures are realities in the cultivation of any relationship—including the Christian's friendship with God. We Christians still possess the old nature, which occasionally raises its ugly head to oppose Christ's values. In this section I will suggest how mentors might address two problems that disciples are likely to encounter on the spiritual journey.

Spiritual Dryness

The first is the common problem of *dryness* in our relationship with God. By spiritual dryness I mean a lack of joy in the Lord, loss of spiritual enthusiasm, and disinterest in prayer. Thomas Green has written two popular books entitled *When the Well Runs Dry* (1979) and *Drinking From the Dry Well* (1991). Notice that the title of the first book contains the word *When*, not *If.* Every Christian experiences dry periods in his or her life. The spiritual director helps the disciple understand that we will have good days and bad days, peaks and troughs. Every relationship experiences the ebb and flow of closeness and distance.

Having said this, spiritual dryness also may be due to *physical* or *mental fatigue.* Because we are integrated beings, a depleted body or mind dulls our emotional responses and depresses our spirits. The wise mentor counsels the disciple to cease striving and seek rest and refreshment. Introducing variety into one's life also helps rejuvenate the soul. So take a walk, listen to music, visit with friends, or play a sport. Francis Houdek offers this helpful counsel.

> When someone's prayer is characterized by aridity, the most helpful thing to do is to encourage the person . . . to observe the livelier sense of God in the larger fabric of life, for God's presence can generally be found in *leisure, nature, and relationships.* . . . Prayer does not change, but a newfound amazement and delight in all the other ways in which God enters the person's actual lived experience arises.[26]

Dryness also may come from *spiritual neglect.* Personal distance from God grows when our spirits are jaded by some besetting sin (see Proverbs 1:28-29, Hosea 5:6), when we suffer a strained or broken human relationship (see 1 John 4:20-21), or when we neglect constructive spiritual disciplines (see 1 Timothy 4:7). Getting our hearts right with the Lord is a major step toward solving the problem of spiritual dryness.

Spiritual Desolation

This second problem is related to the condition known as the "dark night of the soul." John of the Cross's writings actually describe a collection of four dark nights. (I will comment only on John's *passive dark night of the soul*, which is commonly understood as the soul's dark night.)

The "dark night" may be caused by painful trauma, such as death of a loved one. Or it may involve the absence of God without any attending life crisis. In the dark night, we may feel that we have fallen into a black hole with no light to dispel the abandonment and emptiness.

Evangelicals speak little about the dark night, perhaps because we've been trained to think that when we become Christians all our spiritual struggles are over. The dark night, however, is a major theme in Christian spirituality. John of the Cross wrestled with the divine desertion when he wrote his famous work *Dark Night of the Soul.* John called it "night" to distinguish it from the Christian's normal condition of spiritual sight. And he called it "dark" to underscore God's withdrawal of comforting grace. John explained the dark night as a time when we recognize our inner powerlessness and are purified from worldly attachments.

Teresa of Avila experienced the dark night in a period of intense opposition and suffering. She prayed to the Lord, "Why do you treat me so harshly?" God responded, "This is how I treat my friends." Teresa replied, "I understand now why you have so few!"[27]

In 1944 C. S. Lewis wrote his famous book *The Problem of Pain.* Most agree that this book went a long way toward solving the classic problem of how a good and all-powerful God could permit terrible suffering. But in 1961, when his own wife was dying from cancer, the answers Lewis proposed seventeen years earlier no longer made sense. God seemed to have abandoned him, and Lewis became frustrated and angry. The quintessential Christian apologist called God a "Cosmic Sadist" and questioned many of his beliefs. Then one morning, when Lewis awoke, both the grief and doubt had vanished. Lewis wrote about his new perspective in *A Grief Observed.* From this bewildering experience, Lewis learned a great lesson: "You can't see anything properly while your eyes are blurred with tears."[28]

In his challenging book *The Return of the Prodigal Son*, Henri Nouwen describes his own agonizing dark night.

> In the months following the celebration of the thirtieth anniversary of my ordination to the priesthood, I gradually entered into very dark interior places and began to experience immense inner anguish. I came to a point where I could no longer feel safe in my own community and had to leave to seek help in my struggle and to work directly on my inner healing.[29]

Seeking spiritual wholeness, Nouwen meditated on the biblical parable of the prodigal son and Rembrandt's painting of this gospel story. The masterpiece was stimulated by the great artist's own experience of spiritual desolation. Through prolonged meditation on the prodigal, Nouwen was brought into the brightness of renewed relationship with God.

The dark night experience is well supported in Scripture. We have only to consider Job to recognize this is so.

Jesus Himself experienced the dark night—a terrible desolation that fell over Him as He hung in agony on the cross. At Golgotha, the Father turned His back on His own beloved Son and became for Him an absent God. And so Jesus cried out in deep distress, "My God, my God, why have you forsaken me?" (Matthew 27:46).

What an awesome mystery this is that God the Father hid His face from His beloved Son.

The dark night is the result of God's mysterious withdrawal. For a season, God providentially distances Himself, causing the light to become darkness. Spiritually God's absence creates a vacuum that can show us the emptiness of our fleshly attachments, such as our dependence on people and things for a security they cannot give and our reliance on position and money for power that is weak indeed. When we let go of these attachments, then we are propelled toward Christlikeness. And so, through the anguish of the dark night, God performs something like "spiritual surgery" on deeply rooted self-sufficiency, sensuality, and pride. In this light, the dark night is an event the spiritual Christian sees as God-induced—or permitted by God—for his or her ultimate good. It is God's work—painful, but unerringly powerful—in our purification.

How do you minister to a person passing through spiritual desolation? Here are some general directives.

First, assure him of the value of suffering, in the divine economy. To become like Christ, the Christian must be purified by pain. The dark night we find so distressing is a necessary part of our union with Jesus, who experienced the Father's absence and who "learned obedience from the things he suffered" (Hebrews 5:8). In this life, suffering is inevitable, but for the Christian it is always purposeful.

Second, encourage the disciple to cling tenaciously to the Lord in faith. In his dark night, David waited for God's deliverance, even though He seemed worlds away. "I keep right on praying to you, LORD, hoping this is the time you will show me favor" (Psalm 69:13). When the shadows blot out the warmth of the Father's love, remember Job, who confidently exclaimed, "Though he slay me, yet will I hope in him" (Job 13:15, NIV).

Third, help the struggler to emulate the confidence of Jesus, who says, "The one who sent me is with me—he has not deserted me" (John 8:29). The dark night serves notice that God is doing a new work of grace in our lives. In God's good time, the darkness will yield to the brightness and warmth of God's felt love.

Tammy is a talented young woman who came to Christ in her early teens. The church she joined taught that if you *believe* and *do* the right things, all will be well. She must read the Bible, pray, memorize Bible verses, and show up for all the church services. Seeking to be faithful for God, she found herself on a treadmill of activity. When she was stricken with a chronic disease, Tammy entered a period of spiritual confusion and desolation. The sense of God's presence and satisfaction in prayer vanished. She experienced great disappointment with God and considered tossing the Christian faith.

Tammy hit rock bottom when some of her Christian friends told her, "You're not trusting God enough!" and "You're not praying the right way!" But in the darkest moments of the night, Tammy clung to the memory of former days when God was real. In faith, she kept her daily appointment with God and remained in fellowship with His people—even though the Lord remained distant and the Word failed to speak to her.

Finally the darkness dissipated and Christ became real again. She joined a Christian renewal community, read many of the spiritual classics, and explored new prayer forms. Realizing that spirit and body are good creations of God, she began to worship with her entire being. Today Tammy has a contagious relationship with the Lord. She understands that what she experienced was a dark night of the soul, lovingly permitted by God to lead her into a deeper love relationship with Himself.

A Final Word

Dallas Willard, the Christian philosopher and spiritual writer, somewhere offers the following evaluation of spiritual direction in the church throughout history. *"Spiritual direction was understood by Jesus, taught by Paul, obeyed by the early church, followed with excesses in the medieval church, narrowed by the*

Reformers, recaptured by the Puritans, and virtually lost in the modern church."

I personally pray that today we may see a return to the mandate of Scripture and the example of Jesus, and begin to practice soul-care. My hope is that we will take up the ministries of spiritual friendship, spiritual guidance, spiritual mentoring, and spiritual direction on behalf of hungry Christians in search of spiritual transformation.

Try It Yourself

1. A Bible study about a godly mentor.

Examine Naomi's loving mentoring of Ruth, her Moabite daughter-in-law, by reading the entire book of Ruth—it's only four chapters and will take about twenty minutes.

Here's the story in a nutshell. Because of a famine in Judah, Elimelech took his wife, Naomi, and two sons eastward to the land of Moab. Elimelech died, and Naomi's sons married Moabite women. When the famine ended, Naomi planned her return to the family home in Bethlehem. Her daughter-in-law, Ruth, who was now a widow, too, vowed to remain with Naomi and make a new life in the land of the Israelites. In due course, Naomi fashioned a plan to find a new home, a husband, and potentially a son for Ruth to carry on the family line. Naomi, in effect, became Ruth's spiritual friend, guide, and mentor.

The following questions unfold further aspects of the story.

- Can you find evidence in the text that illustrates Naomi's loving concern for Ruth, a foreigner?
- How did Naomi's life and witness point Ruth, a Moabite woman, to the God of Israel?

Reflect on Naomi's plan and her counsel to Ruth, which she hoped would attract the attention of Boaz, a wealthy relative of Naomi's (Ruth 3:1-4,18). Boaz generously agreed to redeem some family land and take Ruth as his wife. In time, Ruth gave birth to a son named Obed—who became the grandfather of David (4:22), from whom descended Jesus Christ.

- How did Naomi's bold counsel to Ruth fit in with God's providential plan?
- How was Naomi, the spiritual friend and mentor, richly blessed through her caring relationship with Ruth (4:14-16)? Discuss how mentoring can be a mutually enriching relationship.

2. Acknowledging spiritual friends and mentors in your life.

Reflect on your life experience for as long as you have been a Christian. Identify, if possible, those who have effectively ministered to you spiritual friendship, spiritual guidance, spiritual mentoring, and spiritual direction. Describe how these caring ministers have enriched your life spiritually.

Consider writing a note to each person, acknowledging his or her role in your spiritual formation. Thank the person for his or her contribution to your growth in Christ.

Prayerfully reflect on the following questions and enter your responses in a diary or journal.

- At this stage of your life, what kind of a spiritual helper (friend, guide, mentor, director) would be of greatest value to you?
- Do you know a person in your circle of contacts who might fulfill this role in your life?
- Will you pray that God will bring to you the spiritual caregiver you need at this stage of your Christian journey? You may be surprised how God answers this prayer you offer to Him.

Suggestions for Further Reading

Barry, William A. *Spiritual Direction and the Encounter with God.* New York: Paulist, 1992.

Biehl, Bobb. *Mentoring: Confidence in Finding a Mentor and Becoming One.* Nashville: Broadman & Holman, 1996.

Dyckman, Katherine and Patrick L. Carroll. *Inviting the Mystic, Supporting the Prophet.* New York: Paulist, 1981.

Peterson, Eugene H. *Working the Angles.* Grand Rapids: Eerdmans, 1987.

Stanley, Paul D. and J. Robert Clinton. *Connecting: The Mentoring Relationships You Need to Succeed in Life.* Colorado Springs: NavPress, 1992.

Wilkins, Michael J. *Following the Master: Discipleship in the Steps of Jesus.* Grand Rapids: Zondervan, 1992.

CHAPTER EIGHT

Redemptive Counseling

"May the God of peace make you holy in every way, and may your whole spirit and soul and body be kept blameless until that day when our Lord Jesus Christ comes again."

1 THESSALONIANS 5:23

"We cannot isolate 'spiritual' problems from 'psychological' problems and treat the latter nonspiritually, because the human soul is a psychospiritual continuum in which psychological stress, physiological conditions and spiritual states are deeply interrelated."

RICHARD F. LOVELACE[1]

"Psychotherapy may lead persons into a place of readiness for spiritual growth and may even help them take significant steps toward God. However, this is not salvation."

DAVID G. BENNER[2]

PSYCHOLOGICAL COUNSELING HAS been under attack in recent years, even psychological counseling done by Christians. In a sense, a civil war has sometimes erupted—even among counselors and therapists themselves—leaving confused Christians, who only know they need help with their inner turmoil, caught in the middle.

Do these positions really need to be at war? Or is there a place for Christian psychological counseling in spiritual care?

The critics claim that under psychology's "corrupting influence," preaching gives way to probing the unconscious, teaching yields to therapy, and Spirit-inspired fear of God collapses into narcissism. The "ego" which psychology focuses on is about "easing God out."[3] Wholesale psychologizing of the faith allegedly reduces the worship of God to idolatry of the self; holiness of heart to psychic wholeness; and sin to sickness or victimization. No aspect of Christianity, it is argued, escapes psychology's pervasive influence.

Further, the critics claim that psychology views life from a humanistic point of view. The entry of secular psychology into counseling is said to corrupt the gospel and lead believers astray. Critics note that Sigmund Freud, the father of psychotherapy, viewed religion as a means of avoiding real life, and religious experience as a sign of mental illness. Nor can we forget how the Nazis and Soviets used psychiatry as tools of terrible human oppression.

And yet, what about those inner conflicts and anxieties that will not yield to "simple obedience," nor vanish while we recite Scripture?

Experts tell us that more than one in five Americans over the age of eighteen suffer from some identifiable psychiatric illness. Certain Christians, such as Jay Adams and David Hunt, claim that all emotional problems (except those caused by organic factors) are the result of personal sin, either of commission or omission. There is no such thing, they insist, as a mental illness.

It is also claimed that the sufficiency of Scripture rules out the need for therapy; the Word of God contains all the resources a Christian needs to live a healthy and wholesome life. One preacher insists that a Christian who consults a psychologist or therapist attacks the sufficiency of the Word of God.[4] Moreover, because the Cross frees us from the power of sin, aren't we trying to add to Jesus' work on Calvary (see 2 Peter 1:3)? And after all, God has given us the Comforter to guide and heal. Didn't John write, "you have received the Holy Spirit, and he lives within you, so you don't need anyone to teach you what is true. For the Spirit teaches you all things, and what he teaches is true" (1 John 2:27).

Why entrust our souls to fallible human guides when we possess the infallible Counselor?

It may be obvious that I disagree with the dismissal of psychological counseling as a tool in spiritual formation. But before we explore the reasons and benefits, it is important to set out some definitions.

Psychology is indeed a broad field, and for that reason alone, this chapter will be focused on a discussion of *counseling psychology in a Christian context.* We'll define the discipline this way: *a ministry where a Christian counselor, employing insights from psychology and listening, relating, and offering advice to another, seeks to restore interior health.*

With this in mind, let's consider how counseling psychology, applied by committed Christian caregivers, can and does bring about emotional health and growth in Christlikeness.

A Biblical Basis for Counseling Psychology

How can psychology, a discipline founded by nonbelievers, offer anything for our spiritual betterment—let alone be used to foster Christlikeness?

Claims for the validity of anything, including counseling psychology, need to be tested by principles drawn from God's Word. So let's begin by evaluating Christian counseling in the light of five biblical doctrines.

General Revelation

From our earlier discussion of dreams, you may recall that *general revelation* communicates to all persons, everywhere, elemental knowledge of God and the world He created. General revelation reaches all people through the data of creation, the implanted moral law, and human experience. Psalm 19 describes God's disclosure through the magnificence of the created order (see verses 1-6).

Paul teaches us much about God's general revelation to all people, at all times, and in all places. Referring to Gentiles who lack the Scriptures, the apostle writes,

> For the truth about God is known to them instinctively. God has put this knowledge in their hearts. From the time the world was created, people have seen the earth and sky and all that God made. They can clearly see his invisible qualities—his eternal power and divine nature. So they have no excuse whatsoever for not knowing God. (Romans 1:19-20)

Add to this Romans 2, which teaches that God communicates moral truth to all persons through their consciences (verses 14-15), and Paul's sermon on Mars Hill (see Acts 17:22-31), in which he reminds the pagan Greeks about truths they embrace from general revelation. Paul believes that from general revelation unbelieving Gentiles comprehend truths about God and His world, short of salvation.

The doctrine of general revelation teaches that all humans comprehend considerable truth across the spectrum of life. F. W. Faber (d. 1863), an evangelical Anglican who became a Roman Catholic, somewhere described the human disciplines of learning as "partial revelations of God." Salvation is impossible without the truths of special revelation. But human existence on earth would be miserable indeed without the insights of general revelation.

If we return to the beginning, to our creation as humans, we find that God has issued there a "cultural mandate." (Later He would issue a "redemptive mandate" through Jesus' command in Matthew 28:19-20 to evangelize and disciple.) But let's focus now on the cultural mandate, long honored in the Hebrew-Christian tradition and first found in Genesis 1:26,28:

> God said, "Let us make people in our image, to be like ourselves. They will be masters over all life—the fish in the sea, the birds in the sky, and all the livestock, wild animals, and small animals." . . . God blessed [Adam and Eve] and told them, "Multiply and fill the earth and subdue it. Be masters over the fish and birds and all the animals."

David also refers to the cultural mandate in Psalm 8:6-8. I encourage you to read these verses.

This mandate means that God has appointed human beings, believing and unbelieving, to serve as His stewards on the earth. The task involves pursuing truth and managing the created order for the good of all creatures and the glory of God. Humans obey the cultural mandate by structuring human institutions and developing disciplines of learning. God never promised this task would be easy (Genesis 3:19).

But prideful independence from God distorts the conclusions of general revelation gathered in the human disciplines. The findings of the physical and social sciences represent truth mixed with error. No body of human learning is entirely true, and none is entirely false. Though I disagree with the Swiss theologian Emil Brunner (d. 1966) on certain points of theology, he offers a valuable insight in his "law of the closeness of relation." That law states: *the closer a discipline approaches the core of the spiritual life, the greater will be the distortion due to sin.*[5]

In the following diagram, the horizontal axis contains the human disciplines, the vertical axis represents the core of the spiritual life, and the dotted vertical lines indicate how far opinions provided by Christians and nonChristians in a given field of learning diverge.

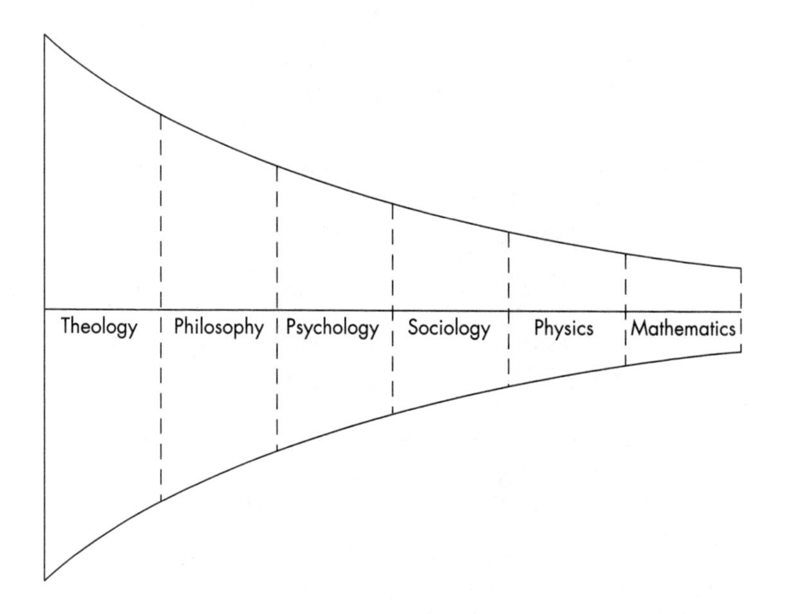

Brunner's law teaches us that a Christian and a Buddhist working an algebra problem can be expected to reach the same solution. But as we move left in the diagram from the physical sciences to the social sciences—such as sociology, psychology, and philosophy—differences of opinion among interpreters increase due to the sin factor. The greatest divergence occurs in theology, where a Christian and a Buddhist will reach radically different conclusions.

Brunner's law helps us understand that all disciplines, including psychology, contain important aspects of truth. But they also contain distortions of truth due to disturbance of judgment by sin.

The bottom line is that *psychology contains much constructive truth mixed with error.* The Christian's task is to identify and welcome what is true in psychology (or in any other human discipline), while rejecting what is inconsistent with the biblical standard of truth.

The Doctrine of the Human Person

The human being, as image of God, is a unity. But this unity is complex, consisting of an inner, immaterial soul-spirit "housed" in a material body. "The LORD God formed a man's body from the dust of the ground and breathed into it the breath of life. And the man became a living person" (Genesis 2:7). Jesus said to His disciples, "Don't be afraid of those who want to kill you. They can only kill your body; they cannot touch your soul" (Matthew 10:28).

The biblical doctrine of the human person as a unity of immaterial soul-spirit in a material body is known as "dichotomy." You might ask, doesn't 1 Thessalonians 5:23 support "trichotomy" (three essential parts to the human being)? I submit that it does not. In this verse, Paul heaps together three closely related terms to communicate the sense of totality. (See also Deuteronomy 6:5, Mark 12:30, Luke 10:27.) Paul prays that believers might be sanctified and preserved *in their entire beings* unto the day of the Lord. Like the Trinity—one God in three persons—the human being is unity with complexity. Because of this, health or hurt in one aspect of the person affects the others.

Consider, too, the fact that soul *(nepeš/psychē)* and spirit *(rûaḥ/pneuma)* are used interchangeably in the Bible (see Job 7:11, Isaiah 26:9, Luke 1:46, compare John 12:27 with 13:21). Soul and spirit are two ways of viewing the inner being of the person. Soul often refers to the self from the human perspective (see Job 30:25, Psalm 42:6, 2 Peter 2:8); spirit, the self from the divine point of view (see Matthew 27:50, Romans 8:16, 1 Corinthians 14:14, 1 John 4:2). This means that the inner person cannot be divided into two essentially different parts—soul and spirit—the former dealing with psychological, the latter with spiritual issues. The Bible, therefore, regards the human person as a "psychospiritual unity."[6] Soul and spirit are two equivalent ways at looking at the one inner being of the person.

The fact is, a person engages God with the same inner structure that he engages himself and others. The person has one *intellect* that contemplates God, as well as self and others. Faulty thinking about self will lead to incorrect ideas about God. The person has one set of *emotions*, which control feelings toward God, self, and others. Hostile emotions toward another human being lead to disordered feelings about God. The person, likewise, has one *relational capacity* that engages God, self, and others. A strained relationship with another person impairs relationship with God. Benner writes, "It appears that people have the same barriers and problems in their relationships with God as they do with other people."[7]

What I'm saying is that emotional disorder does—it *must*—affect spiritual vitality. And psychological woundedness does impair spiritual growth unto maturity. The reverse is also true. Serious spiritual problems can negatively affect our psychological and physical functioning.

Therefore, we need Christian counselors who understand the workings of the soul and who foster spiritual growth by dismantling crippling psychological barriers.

Common Grace

Grace means God's favor extended to the undeserving. Just as there are two kinds of revelation, there are also two forms of grace (common and special). *Special grace* is God's attitude of unmerited kindness that causes Him to be favorable to sinners (see Ephesians 1:5-6). It's also the power of the Spirit in the heart that enables sinners to repent of sins and trust Christ for salvation (see Acts 18:27, Romans 5:20-21).

Common grace, on the other hand, signifies God's goodness that supplies temporal needs (see Psalm 65:9, Matthew 5:45, Acts 14:17), strengthens the light of reason (John 1:9), and enables people to discover truth across the spectrum of human endeavor. Common grace, in short, fosters all that is true, good, and profitable in the human realm. The apostle James writes, "Every generous act of giving, with every perfect gift, is from above, coming down from the Father of lights, with whom there is no variation or shadow due to change" (1:17, NRSV). All the positive contributions of Plato, Shakespeare, and Churchill can be attributed to God's common grace. Likewise, all that is true in the fields of philosophy, psychology, or sociology is due to God's common grace.

John Calvin (d. 1564) noted that through common grace unbelievers discover significant truth from their investigations. In his commentary on Titus 1:12, Calvin writes,

> Those persons are superstitious, who do not venture to borrow anything from heathen authors. All truth is from God; and consequently, if wicked men have said anything that is true and just, we ought not to reject it, for it has come from God.[8]

Calvin believed that knowledge acquired by the unconverted comes from God's Holy Spirit. To reject truth, whatever its source, is to demean the Spirit who imparted it:

> If we regard the Spirit of God as the sole fountain of truth, we shall neither reject the truth itself, nor despise it wherever it shall appear, unless we wish to dishonor the Spirit of God.[9]

Calvin minces no words with Christians who rejected common truth:

> If the Lord has willed that we be helped in physics, dialectics, mathematics, and other like disciplines, by the work and ministry of the ungodly, let us use this assistance. For if we neglect God's gift freely offered in these arts, we ought to suffer just punishments for our sloths.[10]

So Calvin claimed that on the basis of common grace, academic studies aid our understanding of the divine wisdom contained in the Scriptures: People who have "tasted the liberal arts penetrate with their aid far more deeply into the secrets of the divine wisdom."[11]

Consider a comment from the great Reformed theologian Abraham Kuyper (d. 1920):

> By his common grace, God . . . enables men to do good in the broad, nonredemptive sense. It is the source of the good, the true, and the beautiful which remain, in spite of sin, in human life, even in human life which has not been regenerated.[12]

Another Reformed defender of the faith, B. B. Warfield (d. 1921), believed that Christians have nothing to fear from thoughtful investigations into the human disciplines:

> We must not, then, as Christians, assume an attitude of antagonism toward the truths of reason, or the truths of philosophy, or the truths of science, or the truths of history, or the truths of criticism. As the children of light, we must be careful to keep ourselves open to every ray of light. . . . Let us, then, cultivate an attitude of courage as over against the investigations of the day.
>
> The curse of the church has been her apathy to truth, in which she has too often left to her enemies that study of nature and of history and philosophy. . . . She has nothing to fear from truth, but she has everything to fear, and she has already suffered nearly everything, from ignorance.[13]

Christian authorities from earliest times to the present testify that nonChristians perceive significant aspects of truth that serve humankind nonredemptively. This means that Christians will not assimilate *humanistic* psychology into their helping ministries, but they will integrate what is *true, good,* and *edifying,* even if this is discovered by nonChristians. To this cultural task, born of the reality of the Incarnation, God calls His servants.

The Cross and Sanctification

Those who reject counseling psychology as a tool for spiritual growth quote Scripture such as Romans 6. They claim that by a single decision of faith, sin is rendered powerless and victory in Christ is ensured. In other words, sin no longer troubles the souls of surrendered Christians.

Let's look carefully at what the apostle Paul teaches in Romans 6. In Romans 3:21–5:21 Paul expounds the *provision of righteousness* through Christ's justifying work on the Cross. In Romans 6–8 he describes the *impartation of righteousness* through the lifelong process of Holy Spirit sanctification. The apostle's "big idea" in chapter 6 is that, as new creatures in Christ, believers should be servants of righteousness rather than slaves to sin. "Since we have died to sin, how can we continue to live in it?" (verse 2). For Paul, entry into the Christian life marked an end to the tyrannical reign of sin.

Paul further said, "For we died and were buried with Christ by baptism" (verse 4). At conversion believers die with Christ in the sense that the sin principle should no longer dominate them. Moreover "just as Christ was raised from the dead by the glorious power of the Father, now we also may live new lives" (verse 4). In union with the risen Christ, the controlling power of sin is broken. "We are no longer slaves to sin" (verse 6), and "Sin is no longer your master" (verse 14).

Paul never said that dedicated Christians will not have problems. What he did say in Romans 6 is that *sin no longer controls believers in Christ.* This side of glory, believers are buffeted by sin (see 1 John 1:8, James 3:2), because we still possess the old nature (see Romans 6:6, compare Ephesians 4:22, Colossians 3:9). The sin principle is active in Christians, though not controlling. Realistically, the Christian life involves inner struggle with sin that at times can get intense (Romans 7:7-25, Galatians 5:17, 1 Peter 2:11).

The apostle then spells out the tough business that remains for twice-born people. "Consider yourselves dead to sin and able to live for the glory of God through Christ Jesus" (Romans 6:11).

The verb *consider* is present tense, indicating that our decision against sin and for Christ must be reaffirmed continuously. Paul added, "Do not let sin control the way you live; do not give in to its lustful desires" (verse 12). Again the main verb is present tense, implying that our renouncing of sin must be a daily action. In addition, please read verse 13. Spiritual wholeness and maturity normally is not achieved by a single act of surrender.

On the journey to becoming spiritually whole beings, God expects us to use every available means of grace. This includes regular worship in the house of God, the practice of healthy spiritual habits, and the ministry of Christian counselors trained in God's Word and the workings of the soul. God has not spelled out in Scripture all possible means of emotional and spiritual growth. God values physical well-being (see Deuteronomy 7:15, Psalm 103:3, Matthew 8:17). But Scripture certainly does not give details on all the possible means of physical health. Painstaking research through the centuries has produced a multitude of medical discoveries that promote health and extend life. So Christian counseling is one important means God uses to help pilgrim saints put off the "old self" and put on the "new self" in the lifelong process of spiritual and emotional growth (see Ephesians 4:22-24, Colossians 3:9-10).

The Doctrine of Providence

God brings to pass His loving purposes in human lives in two ways. He occasionally produces spiritual and emotional growth by the direct application of supernatural power (Psalm 107:20). We may call this form of providence the "intervention of God." But more often, God produces spiritual and emotional growth through imperfect human helpers. We may call this form of providence the "interaction of God." Remember when the risen Christ struck rebellious Saul blind on the road outside Damascus? The Lord could have healed Saul by the simple touch of divine omnipotence. But instead, Christ directed Saul to an old man, Ananias, who ministered healing to him through the laying on of hands (Acts 9:1-19).

It may seem strange to us that God sometimes uses unbelievers as instruments of His providence. But He does! Cyrus the Great, king of Persia, is a leading example. After defeating Babylon in 539 B.C., pagan Cyrus issued a decree that liberated Israel from captivity and permitted them to rebuild the temple in Jerusalem (see 2 Chronicles 36:22-23, Ezra 1:1-3). Scripture tells us that God called and empowered Cyrus for this important task (see Isaiah 45:1,4,5). The Lord said, "I will raise up Cyrus to fulfill my righteous purpose, and I will guide all his actions . . . I, the LORD Almighty, have spoken!" (Isaiah 45:13). God even calls unbelieving Cyrus my "anointed one" (Isaiah 45:1) and "my shepherd" (Isaiah 44:28)! C. S. Lewis (d. 1963) writes that "people who were not Christians themselves helped me to Christianity."[14]

Reflecting on how God touches lives through others, the great Christian theologian Augustine (d. 430) wrote, "All these things might well have been accomplished by an angel, but human nature would have been lowered in dignity if God had seemed unwilling to transmit His word to men through human means."[15] Because our God is an incarnational God, His usual mode of working is through other people.

C. S. Lewis observes that God could heal bodies and cure souls by the direct application of unlimited power. But "God seems to do nothing of Himself which He can possibly delegate to His creatures. He commands us to do slowly and blunderingly what He could do in the twinkling of an eye."[16] Providentially, the loving God works wholeness through human helpers, including physicians, spiritual directors, and Christian counselors. The preacher who said, "Consulting a psychologist or therapist is an attack on the sufficiency of the Word of God," is on shaky ground biblically and theologically.

With all this in mind, I conclude that Christians who *uncritically* accept the assumptions and conclusions of secular psychology are unwise. But where psychological insights are based on thorough research, where they agree with Scripture and are shown to be practically helpful, they should be accepted as good gifts from God. We Christians delight in what is biblical; we accept truth that is extra-biblical, but we reject what is unbiblical.

Searching out truth in psychology or any discipline requires training and effort. And so with God's assistance, let's move beyond simplistic solutions to complex human and social problems, and fully count on God's help and blessing as we venture into the realm of psychological insight.

Psychology's Contributions to Spiritual Formation

One of the great strengths of Christian counseling is its ability to help the struggler face up to reality. It can help the individual set aside unreasonable defense mechanisms, which hinder emotional and spiritual healing.

A defense mechanism, contributing to an unhealthy soul, can be one of the following:

Denial. A person uses denial to avoid the problem altogether. He may say, "It doesn't matter to me what happens; God will take care of the problem," or even "I'm a Christian, so I don't have a problem."

Rationalization. A person rationalizes in an attempt to use logic to bend or color the truth about his moral responsibility. He may say, "I really needed the money, so I had to cheat," or "I'm only human, and God knows that, so I don't think having an affair is such a big deal."

Projection. The one who uses projection passes off the responsibility to someone else: "My pastor failed us, so I have a right to be bitter and to stay away from Christians." "My son makes me so angry; it's his fault I lose my temper and hit him."

The Christian counselor helps the client face full responsibility for his or her beliefs, attitudes, decisions, words, and actions. He helps the client see self-centeredness, immaturity, sin, and ignorance for what it is, and then to take responsibility in making godly changes. In this way, the Christian counselor helps the client lay claim to—and actually *walk in*—his identity as a child of God. As a spiritual mentor, the counselor shows the client how to rely on God for the godly attitude—and the moral, emotional, and physical strength—to change ungodly behavior into the spiritually healthy behavior of a maturing Christian.

Of the many other examples of psychology's contribution to spiritual health and formation, I will look at four of the most significant.

Psychology Helps Christians Understand Their Uniqueness

Scripture confirms that people are quite different from one another. But psychology addresses the *why* and the *so what*.

My colleague, psychologist Dr. Jim Beck, observes that "The number of questions regarding human personality left unanswered by scriptural revelation is massive."[17] For centuries, philosophers and psychologists have studied personality types. One of the most widely used and tested personality assessment instruments is the Myers-Briggs Type Indicator (MBTI). The MBTI categorizes human personalities in four pairs of preferences that offer sixteen combinations. The four pairs answer the following questions.

Where does one focus attention?
  Extroversion (E) - Introversion (I)
How does one take in information?
  Sensing (S) - Intuition (N)
How does one make decisions?
  Thinking (T) - Feeling (F)
How does one deal with the world?
  Judging (J) - Perceiving (P)

The MBTI informs us that extroverts (entrepreneurs, entertainers) comfortably engage the outer world of persons and things. Their energy comes from social interaction. Introverts (scholars, writers) are more comfortable relating to the world within. They gather energy from solitude and private reflection. Introverts can take heart, for "Western spirituality since Augustine has been mainly developed by Introverts."[18]

Sensing types (professional athletes, craftsmen) gather information from the concrete world through the five senses. They are observant, practical, and realistic. Intuiting types (inventors, detectives) gather information through inner mechanisms of envisioning and intuiting. They are creative, enterprising, and innovative people.

Thinking types (educators, engineers) make decisions more impersonally through rational and logical processes. Because ideas and principles are important to them, they seek to do what is right. Feeling types (therapists, clergy) make decisions on the basis of subjective and emotional considerations. Because values are important, they seek to do what does not offend.

Judging types (accountants, actuaries) function in ways that are structured, orderly, and geared to closure. They deal with issues decisively. Perceiving types (artists) are more spontaneous and flexible. They wait until most of the evidence comes in before acting.[19] Research shows that the "typical" pastor is an ENFJ.

The MBTI and other personality instruments can help us Christians understand our strengths and weaknesses. They can give us insight into how we might better respond to God's working in our lives. Rather than relying on a generic model of spiritual training, the MBTI allows us to structure patterns of spiritual formation suited to people's unique personalities and temperaments.

For example, extroverts flourish through lively interaction with other Christians. Introverts most comfortably relate to God through quiet reflection. Thinkers find spiritual stimulation in theological studies. Feeling types find emotionally uplifting praise music more to their liking. We tend to live out the faith through the grid of our temperamental comfort zone.

The greatest potential for growth, however, will come through the less preferred or weaker function, although overcoming the inertia of habit may be difficult. Jesus said, "You must love the Lord your God with all your heart, all your soul, all your strength, and all your mind" (Luke 10:27)—that is, with every God-created capacity.

High-energy *extroverts* find new potential for growth by practicing the disciplines of biblical meditation, contemplation, and journaling. *Introverts* find new spiritual resources through interpersonal relationships and engaging in group experiences. *Sensates* develop repressed intuition through the practice of contemplative prayer or by listening to others more sensitively. *Intuiting* types grow by being attentive to God's ways in nature and history. They are enriched by drawing on all their God-given senses in worship.

Thinking types grow the heart by disciplines that stir the emotions and draw out feelings. Such might include meditating on the beauty of creation, praying the psalms, or imaginative reflection on biblical stories, such as the prodigal son or the lost sheep. Thinkers become more adaptable by exploring a variety of worship experiences (sacramental, liturgical, and contemplative). *Feeling* types grow as they use their minds more creatively by formulating their biblical world-and-life view. *Judging* types grow as they seek variety in their spiritual experiences. They should be more spacious to the unexpected workings of Providence. *Perceivers* do well to take a more disciplined approach to spiritual formation.

When I consider the uniqueness and complexity of each human being, I recall the words of the psalmist: "Thank you for making me so wonderfully complex! Your workmanship is marvelous" (Psalm 139:14).

Psychology Shows How False Images of God Hinder Spiritual Growth

Parents and authority figures image God for good or ill. How a child views his caregivers determines in large measure how he pictures God. Faithful images of God enhance emotional well-being and spiritual growth. But false or distorted images create emotional barriers to trustful friendship with the Father.

Psychological studies show that if children are raised in a secure, loving, and nurturing environment, they view God as trustworthy. On the other hand, if raised in a cold and critical environment, children develop negative images of God that impede loving relationship with Him. If a child perceives his father to be physically or emotionally distant, he will likely think of God as remote and unavailable. A child who perceives a caregiver as punitive and controlling may view God as a tyrant to be feared. A young woman who was sexually abused may find it difficult to be open and vulnerable to God. Unless dealt with redemptively, false images of God act as formidable barriers to loving relationship with the Father.

A man as saintly as Henri Nouwen struggled with the false image of God as ruthless Power.

> Even my best theological and spiritual formation had not been able to completely free me from a Father God who remained somewhat threatening and somewhat fearsome. All I had learned about the Father's love had not fully enabled me to let go of an authority above me who had power over me and would use it according to his will. Somehow, God's love for me was limited by my fear of God's power, and it seemed wise to keep a careful distance even though the desire for closeness was immense. . . .
>
> This paralyzing fear of God is one of the great human tragedies. . . . As long as the Father evokes fear, he remains an outsider and cannot dwell within me.[20]

A young seminarian I'll call Andy was a talented student who stood near the top of his class. Upon graduation he was appointed senior pastor of a growing church. But before leaving seminary Andy shared with me his sense that God did not love him—in fact, that God was against him. Negative messages communicated by authority figures early in life obscured the clear, biblical teaching that God loved him deeply and accepted him in Christ. Because of his false God-image, Andy failed in ministry and resigned from the church within a couple of years.

Emotional wounds of the past act as anchors, hidden from our sight, that hold us back in our spiritual progress. Although we believe with our minds what the Bible says about God, in our hearts we cannot rest in these realities. A split has occurred between our thoughts and our feelings. We are unable to welcome God as good and loving because of negative experiences at the human level. When treated by a competent Christian counselor using sound psychological and spiritual interventions, false images of God often give way to true images that allow the living water of the Spirit to flow freely.

Psychology Highlights the Destructive Power of False Guilt

Guilt feelings exist in epidemic proportions in Western societies.

While living in England, Elsie and I occasionally visited London. Once while walking through a park, we came across a man standing on a box and preaching. He pointed to passersby with an indicting finger and cried out, "Guilty! . . . Guilty! . . . Guilty!" Some people stared at him curiously; others looked away with embarrassment. But one man was heard to say to a companion, "How did *he* find out!"

Theologians and Christian psychologists identify two forms of guilt: objective or true guilt, and subjective or false guilt. Objective guilt arises from actual violations of God's moral law. For example, if I steal another person's property, God judges me guilty of theft (see Exodus 20:15, Mark 10:19). Confessing the sin, making restitution, and receiving God's forgiveness is the appointed way to silence objective guilt. The guilt we read about in the Bible is usually objective guilt.

False guilt refers to condemnation we feel when we have not violated any divine law, or guilt which persists after confessing our sins. False guilt makes us condemn ourselves when, in fact, God approves us. We read about false guilt in 1 John 3:19-20, and Scripture tells us false guilt may arise from groundless accusations by the Devil (see Revelation 12:10). Sometimes it stems from insensitive domestic or religious upbringing. Children who are shamed by a parent in the presence of peers may be afflicted with false guilt. Moreover, legalistic religion, which lays upon a young person severe taboos, can instill an unhealthy dose of false guilt.

Christian psychology shows that false guilt buries the innocent in self-condemnation, makes receiving of God's forgiveness difficult, and kills prayer and intimacy with God.

My friend Bill, who pastors a large and thriving Baptist church, identifies factors that led to unhealthy self-accusation in his life.

> I was raised in a Christian home, yet it was not a grace-filled environment. I received much discipline with little affirmation and less love, which took its toll emotionally and spiritually. Emotionally, I developed an unhealthy negative conscience that resulted in a heavy perfectionism. Spiritually, I believed that God could never accept me as I was. He could accept me only if I was free from imperfections. Thus, my teen years were filled with tremendous guilt, shame, and insecurity concerning my standing before God. I prayed to receive Christ a thousand times, longing for an acceptance that continually eluded me.

Minirth and Meier observe that the adult guilt-junkie "secretly asks the Lord into his life literally hundreds of times because deep within he does not feel that God could possibly accept him on an unconditional basis."[21]

Believers who are suffering from false guilt easily become disillusioned with God when confession fails to relieve their distress. Wise Christian counseling helps to untangle the web of destructive self-punishment resulting from false guilt and shame. Healing begins in a trusting relationship with a counselor who reflects unconditional love. The embodiment of justice tempered with mercy gives the guilt-ridden soul courage to forgive himself, even as God has forgiven him (Romans 8:1).

It is imperative for the Christian counselor to help the afflicted believer escape the self-centeredness of wrongful "omnipresent" guilt and step into the freeing God-centered, constructive remorse for real sins. Further help can come from the healing prayers offered by gifted members of the body. God's provision for false guilt often comes through the channels of Christian therapy and healing prayer.

Psychology Exposes the Tyranny of Perfectionism and Workaholism

Perfectionism, a common emotional disorder, is the dogma that a person's performance must be flawless to be valued and accepted. Perfectionists think that if the achievement numbers don't compute, God won't accept them. In other words, God gives Himself to those who are totally deserving! Didn't Jesus say, "You are to be perfect, even as your Father in heaven is perfect *teleios* ?" (See Matthew 5:48, Colossians 1:28, and compare Matthew 19:21.)

The Greek word in these Scriptures means "mature" or "complete" (compare 1 Corinthians 2:6, Philippians 3:15). But in his Latin translation of the Bible, Jerome (d. 420) rendered *teleios* as *perfectus*, or "perfect." Building on this misunderstanding, the holiness tradition urges believers to seek a second blessing experience that results in "sinless perfection" here and now.

J. B. Phillips calls this mistaken idea of the Divine the "one hundred percent God."[22] The inevitable shortfall in our performance before a God of absolute perfection may instill a deep sense of unworthiness. In despair of measuring up to an impossible standard, Christians become guilt-laden, depressed, and isolated from social contacts.

Recently I read a newspaper article entitled "Ministerial Burnout Tied to Perfectionism."[23] It reported a recent study showing that 84 percent of the clergy polled expect perfection in themselves; 57 percent feel that other people expect them to be perfect; and 23 percent said they feel uncomfortable unless other people's work is perfect. Fully 10 percent of the clergy in the study believe they have committed the unpardonable sin.

Perfectionism easily leads to workaholism—an addiction to excessive job demands that negatively impacts other areas of one's life. The workaholic is a person who says, "Thank God it's Monday." It is estimated that in the United States there are ten million workaholics, many occupying pulpits and pews. The pastor of a church I once attended communicated to his flock that if they work hard enough, pray long enough, and give sacrificially enough, God *might* favor them with His presence. The message communicated that God's grace hangs on our Herculean performance. Missionaries sometimes are identified as "workers." As a young missionary to Africa, I felt uncomfortable with this label, for it regards servants of Christ as performance machines, valued for what they do, rather than who they are.

People publicly praise the workaholic for his dedication and diligence. But privately the workaholic's life often is in disarray. His compulsion cripples family and other relationships, and his drivenness leaves him with little time or energy for communion with God. Workaholism threatens "burnout" in the form of spiritual lethargy, depression, and chronic physical problems. "If the workaholic is a pastor, his need for control of himself and others will often cause him to become a dictator in his church, imposing rigid regulations upon his congregation. He will pronounce condemnation on anyone (including members of his staff) who disagrees with him or threatens his authority."[24]

The symptoms of workaholism include drivenness to perform, flattening of emotions, inability to give and receive love, and depression. The driven person often is unsettled in his relationship with God, and therefore spiritually unfruitful. Even if the workaholic is a Christian, he is unhappy and unfulfilled. Minirth and Meier estimate that 90 percent of physicians and 75 percent of clergy manifest some measure of these symptoms.

Responsible psychology shows that several personality traits cluster in a destructive pattern: perfectionism, false guilt, workaholism, and even obsessive-compulsive traits. The following figure sets these in relation to one another.

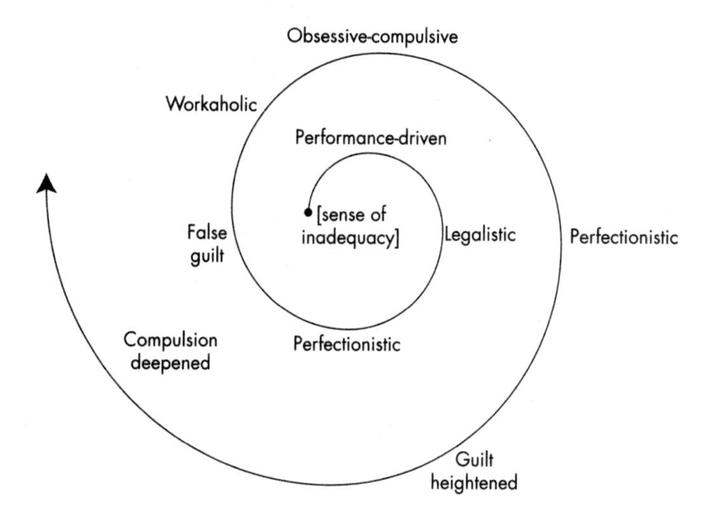

- Conditional acceptance by parents or caregivers, coupled with low self-worth, drives the person to perform in order to be approved (performance-driven).
- The scrupulous person functions out of a rigid set of rules to maximize performance in a search of acceptance (legalism).
- The person is satisfied with nothing less than 100 percent accomplishment (perfectionism).
- Because perfection is unattainable in this life, the person is stricken with feelings of false guilt (neuroticism).
- The person engages in excessive activity to avoid encountering his true self and to assuage felt guilt (workaholism).
- Intensification of workaholism can lead to compulsive perfectionist traits (obsessive-compulsive disorder).

Left untreated and unhealed, the destructive spiral may result in an emotional breakdown. Psychological treatment of perfectionism and workaholism addresses rational, emotional, and behavioral dimensions of the problem. The Christian counselor helps the compulsive to recognize the false thinking at the root of his problem (see Mark 7:20, Philippians 4:8). He must learn that his value to God is not dependent on his performance. There was only one perfect person on planet earth, and His name is Jesus!

The Christian psychological counselor encourages the compulsive person to express his feelings of worthlessness, rejection, and anger to God, thus gradually defusing them of destructive power. The counselor also encourages the sufferer to make decisive lifestyle changes, such as keeping the sabbath rest, cultivating supportive relationships, and enjoying recreational activities.

On this matter, J. B. Phillips puts it well: "God is truly Perfection, but He is no Perfectionist, and one hundred percent is not God."[25] The spiritual writer Thomas Merton (d. 1968) hit the target as well: "Perfection is not a moral embellishment that we acquire outside of Christ, in order to qualify for union with him. Perfection is the work of Christ himself living in us by faith."[26]

I hope you have followed my line of reasoning to its conclusion. Christian counseling that is biblically faithful and skillfully applied fosters emotional and spiritual growth—over time—to perfectionist Christians bound by their compulsion to perform.

The Case of a Courageous Minister

In his stimulating book *A Soul Under Siege: Surviving Clergy Depression*, C. Welton Gaddy tells the story of his painful struggle with mental illness. Gaddy earned several theological degrees, including a doctorate in Christian ethics. He taught at the college and seminary levels and has pastored several large Southern Baptist churches. For years Dr. Gaddy prepared Bible studies and sermons, counseled struggling Christians, preached on television, grew the church, spoke at conferences and conventions, wrote Christian articles and books, served on denominational boards, and so on. Friends and associates describe him as competent, trustworthy, and effective. Some even referred to him as "the next Billy Graham."

With disarming honesty, Dr. Gaddy relates how his own inner responses to the pressures of ministry nearly destroyed him physically, emotionally, and spiritually. Gaddy pushed relentlessly to please others and project the image of a flawless and unflappable minister of the gospel. He felt compelled to be all things to all people. In order to live out this lie, work became his "vocation, avocation, hobby, and means of relaxation."[27] The tension between who he was and what he was supposed to be became unbearable. Nevertheless Gaddy felt that he had to put on a good face, for as church leaders said, "The show must go on." Yes, Gaddy agreed, "The show's the thing!"

As Gaddy puts it, stress, anxiety, relational difficulties, anger toward himself and others, guilt, severe hypertension, depression, and paranoia controlled his life. Happiness and joy evaporated as this minister struggled with deep inner pain. Spiritual vitality gave way to doubt and despair. Parishioners and church leaders urged him to continue producing results. Many denied the possibility of woundedness in the life of their spiritual leader. As his inner world crumbled, his ability to perform church duties sagged. With his family's support, Dr. Gaddy made a courageous decision to "stop the show" and check himself into the mental health unit of a public hospital.

Psychiatric and physiological tests revealed that Gaddy was suffering from long-term depression and related symptoms. He received antidepressant medication, individual psychotherapy, and group counseling. The treatment given by sensitive and supportive therapists (mostly nonChristian) gradually enabled him to drop his defenses, unmask his personal illusions, and peel away the shell that shielded him from his emotions.

Challenged by the transparent honesty of unpretentious fellow patients in the hospital, he learned to admit his deep needs and to risk asking for help. In the psychiatric ward he came to understand his true self as never before. He was given permission to be human—to admit hurt, to make mistakes, and to seek counsel. He grew more comfortable with the idea that he was neither a mechanical robot nor a messiah figure. In his therapy group he claims to have discovered a sense of community—born out of honesty and trust—that was more fulfilling than those he had known in the churches he served.

Gaddy testifies that in this public mental health unit he "found a new drive toward meaning, fulfillment, ministry and joy."[28] A highly educated and experienced minister of the gospel was restored to wholeness by mental health professionals who, like Cyrus, served as God's instruments. Looking back on the years of depression and pain, Gaddy comments, "I need to be reassured that redemptive faith is not a prophylactic unconditionally guaranteed to prevent an impregnation with worry, panic, guilt, depression, and other such negative feelings as futility, purposelessness, and meaninglessness."[29]

Clinical Counseling, Pastoral Counseling, and Spiritual Direction

There is a close relationship between three caring ministries practiced by Christians helpers: counseling psychology, pastoral counseling, and spiritual direction. They relate to each other as three overlapping circles:

Counseling psychology primarily deals with resolution of emotional conflicts, which affect every aspect of the person. Empathy, acceptance, and strength communicated by the Christian therapist plays a large role in the healing process. When the inner conflict that troubles the client is satisfactorily resolved, psychological counseling ends.

Pastoral counseling is usually performed in a local church or hospital ward. It focuses on a presenting problem in the life of the person seeking a helping pastor. The problem may be tension within the family unit, lack of vocational direction, or a serious health problem involving risky surgery. When by God's grace the problem is resolved, pastoral counseling usually ends.

Spiritual direction is the oldest of the three helping ministries. As we've seen, it's the form of soul-care in which a mature and gifted Christian assists another believer to grow in relationship with God, in Christ. As a catalyst for spiritual change, the spiritual director "gets out of the way" and points the disciple under the Spirit's leading to God, the source of all spiritual growth and satisfaction.

It should be clear that all three ministries seek the maturation of the Christian man or woman. Each ministry has its own special focus and task. But because we are integrated beings, the three ministries share some common ground. They are distinct but related ministries that God uses to bring healing and wholeness to His children. In the real world, psychological counseling often deals with the client's relationship with God. Pastoral counseling often addresses emotional obstacles to wholeness. And spiritual direction often confronts problems of daily living. Caregivers cannot be experts in every field. But the more competent they are in these three disciplines, the more effective under God they are likely to be.

Professional Counseling and Lay Caregiving

In his recent book *Connecting: Healing for Ourselves and Our Relationships*, counselor Larry Crabb proposes an alternative to professional counseling for hurting Christians. He suggests that in lieu of standard therapeutic counseling, emotionally troubled folks can be greatly helped as they connect with caring brothers and sisters in Christian communities, who by affirming words release the healing energy of Christ into their souls. There's no doubt that among reasonably healthy folks the ministry of affirming, blessing, and empowering others in the Savior's name can be life-giving and transforming. The transfer of Christ's life from one person in the body to another will go a long way toward healing hurting lives. As Crabb rightly points out, we need much more of this compassionate soul-caring within the community of believers. But regrettably the church has not taken up the challenge and produced the numbers of competent lay caregivers needed to minister healing to the many hurting people in our midst.

We must also recognize that some wounded among us may sense the need to connect with others, but they lack the inner resources to pull this off. What I mean is that severe emotional woundedness prevents some from opening their deepest selves to constructive input from members of the believing community. In other words, some disorders of the soul are so disabling that they are not usually remedied by the sincere affirmations of caring friends. In the case of severely damaged psyches, healing is more likely to occur through the ministry of Christian counselors—ideally in the context of the local church—who are trained in the intricate workings of the soul. Deeply rooted emotional disorders require skillful psychological treatment, even as serious physical illnesses are most effectively remedied by well-trained physicians. The challenging task of soul-care in the church likely will require both a large cadre of equipped and compassionate lay caregivers and a smaller core of professionally trained and godly Christian counselors.

Is "Inner Healing Ministry" Christian?

Many have promoted a form of ministry known as "inner healing prayer" to help relieve spiritual and emotional problems.

But is inner healing, in its various forms, healthy and right for us as Christians?

Inner healing, or healing of memories, as it is sometimes called, is the ministry whereby compassionate Christians, through counsel and prayer, invoke Christ's power to heal the root causes of emotional and spiritual pain. It builds on biblical and psychological insights into the effects of wounding experiences on a person's soul or spirit. "The human spirit can endure a sick body, but who can bear it if the spirit is crushed?" (Proverbs 18:14).

All of us have been wounded to varying degrees by negative life experiences. The wounds that inner healing addresses may be self-inflicted, such as an unforgiving spirit, jealousy, or racial prejudice. Or they may be caused by others, through ridicule or shame, parental divorce, or sexual abuse. A son who receives more criticism than affirmation from his parents may have difficulty loving others, including God. How do we recognize an emotional wound? Whenever a person experiences an inner response inappropriate for a given event, the nerve ends of an emotional wound have been touched. The memories of these wounding experiences may remain with us for life unless redemptively treated.

The Christian ministry of inner healing has been promoted by, among others, Agnes Sanford, Francis MacNutt, John Wimber, John Sanford, David Seamands, and Leanne Payne. John Wimber describes inner healing as "a process in which the Holy Spirit brings forgiveness of sins and emotional renewal to people suffering from damaged minds, wills and emotions."[30] The need for inner healing may be greater than is often recognized, for all of us have sinned and all have been sinned against.

How is healing prayer practiced? The injured person reaffirms his trust in Jesus Christ as Savior and Lord and repents of all known sins. Guided by the Spirit, the prayer minister explores root memories of wounding experiences that cause inner anguish. This should be done carefully to avoid traumatizing a sensitive spirit with painful memories. Through believing prayer, the minister petitions God to heal the specific injury and to fill the life with His love. The minister will recall biblical images and events that illumine the needs of the wounded person.

The minister may lay hands on the head of the person, signifying God's healing and empowering touch (see Acts 8:17). In the Bible, Jesus (see Luke 4:40), Ananias (see Acts 9:17), and Paul (see Acts 28:8) placed hands on people in need of healing. Healing prayer might be accompanied by anointing the head with oil (see Mark 6:13), symbolizing the blessing of the Holy Spirit (see 1 John 2:20,27). James 5:14 reflects the ancient Christian practice of anointing the sick with oil in the context of prayer for healing. Where demonic activity is suspected, the minister quotes Scriptures that affirm Christ's lordship (see Romans 14:9, Philippians 2:11). He dismisses the evil spirit in the powerful name of Jesus and invites the Lord's loving presence. It's a sobering fact that more than one-third of the healings in the Gospels and Acts involved exorcisms of evil spirits (see Matthew 8:16, Luke 4:33).

Inner healing, or healing of memories, as I have described it, is consistent with biblical and theological principles. Consider the following points. *First,* the tragedy of sin injures the entire person—spiritually, physically, and emotionally (see Psalm 32:3-4, 55:4-5). *Second,* God declares Himself to be a healing God: "I am the LORD who heals you" (*Yahweh rōpē',* Exodus 15:26). The Lord healed His people in many ways in the past, and He continues to heal today.

Third, salvation through the Cross renews the person spiritually and emotionally. Isaiah says of the Suffering Servant, "it was our weaknesses he carried; it was our sorrows that weighed him down. . . . But he was wounded and crushed for our sins" (Isaiah 53:4-5). This Scripture teaches that Christ bore sin's guilt and its destructive effects on our lives. I believe there is whole-person healing through the Atonement, but its application is not automatic; God decides when and how to minister His healing balm.

Twenty percent of the Gospel material (727 out of 3,779 verses) deals with Jesus' healing ministry. The Lord's quote from Isaiah 61 in the synagogue at Nazareth implies total person healing: "He's chosen me to . . . set the burdened and battered free" (Luke 4:18, MSG). Jesus cast out demons (see Matthew 9:32, Mark 1:23-27, Luke 13:11-13), cured physical diseases (see Matthew 9:6), and healed people's emotional and spiritual ills. The Lord's act of healing the two demon-possessed men in the land of the Gadarenes (see Matthew 8:28-32) included serious mental illness. The statements of the Evangelists that Jesus healed "various diseases" (see Matthew 4:24, Mark 1:34, NIV) includes emotional brokenness.

I occasionally hear Christians say, "I know in my mind that God loves me, but I don't experience His love from the heart." God is in the business of healing emotional obstacles such as this to our experience of His love.

Fourth, God uses His people as instruments of healing. In the Gospels, "Jesus called together his twelve apostles and gave them power and authority to cast out demons and to heal all diseases" (Luke 9:1). He also entrusted the ministry of healing to the seventy-two disciples (see Luke 10:9). In the early church God healed through the hands of Peter (see Acts 5:15-16, 9:32-35, 36-41), Peter and John (see Acts 3:1-10, 4:7-10), Philip (see Acts 8:6-7) and Paul (see Acts 14:8-10, 19:11-12, 28:8-9). Jesus says to Christians today, "Anyone who believes in me will do the same works I have done, and even greater works, because I am going to be with the Father" (John 14:12).

Do you recall the classic passage in James on healing? "Are you hurting? Pray. . . . Are you sick? Call the church leaders together to pray and anoint you with oil in the name of the Master. Believing prayer will heal you, and Jesus will put you on your feet. And if you've sinned, you'll be forgiven—healed inside and out" (James 5:14-16, MSG). James teaches that confession of sin, together with the prayer of faith, unleashes God's healing power—physically, spiritually, and emotionally. Ministers who pray for healing point the sufferer to God, the loving Source of healing.

So prayer for spiritual and emotional healing is a biblical ministry. Healing prayer is appropriate whenever sin or emotional woundedness binds our spirits or limits our effectiveness for God. Early in his ministry, Augustine believed that the purpose of the New Testament healings was to establish the church on a solid footing. But after witnessing dozens of dramatic healings in his own diocese, Augustine changed his mind. He wrote about his changed view three years before his death, in the essay *Retractions.* After centuries of neglect, the church today is recapturing the grace-filled ministry of healing prayer.

WHAT ABOUT VISUALIZATION?

Some Christian ministers employ visualization in healing prayer. Is this practice faithfully Christian? Christians expressly deny false uses of visualization, such as the attempt to create reality (playing God), manipulate reality (shamanism), or call up inner spirit guides (occultism). Responsible visualization uses the God-created imagination to make present to the senses biblical scenes so they become experientially real and healing. For example, if a Christian feels the need to be more attuned to the needs of others, he might visualize that he is with Jesus as He grieved and wept over Jerusalem (see Luke 13:34-35).

Christian visualization is legitimized by the Incarnation, where Christ assumed our human nature and lived His life in our world. Visualization finds precedent in biblical commands to remember the salvation of the Lord enacted in time and space. For example, before entering the Promised Land, Moses invited the people of Israel to recollect with their mind's eye the display of God's power at the Exodus:

> Don't be afraid of them! Just remember what the LORD your God did to Pharaoh and to all the land of Egypt. Remember the great terrors the LORD your God sent against them. You saw it all with your own eyes! And remember the miraculous signs and wonders, and the amazing power he used when he brought you out of Egypt. (Deuteronomy 7:18-19)

Consider also a later command of Moses: "Remember what the LORD your God did to Miriam as you were coming from Egypt" (Deuteronomy 24:9). He was asking Israel to recall with the imagination the dramatic way God afflicted Miriam with leprosy for her sin (Numbers 12:10).

When the apostle Paul gave instructions concerning the Last Supper—"This is my body, which is given for you. Do this in remembrance of me" (1 Corinthians 11:24)—he encouraged imaginative recollection of Jesus' suffering on the cross. Use of the God-created imagination for holy purposes is implied in other Scripture, such as 2 Corinthians 4:18, Ephesians 3:20, and Philippians 4:8.

The act of imagining Jesus grieving over our sins and touching them with His healing power can make His work more real to the soul. Concreting Jesus' healing work through the faculty of imagination enables us to appropriate more effectively what Jesus longs to do in our lives. Visualization understood in this way is a grace that passes biblical muster!

WRAPPING UP

When a person becomes a Christian, he is delivered from condemnation, not necessarily from emotional illness. God uses Christian psychological counseling—properly interpreted and applied—to bring healing to His children. A biblically framed psychology helps to diagnose emotional and spiritual problems and offers healing solutions.

The body of Christ needs the ministry of Christian psychological counseling. Emotional woundedness does create barriers to the experience of God's love and grace. Psychological problems absorb energy that otherwise might be directed to relationship with God and concern for others. Depressed Christians find it difficult to experience God's goodness, and anxiety-ridden saints are reluctant to serve others. It is the balanced, biblical counselor who can lead his or her clients beyond emotional comfort, knowing that conversion and sanctification of the heart have an ongoing healthy impact by continuing to integrate the human psyche.

I'd like to suggest, in closing this chapter, that in the field of psychology—as in spirituality—Christians should avoid the "all-or-nothing" syndrome. In this line of thinking, if you find one fault in a system you reject the whole thing. The fact is that many human systems, theological as well as psychological, are partially right and partially wrong. Christians must honor what is true but reject what is false, wherever it exists. Knowledge, discernment, and prayer are called for.

When properly interpreted and applied, counseling psychology and theology are friends, not foes. Rather than getting at each other's throats, the two disciplines should be integrated in the God-honoring cause of emotional and spiritual growth.

Mark McMinn, a Wheaton College psychology professor, insists that to be effective in the "care and cure of souls" Christian counselors must be competent in the disciplines of psychology, theology, and Christian spiritual formation. If one leg of this triad is absent, caregiving will collapse like a stool missing a leg.[31] McMinn urges Christian counselors to acquire sound training in the Scriptures, Christian doctrine, the history of the church, and spiritual formation. The demands of soul-care require this kind of "multitasking."[32]

Let me leave you with the following conviction: A godly soul is sown in the act of surrender to Jesus Christ, nourished by healthy spiritual and emotional habits, and supported, when needed, by faithful Christian counseling and healing prayer. Such are the pillars of the pilgrim's spiritual journey.

Try It Yourself

1. Describing your emotional pilgrimage.

Reflect on your life and identify times of emotional distress (anxiety, melancholy, depression) as well as seasons of psychological wholeness (sense of well-being, delight in life, energy for others). Construct a line-drawing of emotional highs and lows in your life. Compare this emotional line-drawing with the spiritual journey line-drawing you did as an exercise in chapter 1.

- How closely do the drawings of your spiritual journey and your emotional journey match?
- What does this tell you about the relationship between a person's emotional health and spiritual well-being?
- With Bible in hand, think through again how your psychological health affects your spiritual well-being, and vice versa.

2. Identifying false images of God you've inherited.

Perhaps you sense in your life stubborn obstacles to a loving relationship with God. The problem may be due to a faulty concept of God. Reflect upon your life, and ask the Spirit to make clear any false images of God that have been subtly communicated to you by a caregiver or other authority figure. Prayerfully recall additional life experiences that have given birth to distorted concepts of God. For example, God may have been pictured to you as a stern judge, a perfectionist, or a distant Deity.

- Which false images of God cause you the most difficulty today?
- How have these false images affected your relationship with God? Your spiritual growth? Your effectiveness in Christian service?
- What do you plan to do about these false images? One helpful approach is to reflect prayerfully on the character of God as revealed in the Bible. You also might engage in a formative reading of a good book on the Divine attributes. If the false images of God persist, seek out a Christian caregiver with whom you can share and pray over your concerns. God may use healing prayer to dispatch the unsettling false images.

Suggestions for Further Reading

Benner, David G. *Care of Souls: Revisioning Christian Nurture and Counsel.* Grand Rapids: Baker, 1998.

Blazer, Dan. *Freud vs. God: How Psychiatry Lost Its Soul and Christianity Lost Its Mind.* Downers Grove, Ill.: InterVarsity, 1998.

Collins, Kenneth J. *Soul Care: Deliverance and Renewal Through the Christian Life.* Wheaton Ill.: Victor, 1995.

Crabb, Larry. *Connecting: Healing for Ourselves and Our Relationships.* Nashville: Word, 1997.

McMinn, Mark R. *Psychology, Theology, and Spirituality.* Wheaton: Tyndale House, 1996.

Payne, Leanne. *The Healing Presence.* Wheaton, Ill.: Victor, 1989.

———. *Restoring the Christian Soul Through Healing Prayer.* Wheaton, Ill.: Crossway, 1991.

Seamands, David A. *Healing of Memories.* Wheaton, Ill.: Victor, 1985.

CHAPTER NINE

Wisdom of the Spiritual Classics

"Since we are surrounded by such a huge crowd of witnesses to the life of faith, let us strip off every weight that slows us down, especially the sin that so easily hinders our progress."

HEBREWS 12:1

"There is a vast storehouse of heavenly and practical wisdom at our disposal in the spiritual classics, ready for us to digest and allow to mould us after the pattern of Jesus Christ."

PETER TOON[1]

WITH THE LOSS OF MEANING AND purpose in society, many are turning *inward* in search of the spiritual. Interestingly we also are witnessing a turn *backward* to more certain times. The search is on to find those stalwart souls who successfully navigated the storms and deserts of life and to learn their insights and answers.

In these confusing times, when the culture is adrift with neither compass nor destination, many Christians also are seeking wisdom from the ancient spiritual writers. Many are revisiting centuries-old treatises and books in hopes of satisfying their spiritual hunger. As Michael Downey observes, "In periods of cultural upheaval and disorientation such as ours, there often emerges a deep appreciation for the merits of earlier periods of history."[2]

The past few years have seen a growing wave of interest in the classics of Christian spirituality. Peter Toon hits the nail on the head with these words: "The wealth of material left to us by men and women who walked closely with God and who were gifted to express the truth of their experiences, is totally overwhelming."[3]

For others of us, the classics are daunting. The language and sentences are awkward, the concepts unfamiliar. An objector might say that these older writings come from unfamiliar denominational traditions. Many were written by desert fathers, mystics, monastics, bishops, saints, and others of unfamiliar pedigree.

Who are these writers? Are they trustworthy communicators of the faith? Can they deepen our faith and strengthen our walk with Christ?

The truth is, we can gain amazing insights about life, suffering, love, loss, God, the church, and our poor, confused selves if we approach the writings of the spiritual masters with open heart and mind.

WHY READ THE SPIRITUAL CLASSICS?

The wonderful fact is, *we are heirs of a two-thousand-year treasury of Christian devotional writing.* We are part of the line of faith that extends back in time for two millennia. The sacred history we share with those who have gone before is a story scripted by the Holy Spirit. Many Christian scholars agree that the long history of Christian spirituality—though occasionally troubled by excesses, even as we are—is evidence of our common hunger to experience and honor God. As modern believers, we read the spiritual classics to enter into conversation with the great personalities of our Christian heritage. And what a valuable resource we have in "all these pioneers who blazed the way" for us (Hebrews 12:1, MSG).

C. S. Lewis was a rabid fan of old books. His contemporaries, like ours, preferred new books to cracked and dusty old ones. The choice between an old or a new book for Lewis was no contest: "A new book is still on its trial. . . . It has to be tested against the great body of Christian thought down through the ages."[4]

A second benefit of reading the classics is that *they acquaint us with the major movements of Christian spirituality.* As we enter the world of the spiritual classics we engage patristic, medieval, Orthodox, Reformation, Roman Catholic, and charismatic writers. Many of us, of course, are leery of certain of these masterpieces, simply because of the labels they bear.

I and a growing crowd of other evangelicals are discovering that each Christian tradition has given us spiritual writings that address the most profound questions and needs of the soul. Downey notes that "the Christian spiritual tradition is like a mountain, containing within it many seams waiting to be mined. Most approaches to spirituality in history mine the same vein over and over again."[5]

If we dismantle faulty and uncharitable stereotypes of other Christian traditions, we may find ourselves wonderfully alert to hear what God's Spirit has spoken to His servants through the centuries.

A third benefit is *the great personal blessing we receive via the writings of spiritually wise men and women.*

For many, however, the question begs: Why read spiritual books from centuries past if we possess the inspired Scriptures? You might as well ask, then, why consult a biblical commentary? (The answer to that is simple: "To benefit from the scholar's insights into the Scriptures after long study and prayer.") Just as we profit from commentaries on the Bible, we read devotional books to be fed by Spirit-illumined writers who struggled to understand growth in the Spirit.

Finally, *the spiritual classics challenge our culturally shaped perspectives on the faith.* All of us, to varying degrees, are captives to our culture. We tend to reflect the norms and values of our social context—blind spots and distortions included. We neglect legitimate elements of biblical faith, and we exaggerate others. For example, Western culture assumes that maximizing wealth is a supreme good. Spiritual writers from other times and traditions may help us distinguish "worldly wealth" from "the true riches of heaven" (Luke 16:11). Moreover, the modern Western lifestyle is too frenzied for our good. Spiritual writers from the past can help us create margin in our lives so that God becomes more real.

C. S. Lewis notes that our age, like every age, suffers blind spots, distorting our perspective on reality. "The only palliative is to keep the clean sea breeze of the centuries blowing through our minds, and this can be done only by reading old books."[6] These older spiritual writers are likely to send us back to Scripture with clearer vision and renewed appetites for deepened relationship with Christ.

Leading Evangelicals Who Valued the Older Spiritual Writers

Many trusted evangelical authorities have read, studied, and applied the wisdom of older spiritual writers to their lives and ministries. Consider three examples of Christian leaders in our tradition who highly valued the spiritual classics.

John Wesley (d. 1791)
John Wesley was a leader of the eighteenth-century revival and an important forerunner of contemporary evangelicalism. Wesley sought to maintain balance between doctrine (belief in biblical truth), mysticism (the experience of God's love), and activism (showing concern for one's neighbor). Scholars say that Wesley succeeded in uniting the Protestant focus on faith and the older Catholic emphasis on holiness of life.

The Bible was John Wesley's primary textbook. But Wesley was also a devoted reader of the spiritual classics. In 1750 he published a fifty-volume series entitled *The Christian Library*. And he did this without a computer and word processing! This huge series consists of selections from leading devotional works through the ages, for the spiritual enrichment of Methodists and other Christians. Wesley's spiritual favorites included the early church fathers; *The Imitation of Christ*, attributed to Thomas à Kempis (d. 1471); *The Interior Castle* by Teresa of Avila (d. 1582); *An Introduction to the Devout Life* by Francis de Sales (d. 1622); *Christian Perfection* by François Fénelon (d. 1715); and *A Serious Call to a Devout and Holy Life* by Wesley's fellow Anglican William Law (d. 1761). He also delighted in the writings of Tauler, Molina, Pascal, Brother Lawrence, and Madame Guyon. Wesley testified that these writings led him to deeper devotion to Christ and to a more serious pursuit of the spiritual path.

At the height of the Methodist revival, Wesley took the time to publish these writers because he believed they were essential for the spiritual nourishment of new believers.

A. W. Tozer (d. 1963)
Tozer, a Christian and Missionary Alliance pastor, is one of us. He was a godly man committed to biblical preaching, missionary outreach, and cultivation of the spiritual life.

Tozer, who had only five years of formal public education, was deeply indebted to spiritual writers from the past. His biographer, David J. Fant, records a list of thirty-five books

Tozer recommended to Christians who desired to pursue "the deep things of God."[7] The following partial list gives the reader an appreciation for the diversity of spiritual writings Tozer treasured.

Athanasius (Eastern father, d. 373)
On the Incarnation

St. Augustine (Western father, d. 430)
Confessions

Anselm (Catholic, d. 1109)
Proslogion

Bernard of Clairvaux (Cistercian, d. 1153)
On the Love of God
Song of Songs

Meister Eckhart (Dominican, d. 1327)
Talks of Instruction

Richard Rolle (Catholic, d. 1349)
Amendment of Life

John Tauler (Dominican, d. 1361)
Sermons

Henry Suso (Dominican, d. 1366)
Book of Eternal Wisdom

Jan van Ruysbroeck (Catholic, d. 1381)
Adornment of the Spirit Marriage

Walter Hilton (Augustinian, d. 1396)
The Goad of Love
The Scale of Perfection

Anonymous (Catholic, fourteenth century)
The Cloud of Unknowing
Theologia Germanica

Julian of Norwich (Catholic, d. 1413)
Revelations of Divine Love

Nicholas of Cusa (Catholic, d. 1464)
The Vision of God

Thomas à Kempis (Catholic, d. 1471)
The Imitation of Christ

John of the Cross (Carmelite, d. 1591)
The Ascent of Mt. Carmel

Francis de Sales (Catholic, d. 1622)
Introduction to a Devout Life

Jacob Boehme (Protestant, d. 1624)
The Way of Christ

Lancelot Andrewes (Anglican, d. 1626)
Private Devotions

Brother Lawrence (Cistercian, d. 1691)
Practice of the Presence of God

Michael Molinos (Catholic, d. 1697)
The Spiritual Guide

François Fénelon (Catholic, d. 1715)
Christian Perfection

Isaac Watts (Protestant, d. 1748)
Poems

Frederick Faber (Catholic, d. 1863)
Poems

Thomas Kelly (Quaker, d. 1941)
A Testament of Devotion

You may note that most of the books on Tozer's list of spiritual favorites were written by Catholic authors. Many are from the medieval period of the church. Only one is written by an American author (Thomas Kelly). And only one is from the twentieth century (also Kelly). While Tozer didn't endorse everything in these books, he judged that their spiritual benefits far outweighed any minor doctrinal defects. In these writings—many of which are mystical—Tozer was attracted to themes of quiet waiting on the Lord, heart-relatedness to Christ, Spirit empowerment, and guiding others along the spiritual path.

How did Tozer's C&MA congregation respond to his frequent appeal to mystical writings in sermons and books? Tozer's biographer relates that lay folk seemed genuinely appreciative of the experiential, Christ-centered piety reflected in these authors. In her study of the "mystical" Tozer, E. Lynn Harris concludes, "Tozer's list of thirty-five recommended works is indeed quite palatable to a Protestant, having much to say to those in the twentieth century wishing a spiritual depth and maturity."[8]

Richard J. Foster

Richard Foster is undoubtedly the most popular living spiritual writer in the evangelical world. The richness and practical relevance of his best-selling books have touched the hearts of Christians everywhere. Foster appreciates all that is edifying in the writings of Christian spirituality through the centuries. He is at home with spiritual authorities in the major branches of Christendom. Wherever truth is found, Foster is prepared to honor it.

In their book *Devotional Classics* (1993), Foster and James Bryan Smith assign the major spiritual writers of the church to five categories: the prayer-filled life, the virtuous life, the Spirit-empowered life, the compassionate life, and the Word-centered life. Foster's latest book, *Streams of Living Water* (1998), refines this scheme into six streams of Christian faith and life that form the core of the RENOVARÉ ministry. Christians achieve wholeness by incorporating into their lives each of these emphases. The six traditions and their most prominent representatives from biblical times to the present are:

The Contemplative tradition: John the Apostle, Gregory of Nyssa (d. 395), Benedict of Nursia (d. 547), Aeldred of Rievaulx (d. 1167), Julian of Norwich (d. 1413), John of the Cross (d. 1591), Brother Lawrence (d. 1691), Madame

Guyon (d. 1717), François Fénelon (d. 1715), Térèsa of Lisieux (d. 1897), Thomas Kelly (d. 1941), Thomas Merton (d. 1968), and Henri Nouwen (d. 1996).

The Holiness tradition: James the Apostle, Tertullian (d. 225), Gregory of Nazianzus (d. 389), John Cassian (d. 435), Bernard of Clairvaux (d. 1153), Thomas à Kempis (d.1471), Richard Baxter (d. 1691), William Law (d. 1761), John Wesley (d. 1791), Hannah Whitall Smith (d. 1911), and Dietrich Bonhoeffer (d. 1945).

The Charismatic tradition: Paul the Apostle, Montanus (2d cent.), Gregory the Great (d. 604), Francis of Assisi (d. 1226), Richard Rolle (d. 1349), George Fox (d. 1691), Charles Wesley (d. 1788), Sundhar Singh (d. 1929), David du Plessis (d. 1987), Oral Roberts (b. 1918), and John Wimber (d. 1997).

The Social Justice tradition: Deacons (1st–20th cents.), John the Almsgiver (d. 619), Vincent de Paul (d. 1660), John Woolman (d. 1772), William Wilberforce (d. 1833), David Livingstone (d. 1873), Florence Nightingale (d. 1910), Mother Teresa (d. 1997), Martin Luther King, Jr. (d. 1968), Desmond Tutu (b. 1931), and Jean Vanier (b. 1928).

The Evangelical tradition: Peter the Apostle, Ignatius of Antioch (d. 107), Athanasius (d. 373), Ambrose of Milan (d. 397), Jerome (d. 420), Augustine (d. 430), Martin Luther (d. 1546), Huldrych Zwingli (d. 1531), John Calvin (d. 1564), George Whitefield (d. 1770), William Carey (d. 1834), Charles Haddon Spurgeon

(d. 1892), Dwight L. Moody (d. 1899), C. S. Lewis (d. 1963), and Billy Graham (b. 1918).

The Incarnational tradition: Jesus of Nazareth (d. 29), Origen (d. 254), John of Damascus (d. 749), Leonardo da Vinci (d. 1519), Michelangelo (d. 1564), John Milton (d. 1674), Johann Sebastian Bach (d. 1750), George Frideric Handel (d. 1759), Fydor Dostoyevski (d. 1881), Dag Hammarskjöld (d. 1961), and Aleksandr Solzhenitsyn (b. 1918).

We readily see that Foster's list of recommended spiritual authors covers every age and many Christian traditions.

Two Pre-Reformation Spiritual Writers

In this section and the next I will look closely at representative spiritual writers to illustrate the riches embedded in the Christian classics. I also offer these writers as wells of spiritual wisdom, whose writings can deepen your devotion to God.

A Patristic Voice: St. Augustine (d. 430)

One leading church historian (Adolf von Harnack) praised Augustine as the greatest man between the apostle Paul and Luther. Augustine's evangelical zeal, profound doctrinal insights, and spiritual passion have had a huge impact on Western Christendom for more than fifteen hundred years.

Born in North Africa, Augustine was converted to Christ at age thirty-two through the prayers of his mother, Monica, and the preaching of Ambrose (d. 397), bishop of Milan. His great intellect, deep spirituality, and heroic sanctity generated a wealth of doctrinal and devotional writings. From among Augustine's vast library we select one theme for reflection: the believer's growth into spiritual maturity in Christ.

In his *Commentary on the Lord's Sermon on the Mount*, Augustine outlines seven steps that lead to maturity in Christ. Augustine weaved together *seven graces of the Spirit* from Isaiah 11:2-3, *seven Beatitudes* from Matthew 5:3-10, and *seven petitions of the Lord's Prayer* in Matthew 6:9-13. Augustine believed that every step forward in the spiritual life is a divine enablement (the Spirit's graces). The power of the Spirit inscribes on the believing heart a new law (the Beatitudes). And the new law, which is the Spirit-enabled life, expresses itself in a habit of prayer (the Lord's Prayer).

A person's decision for Christ is the first step on the path to spiritual maturity. The new Christian experiences holy fear of God, for as the Scripture says, "The fear of the LORD is the beginning of wisdom" (Proverbs 9:10). Because those who fear the Lord are humble in spirit, Augustine linked the grace of *holy fear* (see Isaiah 11:2,3) with the beatitude, "Blessed are the poor in Spirit, for theirs is the kingdom of heaven" (Matthew 5:3). The humble Christian who fears God prays, "Our Father in heaven, hallowed be your name" (Matthew 6:9).

The second step toward maturity in Christ is acquaintance with biblical teaching in a spirit of docility. Through the Scriptures we learn to love God for His own sake and others for God's sake. Because piety reflects itself as meekness, Augustine linked the second grace of the Spirit, *godliness* (see Isaiah 11:2), with the beatitude, "Blessed are the meek, for they will inherit the earth" (Matthew 5:5, NIV). The godly Christian in humility prays, "Your kingdom come" (Matthew 6:10, NIV).

In the third stage the Christian understands sin's damaging effects upon the soul and grieves his unholy condition. So Augustine linked the Spirit's gift of *knowledge* (see Isaiah 11:2) with the beatitude, "Blessed are those who mourn, for they shall be comforted" (Matthew 5:4). Knowing the gulf that exists between his own performance and God's perfections, the Christian prays from the heart, "Your will be done on earth as it is in heaven" (Matthew 6:10, NIV).

The fourth step to maturity involves the hard work of combatting sin and pursuing righteousness. So Augustine connected the Spirit's grace of *fortitude* or *power* (see Isaiah 11:2) with the beatitude, "Blessed are those who hunger and thirst for righteousness, for they will be filled" (Matthew 5:6, NIV). Those who truly hunger for inner rectitude pray, "Give us today our daily bread" (Matthew 6:11, NIV)—that is, the spiritual resources needed to win the battle against sin and Satan.

Stage five, the Spirit's enlightenment, causes love to reign as the rule of one's life, thereby fulfilling the Great Commandment. Love purifies the heart so that it may see God. This vision empowers the Christian to perform loving acts of mercy toward others. Thus, Augustine linked the grace of *counsel* (see Isaiah 11:2) with the beatitude, "Blessed are the merciful, for they will be shown mercy" (Matthew 5:7, NIV). The Christian at this stage of the journey prays, "Forgive us our debts, as we also have forgiven our debtors" (Matthew 6:12, NIV).

In the sixth step to maturity, purity of life, born out of love, opens the Christian's eyes to see the face of God (see Ephesians 1:18) as in a mirror. In other words, faith working through love purifies the heart to behold God. Augustine linked the grace of *understanding* (see Isaiah 11:2) with the beatitude, "Blessed are the pure in heart, for they will see God" (Matthew 5:8, NIV). Because sin blinds our vision of God's face, Christians at this level of maturity pray, "Lead us not into temptation" (Matthew 6:13a, NIV).

In the final stage of our journey, the Christian attains the practical knowledge that is wisdom. Wisdom brings *shalom*, or peace, to the person growing in likeness to Christ. Augustine linked the grace of *wisdom* (see Isaiah 11:2) with the beatitude, "Blessed are the peacemakers, for they will be called sons of God" (Matthew 5:9, NIV). Because Satan's assaults disturb God's *shalom*, Christians earnestly pray, "Deliver us from the evil one" (Matthew 6:13, NIV).

Augustine's seven steps to maturity in Christ weave seven graces, seven beatitudes, and seven petitions into a rich tapestry of prayer, holiness, love, empowerment, contemplation of God, and service. The goal—wisdom—represents the Christian's renewal into the image of Christ.

A Medieval Voice: Bernard of Clairvaux (d. 1153)

Bernard is one of the great figures in the history of the church. In many respects he was a reformer four hundred years before the Reformation. Luther praised Bernard as the most pious of monks and one who preached Christ most exquisitely. Calvin's interest in Bernard was exceeded only by his indebtedness to Augustine. Puritans such as John Owen, Richard Baxter, and Thomas Manton quoted Bernard often. They valued his experiential teaching that brought together reason, piety, and spiritual passion. Bernard of Clairvaux remains a respected spiritual writer 850 years after his death.

Born into a privileged French family, Bernard was taught well in the Scriptures, in logic, and in the secular classics. At twenty-five, Bernard was appointed abbot of the monastery at Clairvaux. He founded an additional sixty monasteries and aided in the establishment of hundreds more. His inspiring preaching motivated thousands of Christians to join monastic communities.

A careful student of Augustine, Bernard stressed God's gracious initiative throughout the course of salvation. Hymns attributed to Bernard have blessed believers through the centuries. They include "Jesus, the Very Thought of Thee," "O Sacred Head Now Wounded," and "Jesus, Thou Joy of Loving Hearts."

On Loving God and the unfinished *Sermons on the Song of Songs* are considered Bernard's greatest spiritual writings. Let's consider his work *On Loving God.* Bernard observed that the triune God is love's fountainhead (see 1 John 4:16). The supreme display of God's love is the eternal Son who became man for our salvation (see 1 John 3:16, compare John 3:16, 1 John 4:9-10). For Bernard, love is God's way to man and man's way to God. In this work, he identifies four degrees of love in the course of the Christian's deepening relationship with God.

The first degree is that *we love ourselves for our own sake.* In the course of nature, a person first loves himself. The law and commandments are summed up in the words, "Love your neighbor as yourself" (Leviticus 19:18, Matthew 22:39, Romans 13:9, Galatians 5:14, James 2:8). Bernard recognized that a person can neither love

God nor others unless he first loves himself. The deepening journey of love must begin here. This first degree admittedly is *immature love*, love of self for self. Because love of self alone does not satisfy the heart, the Christian must reach out to God.

The second degree of love is that *we love God for our own sake*. God in His goodness daily loads us with benefits. He satisfies our needs (see Isaiah 58:11), rescues us from trouble (see Psalm 50:15), and answers our prayers (see Psalm 116:10). Christians look to God and love Him for the consolations He brings into their lives. This second degree of love is a *prudent love*, love of God for self. But the divine favors, however pleasant, fail to quench the heart's deep thirst for God Himself. A higher level of love beckons.

The third degree of love is that *we love God for God's sake*. Having tasted the goodness of the Lord (see Psalm 34:8), our hearts now yearn for the Giver behind the gifts. As we deepen knowledge of the Lord, we find Him altogether lovely (see Song of Songs 5:16). Our hearts now become fixed in love on the God of consolations, rather than the consolations of God. The soul seeks no other reward than God Himself. Loving God for Himself, Christians are enabled to love others as they ought. This is *unselfish love*—love of God for God.

The fourth degree of love is that *we love ourselves for God's sake*. Loving God, we know that we are loved by God. In the security of this knowledge, we can risk abandoning ourselves fully to Him (see Colossians 3:3). Having completely surrendered to God, Christians become one in heart, mind, and will with Him (see 1 Corinthians 6:17). Here Jesus' command becomes a reality: "Love the Lord your God with all your heart, all your soul, all your mind, and all your strength" (see Mark 12:30). This is *perfect love*, love of self for God. This fourth degree of love offers a foretaste of the pure love Christians will enjoy in glory. Bernard explains that this love is realized "when God is loved alone and above all, for now we do not love ourselves except for His sake; He is, Himself, the reward of those who love Him, the eternal reward of those who love Him for eternity."[9]

Bernard of Clairvaux joyfully embraced the historic Christian gospel. He emerges from the pages of history as a man of faith, piety, and action—a great spiritual father of the church. Although we may not agree with every point of his theology, his writings challenge us to go deeper into the loving heart of God.

Two Post-Reformation Spiritual Writers

Of the many spiritual writers in the last four centuries, I chose two to illustrate the spiritual riches contained in less familiar sources.

A Mystical Voice: Teresa of Avila (d. 1582)

Although Teresa lived an active life, she enjoyed deep communion with Christ. Teresa's writings can challenge Christians today to press on to know Jesus Christ more intimately.

Teresa was born in Avila, Spain, in 1515. In her twenties, Teresa became a Carmelite sister (the Carmelites were named after Mount Carmel, where Old Testament saints met God). Teresa was nurtured spiritually on the *Confessions* of St. Augustine and *The Imitation of Christ.* Dissatisfied with the quality of religious life in her order, she established fourteen communities dedicated to prayer and contemplation. Her most important book, *The Interior Castle,* offers powerful insights into the unfolding nature of our spiritual journey in Christ.

Teresa draws on the imagery of a medieval castle with seven rooms to represent the human soul. The gate that provides access to the castle is prayer. The seventh room at the center of the castle is the core of the soul, the place of deepest communion with God. The converted who pass through the castle gate enter upon the spiritual journey. Teresa likens the passage through the castle to the relationship between a lover and his beloved—progressing from spiritual friendship (rooms 1-3), to spiritual courtship (rooms 4-5), to spiritual marriage (rooms 6-7). Let's examine this.

Spiritual friendship: Entering the *first dwelling place*, the new convert engages in devotional readings, mental prayer, and Christian fellowship. The soul experiences some sweetness, but the old self remains in control. The young Christian is attracted to Christ because of the personal benefits or consolations she receives. This person has had an encounter with God, but has not yet developed a relationship with Him. Teresa explained it this way: "In the first room souls are still absorbed in the world and engulfed in their pleasures and vanities, with their honors and pretenses."[10] Matthew 6:21 describes the person in this first room.

Entering the *second dwelling place*, the Christian's life remains focused on external concerns. Faith is feeble and wavering, prayers brief and lukewarm, and service self-centered. Satan attacks the saint by reminding her of her need for financial security and worldly acclaim. Considerable tension exists at the level of inner values. The Christian's soul is torn between going forward with Christ or returning to the world. The Christian remains attracted to the faith for the personal benefits she receives. However she has not yet learned how to abide in Christ (John 15:4-5).

In the *third dwelling place*, the pilgrim strives not to offend the Divine Majesty. She appears to be a "good Christian" outwardly, serving her neighbor; but inwardly she lacks intimacy with God. The spiritual conflict is still lively. She remains torn between earthly honor and surrender to Christ, and may question whether being a Christian is worth the trouble. Most Christians here have not yet experienced deep peace with God through the prayer of the heart. In this third stage, the Christian sometimes experiences a spiritual desert or dark night of the soul. This spiritual drought is God's way of highlighting her need for intimacy with Him. Many Christians fail to progress beyond this point, thinking this is all there is to the Christian life.

Spiritual courtship: In the *fourth dwelling place*, significant spiritual progress occurs as the Christian enhances relationship with

Christ. By allowing the Spirit to draw the faculties inward through the prayer of quiet, the Christian deepens intimacy with the Savior. Now the *heart* becomes the channel for receiving grace. Teresa observed that when two lovers are courting, the heart, not the intellect, is more active. "One should let the intellect go and surrender oneself into the arms of love, for His Majesty will teach the soul what it must do at that point."[11] Here the Christian experiences detachment from the world under the power of a new attraction. As she accepts God's offer of intimacy, a sweet, spiritual fragrance permeates her soul. The beloved now enters the realm of the mystical which, as the Song of Songs teaches, is better experienced than described.

In the *fifth dwelling place*, the Christian becomes so centered in God that a profound experience of communication and communion with Christ occurs. "God so places Himself in the interior of that soul that . . . it can in no way doubt that it was in God and God was in it."[12] Teresa likened the soul's transformation in Christ to that of a silkworm. The silkworm builds its cocoon, is transformed within its tent, and emerges as a beautiful butterfly. Paul describes this spiritual transformation in Colossians 3:3-4. Here are Teresa's words:

> How transformed the soul is when it comes out of this prayer [of quiet] after having been placed within the greatness of God and so closely joined with Him for a little while. . . . Truly, I tell you that the soul doesn't recognize itself. Look at the difference there is between an ugly worm and a little white butterfly; that's what the difference is here. The soul doesn't know how it could have merited so much good.[13]

The soul is so changed by the experience of quietness in prayer that it longs to leave this world and be with Christ (see Philippians 1:21-23). The beloved cannot deny the immediacy of its experience of the Lover's presence ("The LORD is There," Ezekiel 48:35). Teresa believed that relatively few Christians progress to this chamber. The butterfly that has left its cocoon has not yet found its perfect rest. Love for God and the neighbor must grow deeper still.

Spiritual marriage: In the *sixth dwelling place*, love for the heavenly Bridegroom intensifies. The bride understands more fully the scope of her sins and how little she has responded to His love. So passionate is her longing to be united with her heavenly Spouse that her soul is "wounded with love." In anticipation of deeper union, she experiences raptures and visions from Christ, not unlike Moses' experience at the burning bush (Exodus 3:2-6). This stage typically involves physical afflictions and persecutions. The Beloved permits suffering so that the soul may be weaned from earthly attractions and find satisfaction in Him alone. "All these sufferings are meant to increase one's desire to enjoy the Spouse."[14] Many first-century Christians and martyrs likely reached this sixth dwelling place.

The spiritual marriage between God and the soul consummates in the *seventh dwelling place*. In the innermost sanctuary of the castle the Christian becomes one with God, in the sense that two persons become one at marriage. Teresa illustrated the union by the flames of two candles that merge into one. Paul writes about this state in 1 Corinthians 6:17: "The person who is joined to the Lord becomes one spirit with him." Fleeting moments of rapture (as in the previous stage) are elevated into uninterrupted communion with the Beloved. No spiritual dryness, no assault from Satan, now disturbs the relationship. The ego is lost—or rather, fulfilled—in Christ. Christ is married to all aspects of the conscious and unconscious mind. The Christian thinks, wills, and responds with the mind of the Savior. The beloved becomes a free and willing slave of Christ and a servant of the needy.

Teresa wrote, "What God communicates here to the soul in an instant is a secret so great and a favor so sublime . . . that I don't know what to compare it to. I can say only that the Lord wishes to reveal for that moment, in a more sublime manner than through any spiritual vision or taste, the glory of heaven."[15]

How reliable is Teresa's description of the spiritual journey? *The Interior Castle* is a deeply Christ-centered writing. The Christian's calling is to focus on Christ and the needs of others. Teresa also stressed that the Christian merits nothing whatsoever. Everything we enjoy is a gift from God. But what do we make of the mystical phenomena she reports in advanced stages of the journey? Although foreign to us today, perhaps, they appear similar to the spiritual experiences of Moses, Isaiah, Paul, and John in the Bible. To take a more recent example, Baptist preacher C. H. Spurgeon (d. 1892) was no stranger to mystical experiences with accompanying suffering.

> Should you be favored with visions and revelations of the Lord, caught up to the third heaven, admitted into Paradise, and privileged to hear things which it were not lawful for a man to utter, conclude not that you have escaped the rod; rather expect that such high privilege will need heavy afflictions to balance it. If God has given you the great sail and the prosperous wind, he will also give you the heavy ballast to keep your keel deep in the stream.[16]

Teresa wrote *The Interior Castle* to spur Christians onward and upward with Christ. While not endorsing everything, I believe that she offers important insights into the dynamics of the spiritual journey. Teresa reminds us that the Christian life is a process of continual growth, by faith, prayer, and effort, into intimacy with Christ. We Christian pilgrims have much room for spiritual growth and delight in God. As Teresa put it, "The soul [in Christ] is capable of much more than we can imagine."[17] Christians advance spiritually by detaching the heart from lesser loves and surrendering to Jesus (see John 3:30).

Pain and suffering are bedfellows in the life of growing holiness. Finally, unspeakable glory with Christ awaits the sons and daughters of God. As Paul writes, "'No eye has seen, no ear has heard, and no mind has imagined what God has prepared for those who love him.' But we know these things because God has revealed them to us by his Spirit" (1 Corinthians 2:9-10).

A Contemplative Voice: Thomas Merton (d. 1968)

Thinking Christians can't avoid Thomas Merton; he is that imposing a spiritual and prophetic voice of the twentieth century. Some have described Merton as the most influential intellectual and spiritual figure of our time. Merton's writing encourages Christians to touch the heart of God while addressing the needs of a sick and troubled world.

Born into a nominal Protestant background, the French-born Merton professed conversion to Christianity while a student at Columbia University. Merton spent most of his life as a priest in a Trappist monastery in Kentucky. He is the author of some sixty books and hundreds of articles on the spiritual life and related topics. Merton died accidentally of electrocution at age fifty-three while on a lecture tour in Asia.

Merton confessed to being a sinner graciously forgiven by God through faith in Christ. His life's passion was to know the great "I AM" experientially as a lived Reality in the heart. Merton wrote that meditation on Christ's saving love "fills our Christian life with the inexpressible warmth of gratitude and with a transcendent awareness of what it means to be sons of God because the only begotten Son of the Father has loved us even to the point of dying for us on the cross, that we may be united to His love."[18] Merton judged the good news to be the great hope for decaying Western civilization that is Christian only in name. His writings are sprinkled with Scripture texts and citations from Christian theologians and spiritual masters.

At twenty-six, Merton withdrew from secular pursuits to seek the will of God with others in a common life. He followed in the steps of the desert fathers, who centuries ago sought God in the solitude of the wilderness. Through the Trappist regimen, Merton would seek that pearl of great price (see Matthew 13:45-46) and enrich the new man in Christ (see 2 Corinthians 5:17). The centerpiece of the monastic discipline is contemplation, which is about listening to God in silence, being attentive to God in love, and enjoying personal relationship with the Lord. Contemplative prayer is "a way of resting in him whom we have *found*, who loves us, who is near to us, who comes to us to draw us to himself."[19] Through contemplation, Christians draw from the wells of divine love and become refreshing fountains from which others may drink.

Merton developed a burden for the world in its confusion and chaos. The headlines of his day told the story of Auschwitz, Hiroshima, and Vietnam. Merton felt deeply the pain of suffering people around the world. As a Christian, he couldn't isolate himself from social, political, and humanitarian problems wherever they existed. So Merton supported peace and justice movements in the spirit of Christian nonviolence. Yet he firmly believed that personal transformation through Christ is the only viable basis for social transformation. Merton wrote, "We must be transformed interiorly into new men, and then act according to the Spirit given to us by God, the Spirit of our new life, the Spirit of Christ."[20]

Christian service in the public arena, however, must be conducted in a spirit of reflection and contemplation. Merton's ideal for social engagement was *action and contemplation.* His writing reminds us that Mary (the contemplative) and Martha (the activist) were sisters living in the same household. For Merton, "contemplation . . . becomes a reservoir of spiritual vitality that pours itself out in the most telling social action."[21]

Merton claimed that the monastic ideal is for every Christian serious about following Christ in the secular world. What did he mean by this? In the midst of family responsibilities and jobs, lay Christians should cultivate *solitude* for enrichment of their souls. Solitude is not the absence of people; it is awareness of the presence of God. The monastic way in the world is also a life of *community*. Christians unite for kingdom living in the edifying "communion of the saints." Moreover, Christians working in the marketplace *study the Scriptures*, for the written word points us to Christ, the living Word. Worldly monastics are also faithful in *worship*. The liturgical cycle ensures participation in the rich seasons of the church's faith and life. Finally, secular monastics breathe the atmosphere of nourishing *contemplative prayer*.

Later in life, Merton became attracted to the spirituality of the East. He searched for common ground between Christianity and Eastern religions, such as Buddhism and Hinduism. He suspected that Christian contemplation and Zen meditation pursue the same goal—the unmasking of the false or illusory self and the discovery of the true self. Through an immediate intuition or "seeing," Zen mystics and other Eastern masters claim to discover Reality in bursts of sudden enlightenment. In a world crassly consumed with material things, Merton valued Buddhism's emphasis on spiritual concerns. After extensive dialogue with Eastern masters, Merton saw no contradiction between Buddhism and Christianity. When Merton journeyed to the East to visit the Dalai Lama, he said he went not to preach, but to discover truth in dialogue.

How trustworthy, then, are Merton's writings for the evangelical Christian? Are they profitable? As you can see, the picture is mixed.

When Merton writes on Christian issues—such as relationship with Christ and the life of prayer—he remains on rather solid ground. His book *Life and Holiness*, for example, is an uplifting Christian book. Merton says that this book is about "grace, the power and light of God in us, purifying our hearts, transforming us in Christ, making us true sons of God, enabling us to act in the world as his instruments for the good of all men and the glory of God."[22] C. S. Lewis expresses appreciation for some of Merton's works: "I've been greatly impressed by the work of an American Trappist called Thomas Merton—*No Man Is An Island*. You probably know it?"[23]

Things are different when Merton delves into Eastern religions in books such as *Mystics and Zen Masters* (1967). At that point he becomes unreliable. Merton's intentions were to explore similarities between Christianity and Buddhism so that there could be dialogue between the two faiths (an ancient practice in the church). But he drifted from biblical moorings by accepting Buddhism as a legitimate path to God. On biblical grounds, I cannot accept Merton's later view of the equality of Buddhism and Christianity. Buddhism rejects the idea of a personal Creator God with whom one may have fellowship. Essentially Buddhism is a system of nihilism, for as Zen masters admit, "Zen teaches nothing." The Zen god is Enlightenment—the extinction of desire and, indeed, of personal identity. If Buddhist claims were true, the Father would not have sent His Son into the world to die on the cross and rise from the grave. If Buddhism were a path to salvation, Jesus would not have said, "I am the way, the truth, and the life. No one can come to the Father except through me" (John 14:6). The Dalai Lama even remarks, "Buddhism is Buddhism, and not Christianity."

I trust that you sense my ambivalence toward this influential, twentieth-century spiritual writer.

Wrapping Things Up

The spiritual classics are certainly of secondary importance to the Bible. But the gifted writers of the classics often open our eyes to spiritual truths in Scripture that we may have overlooked. As such, these older writings can be powerful resources for restoring our spiritual lives—not only in the area of soulcare, but by restoring a strong theology of sanctification and our progress in spirit.

Alister McGrath observes that his own evangelical tradition has been a potent force for theology and evangelism in the twentieth century, then adds that "evangelicalism . . . lacks a *spirituality* to give its *theology* staying power. There is a serious weakness here" (emphasis added).[24] Roman Catholics and high Anglicans, on the other hand, often neglect conversion through a personal decision of faith. Evangelicals offer better theological interpretations of the Christian faith, for ours is a doctrinal spirituality. But Christian renewal traditions often engage the heart of God more profoundly, for theirs is an affective spirituality. Believers in the body need to learn from each other's strengths and appropriate the riches of each other's traditions.

You and I may be tempted to believe that our denomination has a privileged corner on the truth. Such an opinion betrays a lack of understanding. Allow me to cite three respected evangelicals who encourage us to listen to, and learn from, faithful voices in other Christian traditions.

In his stimulating little book *Your God Is Too Small*, J. B. Phillips writes,

> No denomination has a monopoly of God's grace, and none has an exclusive recipe for producing Christian character. It is quite plain to the disinterested observer that the real God takes no notice whatever of the boxes; "the Spirit bloweth where it listeth" and is subject to no regulation of man.[25]

C. S. Lewis has this to add on the subject:

> Christianity is the total plan for the human machine. We have all departed from that total plan in different ways, and each of us wants to make out that his own modification of the original plan is the plan itself. You will find this again and again about anything that is really Christian: every one is attracted by bits of it and wants to pick out those bits and leave the rest. That is why. . . people who are fighting for quite opposite things can both say they are fighting for Christianity.[26]

Eugene Peterson says, "Every religious tradition has its dead spots." But likewise, "every denomination has a rich spiritual tradition to be discovered and explored."[27] These trusted Christian leaders point up the need to pool our resources in order to achieve the spiritual wholeness God intends for His people.

Richard Lovelace hits the bulls-eye when he writes,

> We need to listen carefully to other kinds of Christians. Mainline Protestants, Roman Catholics, and Orthodox believers have preserved biblical values that we lack. And they often have clear insights about our faults that could help us toward repentance.
>
> We need to listen to . . . the body of tradition that has nourished other movements. The early fathers, the medieval mystics, the spiritual doctors of the Reformation and Counter-Reformation, the leaders of the awakening eras, the uneven prophets of liberal social reform—all of these can force us back toward biblical balance and authentic spirituality.[28]

As we read the spiritual classics with open minds and hearts, we learn to appreciate the unity of God's believing people through the centuries. As I read Christian writers from past centuries, I am humbled by the spiritual graces found there. I learn that what unites true believers in the body of Christ is greater than what divides us. J. I. Packer speaks of a hope that evangelicals will overcome resistance to other traditions and return to "an historic Christian emphasis—Patristic, Medieval, Reformational, Puritan, Evangelical—with which the Protestantism that I know has largely lost touch."[29]

As a final thought, I'd like to suggest that reading the spiritual classics may be one way God will reconcile estranged Christians. In the last meal He shared with the disciples, Jesus spoke in a loud voice to the Father, and said,

> "My prayer for all of them is that they will be one, just as you and I are one, Father—that just as you are in me and I am in you, so they will be in us, and the world will believe you sent me.
>
> "I have given them the glory you gave me, so that

> they may be one, as we are—I in them and you in me, all being perfected into one. Then the world will know that you sent me and will understand that you love them as much as you love me." (John 17:21-23)

In a spirit of unity, I encourage you to read the classics.

Try It Yourself

1. An exercise in discriminating reading.

Identify a spiritual book written by an author from a Christian denomination or tradition different from your own. You will find many possibilities given in the resource books listed in the section that follows. I suggest that evangelicals read an author such as Thomas à Kempis, Brother Lawrence, Henri Nouwen, or Jean Vanier. Read the chosen book thoughtfully and prayerfully.

- What new insights about God's goodness and the spiritual life have you discovered? How may these gems uplift and enrich your own spiritual life?
- We are all fallible humans, products of our culture and context. Do you find any statements or practices in the book you have read with which you disagree?
- Now make a preliminary judgment. Do the spiritual insights and benefits of the book you have read outweigh any theological problems you may have detected? Christians need to read every author critically, discerning what is true from what may be false.

2. Where are you on the spiritual journey?

Reread the summary of the stages of the spiritual journey described by Teresa of Avila in her work *The Interior Castle.* If you have time, read the book itself. It's not too long or difficult.

- Does Teresa's interpretation of the seven stages of the Christian's spiritual progress shed light on where you might be on the spiritual path?
- Does her description of the journey to deepening relationship with Christ offer you hope for growth?
- Ask a trusted friend to read Teresa's description of the spiritual journey. Invite your friend to suggest which "room" in the castle he or she believes you currently occupy. Does your friend's assessment agree with your own? Reverse roles. Offer your assessment of where you think your friend is spiritually. Spend some time in prayer for each other's spiritual growth and usefulness.

Suggestions for Further Reading

Foster, Richard J. and James Bryan Smith. *Devotional Classics: Selected Readings for Individuals and Groups.* San Francisco: HarperSanFrancisco, 1993.

Hazard, David. *Rekindling the Inner Fire Devotional Series.* Minneapolis: Bethany, 1991–.

Hinson, E. Glenn. *Seekers After Mature Faith: A Historical Introduction to the Classics of Christian Devotion.* Waco, Tex.: Word Books, 1968.

Miller, Calvin. *Walking with the Saints: Through the Best and Worst Times of Our Lives.* Nashville: Thomas Nelson, 1995.

Toon, Peter. *Spiritual Companions: An Introduction to the Christian Classics.* Grand Rapids: Baker, 1990.

Shelley, Bruce L. *All the Saints Adore Thee: Insights From Christian Classics.* Grand Rapids: Zondervan, 1988.

CHAPTER TEN

Getting On with the Spiritual Journey

"I want you to get out there and walk—better yet, run!—on the road God called you to travel. I don't want any of you sitting around on your hands. I don't want anyone strolling off, down some path that goes nowhere."

EPHESIANS 4:1 (MSG)

"On earth we are wayfarers, always on the go. This means that we have to keep on moving forward. Therefore, be always unhappy about where you are if you want to reach where you are not.

If you are pleased with what you are, you have stopped already. If you say, 'It is enough,' you are lost. Keep on walking, moving forward, trying for the goal."

ST. AUGUSTINE[1]

IN THE COURSE OF THIS BOOK, I HAVE presented my case for restoring the heart of Christian spirituality.

One perspective I hope you've gained is that believers need not pursue Christlikeness by walking identical paths. And I hope you will test for yourself some of the ways God has made His presence known in and through Christians through the ages. Above all, I wish to challenge you, my fellow believers, to pursue spiritual health and maturity.

Reflecting on Christian spirituality through the centuries, Michael Downey offers these wise words:

> The most helpful approaches to history and tradition are those which do not attempt to convey the same insights over and over again, or look at history in an attempt to validate what is already held to be true. Rather, the most helpful views of history and tradition are those which attempt to take history seriously, seeking to understand persons, movements, writings in their own context.[2]

I have tried not to bore you by rehashing old positions. Rather, I've sought to be faithful, visionary, and perhaps prophetic in my summons to spiritual renewal. God knows the positive intentions of my heart.

IS YOUR SOUL SATISFIED?

Today we bend over backwards in search of meaning and satisfaction.

The ancient book of Ecclesiastes speaks directly to this crying human need. Solomon, who experienced everything life had to offer, found that nothing satisfies the heart apart from God. Not knowledge (see Ecclesiastes 12:12), not human wisdom (1:16-18, 2:12-15), not work and labor (2:17-23), not pleasure

(2:1-2, 7:4), not sexual escapades (2:8), not silver and gold (2:8, 5:10-16), and not houses and land (2:4-6). One of America's wealthiest men was asked, "How much will it take to satisfy you?" His answer, "Just a little bit more!" Ecclesiastes anticipated this response millennia ago. "Those who love money will never have enough. How absurd to think that wealth brings true happiness!" (5:10). Walk along the main street of any affluent town or city in America. The people you see decked out in their finery have so many *things*, but so little *joy*. The glazed expressions on their faces reveal the hollowness of their hearts.

Apart from a living relationship with God, everything is "chasing after wind," says Ecclesiastes (nine times: 1:14, 2:11, 4:4). Nothing satisfies. "'Everything is meaningless,' says the Teacher, 'utterly meaningless!'" (thirty-five times: 1:2, compare 9:9, 12:8). So unsatisfying is life without God that the Teacher concludes that men and women are better off dead (4:2)—better off if we'd never been born (4:3).

The reality is this: God has sculpted us humans for eternity (3:11), and the crumbs of time fail to satisfy our undying souls. Life that isn't centered on God and lived in communion with Him consistently disappoints.

Fortunately the Teacher does not leave us despairing. In God, our hearts find satisfaction and meaning (2:24-26, 5:18-20). David, Solomon's father, puts it this way: "Your unfailing love is better to me than life itself; how I praise you! . . . You satisfy me more than the richest of foods." (Psalm 63:3,5). The only thing that fulfills us is "the bread of heaven" (Psalm 105:40, NIV). Jesus is that bread (see John 6:41), and as the Father teaches us to know and rest in Him, as Jesus did, our souls are satisfied.

So I ask, Is your heart really satisfied? Is the hole in the core of your soul filled with the living God—with His grace and goodness?

Do You Long to Be Filled?

All spiritual longing is a sign of life and hope. Paul expresses the hunger in his heart this way: "I want to know Christ and the power of his resurrection and the fellowship of sharing in his sufferings, becoming like him in his death" (Philippians 3:10, NIV).

Catherine of Siena (d. 1380) describes an imaginary dialogue between herself and God. During the conversation the Lord says to her, "This life, this desire, this possession, this love, this seeing, this having, this joy, begins here and now for those who desire me."[3] Catherine opened her heart to God and enjoyed deep, lifelong devotion to the Lord. Her relationship with Christ overflowed like a river in selfless service to the poor and needy.

God makes His home wherever He is invited and welcomed. If you truly hunger and thirst for God, you can be confident that He will join Himself to your heart. Jesus promises this: "God blesses you who are hungry now, for you will be satisfied" (Luke 6:21). The crucial first step is to open our hands and unlock our hearts so as to be filled.

Teresa of Avila wrote about the need for believers to surrender themselves unconditionally into God's loving arms:

> There is no secret, occult or mysterious formula. Our whole welfare consists solely in doing the will of God. God will not force our wills. God will take only what we give. But God will not be ours entirely until we yield ourselves to God.

She added,

> The point is that we should make a gift of our hearts, emptying them of ourselves that they may be filled with God. What power lies in this gift! Our almighty Father becomes one with us and transforms us, uniting Creator and creature.[4]

Have you ever fully surrendered yourself into the Divine embrace? Do so now! Freely receive Him, not piecemeal, bit by bit, but wholesale, bucket by bucket.

A New Habit of Being

To experience continual soul restoration you are now aware that you can benefit from the practice of spiritual habits or disciplines. Just as regular physical exercise produces healthy bodies, a spiritual regimen fosters maturity in the soul. Spiritual growth requires discipline and training.

A popular proverb says, "Sow an action and you reap a habit; sow a habit and you reap a character." Growing Christians do well to cultivate, each in his or her own way, disciplines of quietness, meditation, verbal and nonverbal prayer, spiritual reading, and the like. Spiritual progress occurs through the synergy of God's initiative and our trusting response. As Paul writes, "Continue to work out your salvation with fear and trembling, for it is God who works in you to will and to act according to his good purpose" (Philippians 2:12-13, NIV). The breathtaking reality in all this, as Augustine observed, is that we would not be searching unless we had first been found of the Lord!

Remain Focused on Christ

Christ is not merely one aspect of the Christian life; He, and the formation of His life in us, is its sum and substance. The phrase "Christianity is Christ" is far more than a hollow slogan. Spiritual wholeness develops through Christ, with Christ, and in Christ. That is, *through* Him in justification and reconciliation (see Romans 5:9), *with* Him in devotion and service (see Matthew 28:20), and *in* Him by personal identification and vital union (see John 14:20, 2 Corinthians 5:17).

Do you want to be restored and renewed spiritually? Then become a Christ-seeking and Christ-centered person. Luther described the Christian as a "little Christ." C. S. Lewis developed this idea, saying, "God looks at you as if you were a little Christ: Christ stands beside you to turn you into one."[5]

We become little Christs by continuous association with the Savior. As we focus on Christ and dwell in His presence, His graces invade the threshold of our personalities and transform us from within. In heaven, Christians will be in Christ's presence forever. Why not become well acquainted with Him this side of glory? Francis of Assisi became a little Christ. His biographer says of this great medieval saint: "He was always thinking about Jesus; Jesus was in his mouth, in his ears, in his eyes, in his hands; Jesus was in his whole being."[6]

We become little Christs by following the Lord in faithful discipleship. By dying to ourselves and trusting our futures to Him, love deepens. Jesus says, "If you love your father or mother more than me, you are not worthy of being mine. If you refuse to take up your cross and follow me, you are not worthy of being mine" (Matthew 10:37-38). *The Imitation of Christ* offers these memorable words:

> Jesus has many lovers of His heavenly kingdom, but few actually carry His cross. He has many who like consolation; few desire tribulation. Many wish to feast with Him; few want to fast with Him. All want to rejoice with Him; few will endure for Him. . . . Many respond to His miracles; few share the disgrace of His cross.[7]

Teresa of Avila added, "To be truly spiritual is to make ourselves slaves of Christ branded with the cross. God can give us no greater grace than to give us a life such as was led by Jesus."[8]

Finally, we become little Christs by imitating Jesus as He is revealed in the Gospels. Writing to the Corinthians, Paul says, "You should follow my example, just as I follow Christ's" (1 Corinthians 11:1). Growing Christians are those who thoughtfully meditate on Christ's devotion to the Father. They prayerfully ponder Christ's virtues, values, actions, and interactions with people.

François Fénelon (d. 1715) said, "We must imitate Jesus. This is to live as he lived, to think as he thought, to conform ourselves to his image, which is the seal of our sanctification."[9] I quote again from *The Imitation of Christ*: "Imitate Christ in life and behavior. This is the way we find light and avoid darkness. . . . The clue to understanding Christ? Conform one hundred percent to His life."[10]

Seek the Fullness of the Spirit

As believers, we are loved by the Father, redeemed by the Son, and renewed by the Holy Spirit. Yet a recent survey reveals that when Christians in the United States think of God, only 33 percent regard Him as Trinity.[11] We, most of all, have a hard time understanding His movements in and around us as Spirit.

As we've mentioned elsewhere, reacting against certain emotional excesses has caused evangelicals to neglect the person and ministry of the Spirit. This, in spite of the fact that the New Testament mentions the Holy Spirit more than three hundred times. By default, the Spirit has become the forgotten member of the Godhead—a kind of junior assistant to Jesus. A leader of one of the largest evangelical denominations in the country admitted to me, "Our churches are scared stiff of the Holy Spirit."

Authentic spirituality flows from the Holy Spirit, who is the personal power of God in believing lives (see Luke 24:49, Acts 1:8). Paul writes, "When we brought you the Good News, it was not only with words but also with power, for the Holy Spirit gave you full assurance that what we said was true" (1 Thessalonians 1:5). As the *Unction* from on high, the Spirit invades the stronghold of our hearts and takes captive the sinister forces of the flesh. As *Enabler* of the Godhead, He makes powerless religion "power-full." Paul makes the awesome claim that the power that raised Christ from the grave inhabits every believer (see Romans 8:11). As *Fire*, He ignites us to live lives that are supranatural rather than natural, heavenly rather than earthly, and spiritual rather than carnal. When the Spirit comes upon us, unreality gives way to reality, frustration to fulfillment, and sadness to satisfaction.

Even a cursory reading of the Gospels shows that the incarnate Son of God was entirely dependent upon the Spirit during His earthly ministry. Following His temptation by the Devil, Jesus entered the synagogue in Nazareth and read from Isaiah 61: "The Spirit of the Lord is upon me, for he has appointed me to preach Good News to the poor. He has sent me to proclaim that captives will be released, that the blind will see, that the downtrodden will be freed from their oppressors. . . ." (Luke 4:18). If God's Son relied upon the Spirit to fulfill His earthly calling, how much more ought we!

Jesus' followers, as we read in the book of Acts, lived and died in the power of the Spirit. The key to the missionary expansion of the church is the simple fact that believers were "filled with the Holy Spirit" (Acts 2:4, 4:8, 9:17) or "full of the Holy Spirit" (Acts 6:3, 7:55, 11:24). Empowered by the Spirit, missionaries preached the Word boldly (see Acts 4:31), saw sinners convicted and converted (see 2:37, 11:24), cast out demons (see 5:16, 8:7), and experienced supernatural deliverances (see 12:3-17, 16:25-26). The Apostles' Creed contains the line, "I believe in the Holy Spirit." But as one authority observes, "Long before the Holy Spirit became an article of the Creed, he was a reality lived in the experience of the primitive church."[12]

Scripture teaches that the Spirit is God's "gift" to His people (see Acts 2:38, 10:45, 11:17). When a trusted person offers me a gift, I gladly receive it. Let's not be afraid to accept the enormous gift of God's Spirit! The Word tells us how we should respond to this gracious gift. We should not resist the Spirit (see Acts 7:51) nor quench the Spirit (see 1 Thessalonians 5:19). Neither should we grieve God's Spirit through disobedience. "Don't grieve God. Don't break his heart. His Holy Spirit, moving and breathing in you, is the most intimate part of your life, making you fit for himself. Don't take such a gift for granted" (Ephesians 4:30, MSG). And certainly we must not insult the Spirit by treading God's beloved Son underfoot (see Hebrews 10:29).

Without question, Scripture enjoins us to embrace the gifts of the Spirit (see Romans 12, 1 Corinthians 12–14, Ephesians 4). The Spirit bestows these *charisms* not to stir up controversy but to edify the body and equip believers for effective service. Paul urges Timothy to "fan into flames the spiritual gift God gave you when I laid my hands on you" (2 Timothy 1:6). God skillfully arranges spiritual gifts in the church like the pieces of an intricate jigsaw puzzle (see 1 Corinthians 12:18). Every piece has a place in the divine scheme of things.

God, in fact, commands us to be filled with the Spirit: "Let the Holy Spirit fill and control you" (Ephesians 5:18). In addition, we must allow the Spirit to guide us into the Father's will (see Acts 8:29, Romans 8:14, Galatians 5:18). "If we are living now by the Holy Spirit, let us follow the Holy Spirit's leading in every part of our lives" (Galatians 5:25). Finally, we are told to "yield" ourselves so the Spirit may produce His fruit in us: "When the Holy Spirit controls our lives, he will produce this kind of fruit in us: love, joy, peace, patience, kindness, goodness, faithfulness, gentleness, and self-control" (Galatians 5:22-23). Every one of us is offered the hope that the same spiritual fruit seen in Jesus' life can be seen in ours as well (see Matthew 7:15-20).

Our satisfaction, then, comes as we welcome the life-giving Spirit each day—for He is the invisible "water" that flows from Jesus, the Vine, into us, the branches. And He flows to us as God's gift to open hearts.

Simon was a sorcerer who professed belief in Christ. When Simon saw the mighty works done by the apostles, he tried to buy the Holy Spirit with money (see Acts 8:9-24). How foolish! The Spirit of God cannot be purchased at any price. He indwells Jesus' followers as the pure gift of the Father's love, accepted by faith and enjoyed without measure.

Our spiritual restoration, then, is all about allowing God's Holy Spirit to be joined to our human spirits. When the Spirit inhabits the sanctuary of our hearts, we experience a gradual transformation from within. "As the Spirit of the Lord works within us, we become more and more like him and reflect his glory even more" (2 Corinthians 3:18). The Spirit bears us into the deep heart of God and makes Christ real to our souls. Think of it! *The Spirit makes us qualitatively new in holiness and godliness.* And so, in time, it is said of us, "those who become Christians become new persons. They are not the same any more, for the old life has gone. A new life has begun!" (see 2 Corinthians 5:17).

Prior to His conversion, Augustine lived a morally decadent

life. After becoming a Christian, he was met on the street by a former mistress. Seeing her, he turned away, but she called out to him, "Augustine, it is only I." He continued on his way, responding, "Yes, but it is not I."[13]

If we want to be so in love with God, so "new" that we can turn from our deadness and our sins, we must come under the influence of the Spirit of God. A. W. Tozer said that Spirit-less religion is as deadly as heresy. As in the example from Augustine's life, we become filled with the Spirit as we surrender our wills to God.

Take a moment to meditate on a verse from Isaac Watts' uplifting hymn "Come Holy Spirit, Heavenly Dove," written in 1709:

> Come, Holy Spirit, heavenly dove
> with all thy quickening powers,
> Come, shed abroad a Savior's love
> in these cold hearts of ours.

Keep Your Theology Straight

Throughout this book I have pled for balance in living out the gospel. The history book and the daily newspaper show how easily we become unbalanced. As noted earlier, Christian spirituality involves the whole person: head, heart, and hands—or knowing, being, and doing. The mind's understanding of God from the Word must seep down to the heart so that we engage Christ intimately in a transforming relationship of love. The spiritual vision and passion fired by knowledge of the heart then propels us into the world as the hands, feet, and lips of Jesus. In this way we fulfill our calling as knowers of God's Word, lovers of Jesus, and doers of the Father's will.

Back to theology. Isolated from spirituality, theology can become dry and barren. Isolated from theology, spirituality can drift into platitudinous piety. Theology and spirituality must be bound together in mutually nourishing relationship.

Some forms of spirituality betray an unsettling indifference to theology. We must take seriously biblical warning against doctrinal laxity (see 1 Timothy 1:10; 6:3,20). As we deepen our spiritual lives, we must remain firmly rooted in the historic Christian message. We must preserve the pattern of truth set forth in the Apostles' and Nicene creeds. We must cling to the teachings of Christ and the convictions of faithful theologians past and present such as Augustine, Luther, Calvin, Edwards, Spurgeon, and Packer.

In pursuing heart satisfaction and spiritual renewal, we must avoid the peril of *postmodernism* which denies absolute truth and morality. We must reject the ruse of *relativism* which claims that people come to God in a fashion dictated by their particular culture. And we must guard against the scourge of *syncretism* which joins nonChristian spiritual paths to God's exclusive way of life in Christ.

In our quest for spiritual renewal we must be zealous for doctrinal purity. On our journey to Christian maturity, we must faithfully work at integrating theology and spirituality (psychology as well). Under God, we must be faithful theologians and godly saints. The apostle Paul warns the Corinthians to be alert to "a different Jesus than the one we preach, or a different Spirit than the one you received, or a different kind of gospel than the one you believed" (2 Corinthians 11:4). Paul urged his coworker Titus to "promote the kind of living that reflects right teaching" (Titus 2:1).

Plotting Our Course

As a young man, Francis was praying in the small, rundown chapel of St. Damien in Assisi. While worshiping, he felt lifted by the Holy Spirit and heard the voice of God saying, "Renew my church."

Taking this message literally, this obscure man began to restore the deteriorating chapel with materials begged and borrowed. After a while, Francis realized that God was calling him to something much more important than physical restoration of a building. God was beckoning him to renew the spiritual life of the people—the temple of the living God. Francis obeyed the heavenly call and launched a significant, Christ-centered reform movement that reached far beyond the town of Assisi. It spilled out of the walls of churches and ministered to the poor and those "untouchables" of medieval Europe, the lepers. By following the Holy Spirit, Francis was so transformed in Christ-likeness that he has been beloved by the church for all time.

But Francis began as a spoiled brat, a party boy, who threw away his father's hard-earned money on his lazy, drunken friends. Francis did not always walk with God.

I use Francis of Assissi as an example here to give us several vectors that point us toward our destination.

First of all, transforming spiritual renewal is not for an elite minority only—the province of ministers, monks, and clerics. It's the privilege of rank-and-file, rubber-meets-the-road Christians. The blessings of salvation are the birthright of every soul who believes. Having left Egypt, the land of bondage, every Christian is summoned to enter Canaan, the land of blessing and bounty.

Second, Christian spirituality is an enterprise that integrates the whole person. The one who has found restoration through prayer and personal devotion to Christ will find himself compelled to serve his neighbor, for the spiritually renewed life is anything but self-absorbed. I imagine the spiritual Christian as the true "ex-centric." He reaches out to care for the poor, those calling for justice, the foreigner, and the environment. "O people, the LORD has already told you what is good, and this is what he requires: to do what is right, to love mercy, and to walk humbly with your God" (Micah 6:8). Our quest for spiritual renewal will cause us to embrace the full range of life's needs and activities.

Third, spiritual renewal calls for self-denial. Following the example of Jesus and people like Francis, growing Christians resolve to lay down their lives for God and others. "Jesus says to His disciples, 'If any of you wants to be my follower, you must put aside your selfish ambition, shoulder your cross, and follow me. If you try to keep your life for yourself, you will lose it. But if you give up your life for me, you will find true life'" (Matthew 16:24-25).

As you and I move into deeper relationship with Jesus, the

Spirit will burden us to leave behind a trail of blessing for others (1 Corinthians 10:24).

Fourth, the spiritual path requires openness to change. The One we serve is the living, active, and dynamic Lord. Francis learned, as God directed and expanded his vision, that we follow the God of the unexpected and the new. We grow and mature as we learn to be receptive to fresh insights, new leadings, and the call of God that challenges our comfort zones. God is always preparing us for challenge and change. Growing Christians must give God permission to lead them into unexplored spiritual territory. While never comfortable, change is essential to progress.

Fifth, spiritual restoration calls for courage. For the kingdom's sake, the spiritual Christian should be a calculated risk-taker. If we fail to take prudent risks, we limit the Spirit's working in our lives. Teresa of Avila offers this word of challenge. "Our Lord seeks and loves courageous souls. Let us not fail to reach our spiritual destiny because we have been too timid, too cautious in our desires, because we sought too little."[14]

Finally, transformation occurs in the context of community. In our Western preoccupation with rugged individualism, we neglect an important pillar of growth, which is the "communion of the saints." Paul writes, "We who believe are carefully joined together, becoming a holy temple for the Lord. Through him you Gentiles are also joined together as part of this dwelling where God lives by his Spirit" (Ephesians 2:21-22).

Behind each growing saint stand other committed and obedient saints. If you are not part of a spiritually flourishing community—a community using creative resources for spiritual development—ask God to lead you to a worshiping people who share your passion for renewal of life and action.

A Season of Blessing

God has His appointed times and seasons of blessing. Some believe that we may be in the early stages of a period of significant spiritual revitalization. I want to be a part of the glorious things

God is doing, and yet will do, through His Spirit. What about you?

If you have been hungering for satisfaction in God, the season of blessing is now. And the path has been mapped out before you. Will you join those of us who are pressing on to grow deeper in Christ?

As we close, I would like to offer this prayer:

> *Gracious Father, I thank you that You stir our hearts with a restlessness that will not cease until we seek our satisfaction only in You!*
>
> *I ask, Lord, that You will continue to shape each one of us as vessels for Your Spirit so that more and more each day we radiate the goodness, the love, and the righteous strength of Your Son, Jesus Christ! Restore our oneness as a community of believers. Help us to be faithful in training our souls to follow after You, and make us quick to sense Your directions as You lead us to serve You in this troubled world.*
>
> *Draw us to Yourself, Father, and give us a fresh vision of Your eternal goodness each day so that our strength is found in worshiping only You. Amen.*

Try It Yourself

1. Personalizing your spiritual plan.

As you reflect on this book, and particularly the last chapter, prayerfully formulate your personal plan for spiritual growth in Christ. Include clear spiritual goals as well as the means by which you hope to achieve these goals. Remember that without a goal you are likely to hit nothing. One leading objective might be to develop a more intimate relationship with Christ. To achieve this goal you might carve out thirty minutes at the beginning of each day for quietness, Bible meditation, the practice of various prayer forms, and writing in a journal.

Enter your spiritual growth plan in your journal. In addition, periodically record areas of spiritual progress, answers to prayer, problems you encounter. Reread your journal entries on a regular basis. Happy journaling!

For accountability purposes, I strongly suggest that you discuss your growth plan with a spiritual friend or mentor. If you're part of a support group, share it with them, too. Have your friend or support group review your progress on a regular basis.

- What elements have you included in your spiritual plan?
- Are the means you have chosen adequate to achieve your goals?
- Identify what specific changes in your lifestyle must be made for you to achieve your spiritual goals.

Suggestions for Further Reading

Chan, Simon. *Spiritual Theology: A Systematic Study of the Christian Life.* Downers Grove, Ill.: InterVarsity, 1998.

Jones, Timothy. *21 Days to a Better Quiet Time with God.* Grand Rapids: Zondervan, 1998.

Mulholland, M. Robert. *Invitation to a Journey: A Road Map for Spiritual Formation.* Downers Grove, Ill.: InterVarsity, 1993.

Thomas à Kempis. *The Imitation of Christ,* ed. Donald E. Demaray. Grand Rapids: Baker, 1983.

Tozer, A. W. *The Divine Conquest.* New York: Revell, 1950.

Notes

Chapter One

1. Mark R. McMinn, *Psychology, Theology, and Spirituality in Christian Counseling* (Wheaton, Ill.: Tyndale House, 1996), p. 258.
2. Robert A. Johnson, *Inner Work: Using Dreams and Active Imagination for Personal Growth* (San Francisco: Harper & Row, 1986), p. 133.
3. Richard J. Foster, *Celebration of Discipline* (San Francisco: Harper & Row, 1988), p. 7.
4. Augustine, *Confessions*, 7.10. Cited in *Augustine Day by Day* (New York: Catholic Book Publishing Co., 1986), p. 33.
5. Augustine, 1.13. Cited in *Augustine Day by Day*, p. 33.

Chapter Two

1. Brennan Manning, *Abba's Child: The Cry of the Heart for Intimate Belonging* (Colorado Springs, Colo.: NavPress, 1994), pp. 38-39.
2. *The Orange County Register*, April 23, 1995.
3. "Buddhist Practices Make Inroads in the US," *The Christian Science Monitor* (November 3, 1997), p. 9.
4. Cited by Timothy Jones, "Great Awakenings," *Christianity Today* (November 8, 1993), p. 24.
5. Harvey Cox, *Fire From Heaven* (Reading, Mass.: Addison-Wesley, 1995), p. 301.
6. "Rooms for Reflection," *USA Weekend*, April 3-5, 1998.
7. *The Denver Post*, August 4, 1997, pp. 1F-2F.
8. Augustine, *Confessions*, 3.1. Cited in *Augustine Day by Day* (New York: Catholic Book Publishing Co., 1986), p. 112.
9. Henri Nouwen, *Making All Things New* (San Francisco: Harper & Row, 1981), p. 36.
10. A. W. Tozer, *The Pursuit of God* (Harrisburg, Penn.: Christian Publications, 1982), p. 50.
11. See William D. Hendricks, *Exit Interviews: Revealing Stories of Why People Are Leaving the Church* (Chicago: Moody, 1993).
12. Dallas Willard, *The Spirit of the Disciplines* (San Francisco: HarperSanFrancisco, 1988), p. 18.

13. "Buddhist Practices Make Inroads in the US," p. 9.
14. Alister McGrath, *Evangelicalism and the Future of Christianity* (Downers Grove, Ill.: InterVarsity, 1995), chap. 8.
15. Augustine, *Soliloquies*, 1.15. Cited in *Augustine Day by Day*, p. 130.
16. Manning, p. 141.
17. Alister McGrath, *Spirituality in an Age of Change* (Grand Rapids: Zondervan, 1994), p. 9.
18. As reported in the news item, "Toronto Blessing: Is It a Revival?" *Christianity Today* (May 15, 1995), p. 51.
19. C. S. Lewis, "Introduction," to St. Athanasius, *The Incarnation of the Word of God* (New York: Macmillan, 1946), pp. 6, 7, 9.
20. Charles Hummel, *Fire in the Fireplace* (Downers Grove, Ill.: InterVarsity, 1993), p. 93.
21. Augustine, *Confessions*, 10.26. Cited in *Augustine Day by Day*, p. 78.

Chapter Three

1. Quoted by James L. Snyder, *In Pursuit of God: The Life of A. W. Tozer* (Camp Hill, Penn.: Christian Publications, 1991), p. 159.
2. Gordon S. Wakefield, ed., *The Westminster Dictionary of Christian Spirituality* (Philadelphia: Westminster, 1983), p. 361.
3. C. S. Lewis, *The Screwtape Letters*, in *The Best of C. S. Lewis* (Grand Rapids: Baker, 1969), p. 54.
4. Thomas Moore, *Care of the Soul: A Guide for Cultivating Depth and Sacredness in Everyday Life* (New York: HarperCollins, 1992), p. xv.
5. Moore, p. xvii.
6. Augustine, *Confessions*, 1.1. Cited in *Augustine Day by Day* (New York: Catholic Book Publishing Co., 1986), p. 177.
7. "The Global Network's purpose is to support and connect people of all cultures, talents, and beliefs who are dedicated to personal and global transformation by unfolding the infinite possibilities inherent in the human spirit for healing, self-knowledge and the expansion of happiness and love." (from www.chopra.com/gnabout.htm)
8. "Deepak's Instant Karma," *Newsweek* (October 20, 1997), p. 56.
9. Francis Schaeffer, *True Spirituality* (Wheaton, Ill.: Tyndale, 1972), p. 14.
10. Henri Nouwen, *A Cry for Mercy* (New York: Doubleday/Image, 1983), p. 15.
11. See Richard J. Foster, *Celebration of Discipline* (San Francisco: Harper & Row, 1978), p. 27.

12. Richard F. Lovelace, "Evangelical Spirituality: A Church Historian's Perspective," *Journal of the Evangelical Theological Society* 31/1 (March 1988), p. 35.
13. Michael S. Horton, *In the Face of God* (Dallas: Word, 1996), p. 21.
14. Michael S. Horton, "The Subject of Contemporary Relevance," in *Power Religion*, ed. Michael S. Horton (Chicago: Moody, 1992), p. 337.
15. Horton, *In the Face of God*, p. 198.
16. *John of the Cross, Spiritual Canticle*, trans. E. Allison Peers (Garden City, N.Y.: Doubleday/Image, 1961), pp. 55-56.
17. *John of the Cross, Ascent of Mt. Carmel*, trans. E. Allison Peers (Garden City, N.Y.: Doubleday/Image, 1958), pp. 163-64. Bonaventure (d. 1274), whose Augustinian views on theology helped pave the way for the Reformation, wrote the following about the soul's ascent to God: "No one can be made happy unless he rise above himself, not by an ascent of the body, but of the heart. But we cannot rise above ourselves unless a higher power lift us up. No matter how much our interior progress is ordered, nothing will come of it unless accompanied by divine aid. . . . Prayer is the mother and source of the ascent." *The Soul's Journey into God* (New York: Paulist, 1978), in *Classics of Western Spirituality*, pp. 59-60.
18. See John Wesley's sermon, "On the Wedding Garment" (1790): "Religion does not consist in orthodoxy or right opinions. . . . A man may assent to all the three creeds—that called the Apostles', the Nicene, and the Athanasian—and yet 'tis possible he may have no religion at all."
19. Stephan Charnock, quoted in *The Golden Treasury of Puritan Quotations*, compiled by I. D. E. Thomas (Chicago: Moody, 1975), p. 163.
20. Brennan Manning, *Abba's Child: The Cry of the Heart for Intimate Belonging* (Colorado Springs: NavPress, 1994), p. 156.
21. David Hesselgrave, *Communicating Christ Cross Culturally* (Grand Rapids: Zondervan, 1978), p. 231.
22. C. J. H. Hingley, "Evangelicals and Spirituality," *Themelios 15* (April-May, 1990), p. 87.
23. Hingley, p. 89.

Chapter Four

1. A. W. Tozer, *The Pursuit of God* (Harrisburgh, Penn.: Christian Publications, 1982), p. 36.
2. A. W. Tozer, as quoted by James L. Snyder, *In Pursuit of God: The Life of A. W. Tozer* (Camp Hill, Penn.: Christian Publications, 1991), p. 220.
3. C. S. Lewis, *Mere Christianity* (London: Geoffrey Bles, 1952), p. 130.

4. See William D. Hendricks, *Exit Interviews: Revealing Stories of Why People Are Leaving the Church* (Chicago: Moody, 1993), chaps. 1 and 19.
5. Morton Kelsey, *Christo-Psychology* (New York: Crossroad, 1982), p. 11.
6. Tozer, *Pursuit of God*, p. 13.
7. Augustine, *Confessions*, 3.1. Cited in *Augustine Day by Day* (New York: Catholic Book Publishing Co., 1986), p. 112.
8. Lynn DeShazo, 1995 Integrity's Hosannah! Music/ASCAP.
9. Abraham Kuyper, *Near Unto God*, edited and adapted by James C. Schaap (Grand Rapids: CRC Publications, 1997), p. 16.
10. For example, Michael Downey, *Understanding Christian Spirituality* (New York: Paulist, 1997), p. 91.
11. C. S. Lewis, *Surprised By Joy* (New York: Harcourt, Brace, 1956), p. 177.
12. J. B. Phillips, *Your God Is Too Small* (New York: Macmillan, 1961), p. 91.
13. Meister Eckhart (d. 1327), as quoted by David Manning White, *The Search for God* (New York: Macmillan, 1983), p. 125.
14. William A. Barry and William J. Connolly, *The Practice of Spiritual Direction* (San Francisco: HarperCollins, n.d.), p. 75.
15. Peter Kreeft, *Christianity for Modern Pagans* (San Francisco: Ignatius Press, 1993), p. 325.
16. A. W. Tozer, *Man: The Dwelling Place of God* (Harrisburg, Penn.: Christian Publications, 1966), p. 52.
17. A. W. Tozer, *That Incredible Christian* (Harrisburg, Penn.: Christian Publications, 1964), p. 85.
18. C. S. Lewis, *A Grief Observed* (New York: Seabury, 1961), p. 59.
19. Winfried Corduan, *Mysticism: An Evangelical Option?* (Grand Rapids: Zondervan, 1991), p. 32.
20. Anthony Campolo, *How to Be Pentecostal Without Speaking in Tongues* (Dallas: Word, 1991), p. 48.
21. According to Richard F. Lovelace, *Dynamics of the Spiritual Life* (Downers Grove, Ill.: InterVarsity, 1979), p. 22, mysticism is "a non-technical term denoting movements stressing Christian experience and encounter with God." A. W. Tozer, in Snyder, *In Pursuit of God*, p. 157, simply states that a mystic is a believer who practices the presence of God.
22. Augustine, *Confessions*, 12.16. Cited in *Augustine Day by Day*, p. 172.

23. Donald G. Bloesch, *The Struggle of Prayer* (Colorado Springs: Helmers & Howard, 1988), p. 7. Bloesch adds, p. 10, n. 14: "Those who stand in the Reformation tradition will acknowledge that a Christian can at the same time be a mystic, but they will insist that this means a radically qualified mysticism, qualified by faith in the self-revelation of a divine mediator in human history."
24. Chuck Colson, "A Pilgrim's Progress: Chuck Colson Speaks Out on . . . Chuck Colson," *Jubilee* (Summer, 1998), p. 9.
25. See Frank Whaling, ed., *John and Charles Wesley*, in *The Classics of Western Spirituality* (New York: Paulist, 1981), p. 5.
26. Charles Wesley, "Love Divine, All Loves Excelling," *Presbyterian Hymnal* (Louisville, Ky.: 1990), no. 376.
27. A. W. Tozer, as quoted by George Sweeting, ed., *Great Quotations and Illustrations* (Waco, Tex.: Word, 1985), p. 140.
28. Charles Wesley, in Whaling, *John and Charles Wesley*, p. 279.
29. Tozer, as quoted by Snyder, p. 157.
30. John Murray, *Redemption Accomplished and Applied* (Grand Rapids: Eerdmans, 1955), p. 167.

Chapter Five

1. Dietrich Bonhoeffer, *Meditating on the Word*, ed. David McI. Gracie (Cambridge, Mass.: Cowley, 1986), p. 30.
2. As reported in the article, "How the World Sees Us," *The Denver Post*, June 15, 1997.
3. Thomas Moore, *Care of the Soul* (New York: HarperCollins, 1992), p. 286.
4. Morton T. Kelsey, *Adventure Inward* (Minneapolis: Augsburg, 1980), p. 49.
5. Henri Nouwen, *With Open Hands* (Notre Dame, Ind.: Ave Maria, 1972), p. 36.
6. Thomas à Kempis, *The Imitation of Christ*, ed. Donald Demaray (Grand Rapids: Baker, 1982), p. 93.
7. John of the Cross, "The Sayings of Light and Love," *The Collected Works of St. John of the Cross*, trans. Kieran Kavanaugh and Otilio Rodriguez (Washington, D.C.: ICS Publications, 1991), p. 92.
8. Mother Teresa, as quoted by Bruce L. Shelley, in *All the Saints Adore Thee* (Grand Rapids: Zondervan, 1988), p. 111.
9. Donald G. Bloesch, "Prayer," *Evangelical Dictionary of Theology*, ed. Walter A. Elwell (Grand Rapids: Baker, 1984), p. 867.

10. John Calvin, *Institutes of the Christian Religion, The Library of Christian Classics*, vol. 21, ed. John T. McNeill (Philadelphia: Westminster, 1960), pp. 853-854 [book III, chap. 20, par. 4]
11. Morton T. Kelsey, *The Other Side of Silence* (New York: Paulist, 1976), p. 97.
12. Henri Nouwen, *A Cry For Mercy* (New York: Doubleday/Image, 1983), Saturday, March 17, p. 47.
13. Jonathan Edwards, *Images or Shadows of Divine Things*, ed. Perry Miller (Greenwood Press: Westport, Conn.: 1977), p. 133.
14. Kelsey, *The Other Side of Silence*, p. 100.
15. Peter Toon, *Meditating as a Christian* (London: Collins, 1991), p. 100. The British evangelical C. G. H. Hingley agrees that such exercises can be valuable preparation for prayer ("Evangelicals and Spirituality," *Themelios* 15, April-May 1990, p. 87).
16. J. I. Packer, *Knowing God* (Downers Grove, Ill.: InterVarsity, 1973), p. 23.
17. Richard Baxter, *The Saints' Everlasting Rest* (New York: American Tract Society, 1758), pp. 405-406.
18. Baxter, p. 429.
19. Bonhoeffer, p. 32
20. Toon, p. 62.
21. Toon, p. 183.
22. Frederick W. Faber (1814-1863), *Presbyterian Hymnal* (Louisville, Ky.: Westminster/John Knox, 1990), no. 298.
23. Isaac Watts (1674-1748), *Presbyterian Hymnal*, no. 172.
24. John Calvin, *Institutes of the Christian Religion, The Library of Christian Classics*, vol. 20, p. 112 [book I, chap. 11, par. 12].
25. Leland Ryken, *Culture in Christian Perspective* (Portland: Multnomah, 1986), p. 33.
26. "Sacred Images all the Rage in Secular Shops," *The Denver Post*, December 24, 1997, p. B1.
27. Henry Ward Beecher, as quoted by George Sweeting, ed., *Great Quotes and Illustrations* (Waco, Tex.: Word, 1985), p. 149.
28. Francis Schaeffer, *Art and the Bible* (Downers Grove, Ill.: InterVarsity, 1973), p. 61 and flyleaf.
29. Oswald Chambers, *My Utmost for His Highest* (New York: Dodd & Mead, 1943), p. 42 [Feb. 11th].

30. The U.S. District Court, Newark, N.J., on October 29, 1977, and the U.S. Court of Appeals, Philadelphia, PA, on February 2, 1979. See "U.S. Court of Appeals Rules Against TM Movement," *Spiritual Counterfeits Project* (Feb. 6, 1979).
31. See Gordon R. Lewis, *What Everyone Should Know About Transcendental Meditation* (Glendale, Calif.: Regal, 1975), pp. 64-65.

Chapter Six

1. Thomas Merton, "The Inner Experience: Christian Contemplation," *Cistercian Studies* 18.3 (1983), p. 210.
2. Henri Nouwen, *The Way of the Heart* (New York: Seabury, 1981), p. 81.
3. John Calvin, *Institutes of the Christian Religion, The Library of Christian Classics,* vol. 21, ed. John T. McNeill (Philadelphia: Westminster, 1960), p. 897 [book III, chap. 20, par. 33].
4. Cited by Avery Brooke, "What is Contemplation?" *Weavings* 7.4 (July/August, 1992), p. 10.
5. R. Paul Stevens, "Poems for People Under Pressure: The Apocalypse of John and the Contemplative Life," *Alive to God* (Downers Grove, Ill.: InterVarsity, 1992), p. 87. Basil Pennington, *Centering Prayer* (Garden City, New York: Doubleday/Image, 1980), p. 86, gives a helpful definition of contemplation: "An opening, a response, a putting aside of all the debris that stands in the way of our being totally present to the present Lord, so that he can be present to us."
6. John Cassian, *Conferences* I.8, in *The Classics of Western Spirituality* (New York: Paulist, 1985), p. 43.
7. Anselm, *Proslogion,* chap. 1. In *St. Anslem's Proslogion,* trans. by M. J. Charlesworth (Notre Dame: University of Notre Dame Press, 1979), p. 111
8. John Owen, *The Works of John Owen,* ed. William H. Goold (London & Edinburgh: Johnstone & Hunter, 1850-57), vol. 1, p. 286.
9. Richard Baxter, *The Saints Everlasting Rest* (New York: American Tract Society, 1758), p. 421.
10. Baxter, p. 429.
11. Baxter, p. 430.
12. Baxter, p. 334.
13. Baxter, p. 473.
14. Brother Lawrence, *The Practice of the Presence of God,* ed. Donald E. Demaray (New York: Alba House, 1997), pp. 19-20.
15. Brother Lawrence, p. 52.

16. Brother Lawrence, p. 54.
17. Brother Lawrence, p. 56.
18. Ole Hallesby, *Prayer* (Minneapolis: Augsburg, 1931), pp. 146-147.
19. James M. Houston, "Spirituality," *Evangelical Dictionary of Theology*, ed. Walter A. Elwell (Grand Rapids: Baker, 1984), p. 1050, writes, "Why Puritanism collapsed as a cultural force is a complex issue, but one suggestion is that prayer was vocalized like the preaching that was central to its witness. Meditation did have a significant emphasis . . . but the contemplative life was suspect by its associations with popery. It might have had a richer, more sustained spirituality if the contemplative life had also been considered."
20. Thomas Merton writes, "The poet enters into himself in order to create. The contemplative enters into God in order to be created." *Seeds of Contemplation* (Westport, Conn.: Greenwood Press, 1979), p. 71.
21. A. W. Tozer, *Pursuit of God* (Camp Hill, Penn.: Christian Publications, 1982), pp. 96-97.
22. Augustine, *Soliloquies*, 2.1.1, in *The Nicene and Post Nicene Fathers* vol. 7 (Peabody, Mass.: Hendrickson, 1994), p. 547
23. Joel S. Goldsmith, *Practicing the Presence* (San Francisco: Harper & Row, 1958) offers a pantheistic perspective on contemplation.
24. *Rejoice in the Lord* (Grand Rapids: Eerdmans, 1985), p. 244.
25. "A Matter of Faith," *Dallas Morning News*, November 2, 1997.
26. Larry J. Peacock, "Knee-Bent Wonder: The Art of Contemplative Simplicity," *Weavings* 3 (May/June, 1990), pp. 31-33.
27. Richard Lovelace, *Dynamics of Spiritual Life* (Downers Grove, Ill.: InterVarsity, 1979), p. 345.
28. Baxter, *The Saints' Everlasting Rest*, ch. 13, sect. 4. Cited in *The Westminster Dictionary of Christian Spirituality*, ed. Gordon S. Wakefield (Philadelphia: Westminster, 1983), p. 39.
29. C. S. Lewis, *Mere Christianity* (New York: Macmillan, 1976), p. 65.
30. C. S. Lewis, *Miracles* (New York: Macmillan, 1948), p. 194.
31. Robert A. Johnson, *Inner Work* (San Francisco: Harper & Row, 1986), pp. 100-101.
32. The Web address of this organization is www.gracecom.org.
33. "Newest Path to Happiness: Labyrinth," *Denver Post*, May 10, 1998, pp. 2, 23.
34. Lauren Artress, *Walking a Sacred Path: Rediscovering the Labyrinth as a Spiritual Tool* (New York: Riverhead Books, 1995), p. 3. This is a good modern introduction to the Labyrinth, although written from a liberal Episcopalian perspective.

35. Artress, p. 67.
36. Artress, p. 52.
37. Artress, p. 22.
38. Tozer, pp. 9-10.
39. Cited in Alan Jones, *Exploring Spiritual Direction* (San Francisco: Harper & Row, 1982), p. 125.
40. Augustine, *City of God*, 19.19, in *The Fathers of the Church*, vol. 24 (Washington, D.C.: Catholic University of America Press, 1954), p. 230
41. Clark Pinnock, *Flame of Love* (Downers Grove, Ill.: InterVarsity, 1996), pp. 121-122.

Chapter Seven

1. Douglas Webster, *Finding Spiritual Direction* (Downers Grove, Ill.: InterVarsity, 1991), p. 13.
2. Richard J. Foster, *Celebration of Discipline* (HarperSanFrancisco, 1988), p. 185.
3. "The Unique Journey of 'Spiritual Companioning,'" *USA TODAY* (Aug. 11, 1998), 8D. As of this writing, the key phrase "spiritual guide" will connect you to thousands of sites on the World Wide Web.
4. Michael J. Wilkins, *Following the Master: Discipleship in the Steps of Jesus* (Grand Rapids: Zondervan, 1992), p. 279.
5. Aelred of Rievaulx, as quoted by Jerome M. Neufelder and Mary C. Coelho, eds., in *Writings on Spiritual Direction* (New York: Seabury, 1982), p. 33.
6. Cited in James Melvin Washington, ed., *A Testament of Hope: The Essential Writings of Martin Luther King, Jr.* (San Francisco: Harper & Row, 1986), p. 517
7. Richard J. Foster, *Prayer: Finding the Heart's True Home* (HarperSanFrancisco, 1992), pp. 252-253.
8. Thomas à Kempis, *The Imitation of Christ*, ed. Donald E. Demaray (Grand Rapids: Baker, 1982), p. 18 [I.4].
9. John of the Cross, *Spiritual Maxims and Sentences*, as quoted by Neufelder and Coelho, p. 5.
10. Jeremy Taylor, as quoted by Reginald S. Ward, in *A Guide for Spiritual Directors* (Oxford: Mowbray, 1958), p. 9.
11. Eugene H. Peterson, "The Summer of My Discontent," *Christianity Today* (Jan. 15, 1990), p. 30.
12. Eugene H. Peterson, *Working the Angles: The Shape of Pastoral Integrity* (Grand Rapids: Eerdmans, 1987), p. 1.

13. James Houston, "The Independence Myth," *Christianity Today* (Jan. 15, 1990), p. 32.
14. Bernard of Clairvaux, as quoted by Joseph de Guibert, in *The Theology of Spiritual Life* (New York: Sheed and Ward, 1956), p. 155.
15. Houston, p. 32.
16. Baron Friedrich von Hügel, *Essays and Addresses on the Philosophy of Religion*, as quoted by Neufelder and Coelho, p. 8.
17. C. Welton Gaddy, *A Soul Under Siege: Surviving Clergy Depression* (Philadelphia: Westminster/John Knox, 1991), p. 56.
18. Michael Ramsey, *The Charismatic Christ* (New York: Morehouse-Barlow, 1973), p. 46.
19. John of the Cross, "The Living Flame of Love," stanza 3, *The Collected Works of St. John of the Cross*, trans. K. Kavanaugh and O. Rodriguiez (Washington, D.C.: ICS Publications, 1991), p. 685.
20. Teresa of Avila, as quoted by Neufelder and Coelho, p. 43.
21. John Cassian, *Conferences*, I.20, in *The Classics of Western Spirituality* (New York: Paulist, 1985), p. 55.
22. *The Denver Post*, September 15, 1998.
23. Dietrich Bonhoeffer, *Life Together* (New York: Harper & Row, 1954), pp. 97-99.
24. Henry T. Blackaby and Claude V. King, *Experiencing God* (Nashville: Broadman & Holman, 1994), p. 31.
25. Denis Duncan, ed., *365 Meditations by J. B. Phillips for This Day* (Waco, Tex.: Word, 1974), pp. 32-34.
26. Francis J. Houdek, *Guided by the Spirit* (Chicago: Loyola, 1995), p. 88-89.
27. Teresa of Avila, *The Interior Castle, The Classics of Western Spirituality* (New York: Paulist, 1979), p. xvii.
28. C. S. Lewis, *A Grief Observed* (New York: Seabird, 1961), p. 37.
29. Henry J. M. Nouwen, *The Return of the Prodigal Son* (New York: Image, 1993), p. 21.

Chapter Eight

1. Richard F. Lovelace, *Dynamics of Spiritual Life* (Downers Grove, Ill.: InterVarsity, 1979) p. 220.
2. David G. Benner, *Psychotherapy and the Spiritual Quest* (Grand Rapids: Baker, 1988), p. 158.
3. Kenneth J. Collins, *Soul Care: Deliverance and Renewal Through the Christian Life* (Wheaton, Ill.: Victor Books, 1995), p. 36.

4. Cassette tape sermon by Gil Rugh, "Psychology: The Trojan Horse." Produced by Indian Hills Community Church, Lincoln, Nebraska.
5. Emil Brunner, *Revelation and Reason* (London: SCM Press, 1947), pp. 383-385.
6. Benner, pp. 108-111.
7. Benner, pp. 116-117.
8. John Calvin, *Commentaries on the Pastoral Epistles* (Grand Rapids: Eerdmans, 1959), pp. 300-301.
9. John Calvin, *Institutes of the Christian Religion, The Library of Christian Classics*, vol. 20, ed. John T. McNeill (Philadelphia: Westminster, 1960), pp. 273-274 [book II, chap. 2, par. 15].
10. Calvin, *Institutes*, p. 275 [book II, chap. 2, par. 16].
11. Calvin, *Institutes*, p. 53 [book I, chap. 5, par. 2].
12. See Frank Vandenberg, *Abraham Kuyper* (Grand Rapids: Eerdmans, 1960), p. 207.
13. B. B. Warfield, "Incarnate Truth," *In Selected Shorter Writings*, 2 vols. (Nutley, N.J.: Presbyterian & Reformed, 1970-73), vol. 2, pp. 463-465.
14. C. S. Lewis, *Mere Christianity* (London: Geoffrey Bles, 1952), p. 150.
15. Augustine, *Christian Instruction*, Prologue, 6, in *The Fathers of the Church*, vol. 2 (Washington, D.C.: Catholic University of America Press, 1947), pp. 23-24.
16. C. S. Lewis, "The Efficacy of Prayer," *His* (May 1959), p. 8.
17. James Beck, *Jesus and Personality Theory* (Downers Grove, Ill.: InterVarsity, 1999), p. 19.
18. Roy M. Oswald and Otto Kroeger, *Personality Type and Religious Leadership* (Washington, D.C.: The Alban Institute, 1988), p. 107.
19. The reader can gain a good sense of his or her type by doing the questionnaire in Oswald and Kroeger, pp. 10-16.
20. Henri J. M. Nouwen, *Return of the Prodigal Son* (New York: Doubleday/Image, 1992), p. 121. In the same spirit, Thomas Merton writes, "If we believe God is a stern, cold lawgiver who has no real interest in us, who is merely a ruler, a lord, a judge and not a father, we will have great difficulty in living the Christian life." *Life and Holiness* (Garden City, N.Y.: Doubleday, 1964), p. 31.
21. Frank Minirth et al., *The Workaholic and His Family* (Grand Rapids: Baker, 1984), p. 56.
22. J. B. Phillips, *Your God Is Too Small* (New York: Macmillan, 1961), p. 30.
23. As reported in *The Denver Post*, February 21, 1998, pp. 1,6.
24. Minirth et al., pp. 133-134.
25. Phillips, p. 32.

26. Merton, p. 65.
27. C. Welton Gaddy, *A Soul Under Siege: Surviving Clergy Depression* (Louisville: Westminster/John Knox, 1991), p. 27.
28. Gaddy, p. 139.
29. Gaddy, p. 26.
30. John Wimber, *Power Healing* (San Francisco: HarperCollins, 1987), p. 80.
31. Mark R. McMinn, *Psychology, Theology, and Spirituality in Christian Counseling* (Wheaton: Tyndale House, 1996), pp. 9-12. McMinn, p. 11, adds, "Only those counselors aware of psychological symptoms, theological principles, and spiritual formation will be able to discern the best treatment" for hurting people.
32. McMinn, p. 270.

Chapter Nine

1. Peter Toon, *Spiritual Companions* (Grand Rapids: Baker, 1990), p. 1.
2. Michael Downey, *Understanding Christian Spirituality* (New York: Paulist, 1997), p. 53.
3. Toon, p. 5.
4. C. S. Lewis, "Introduction" to St. Athanasius, *The Incarnation of the Word of God* (New York: Macmillan, 1946), p. 6.
5. Downey, p. 68.
6. Lewis, "Introduction," p. 7.
7. The list appears in E. Lynn Harris, *The Mystic Spirituality of A. W. Tozer* (San Francisco: Mellen Research University Press, 1992), appendix A, p. 139. I have omitted several names and titles from Tozer's list because of their unfamiliarity to today's readers.
8. Harris, p. 133.
9. *Bernard of Clairvaux: Selected Works*, trans. G. R. Evans, in *The Classics of Western Spirituality* (New York: Paulist, 1987), pp. 199-200.
10. Teresa of Avila, *The Interior Castle*, in *The Classics of Western Spirituality* (New York: Paulist, 1979), p. 44.
11. Teresa of Avila, p. 81.
12. Teresa of Avila, p. 89.
13. Teresa of Avila, p. 93.
14. Teresa of Avila, p. 126.
15. Teresa of Avila, p. 178.
16. C. H. Spurgeon, "A Wafer of Honey," *Spurgeon's Expository Encyclopedia*, 15 vols. (Grand Rapids: Baker, 1978), vol. 8, p. 289.
17. Teresa of Avila, p. 42.

18. Thomas Merton, *Life and Holiness* (Garden City, N.Y.: Doubleday/Image, 1964), pp. 64-65.
19. Thomas Merton, *Contemplative Prayer* (Garden City, N.Y.: Doubleday/Image, 1971), p. 29.
20. Merton, *Life and Holiness*, p. 57.
21. Thomas Merton, "The Contemplative Life," *Dublin Review 223* (Winter 1949), p. 32.
22. Merton, *Life and Holiness*, p. 7.
23. C. S. Lewis, *Letters to an American Lady* (Grand Rapids: Eerdmans, 1967), p. 99.
24. Alister McGrath, "Borrowed Spiritualities," *Christianity Today* (Nov. 8, 1993), p. 20.
25. J. B. Phillips, *Your God Is Too Small* (New York: Macmillan, 1961), p. 39.
26. C. S. Lewis, *Mere Christianity* (New York: Macmillan, 1960), p. 80 [book III, chap. 3].
27. Eugene Peterson, "Spirit Quest," *Christianity Today* (Nov. 8, 1993), p. 30.
28. Richard F. Lovelace, "Evangelical Spirituality: A Church Historian's Perspective," *Journal of the Evangelical Theological Society* 31/1 (March, 1988), p. 35.
29. J. I. Packer, *A Quest for Godliness: The Puritan Vision of the Christian Life* (Westchester, Ill.: Crossway, 1990), p. 13.

Chapter Ten

1. Augustine, *Sermon*, 169.18. Cited in *Augustine Day by Day* (New York: Catholic Book Publishing Co., 1986), p. 17.
2. Michael Downey, *Understanding Christian Spirituality* (New York: Paulist, 1997), p. 72.
3. Catherine of Siena, *Set Aside Every Fear*, compiled by John Kirvan (Notre Dame: Ave Maria, 1997), p. 193.
4. Teresa of Avila, *Let Nothing Disturb You*, compiled by John Kirvan (Notre Dame: Ave Maria, 1996), pp. 180-181.
5. C. S. Lewis, *Mere Christianity* (London: Geoffrey Bles, 1952), p. 153.
6. "St. Francis of Assisi," *The Westminster Dictionary of Christian Spirituality*, ed. Gordon S. Wakefield (Philadelphia: Westminster, 1983), p. 157.
7. Thomas à Kempis, *The Imitation of Christ*, ed. Donald E. Demaray (Grand Rapids: Baker, 1982), pp. 103-104 [book II, chap. 11].
8. Teresa of Avila, pp. 186–187.

9. Cited in Sherwood Wirt, ed., *Spiritual Disciplines* (Westchester, Ill.: Crossway, 1983), p. 75.
10. Thomas à Kempis, p. 11 [book I, chap. 1].
11. "Living in the Holy Spirit," *Newsweek* (April 13, 1998), p. 59.
12. E. Schweitzer, as quoted by Léon Joseph Suenens, in *Ecumenism and Charismatic Renewal* (Ann Arbor, Mich.: Servant, 1978), p. 28.
13. See C. Douglas Weaver, ed., *From Our Christian Heritage* (Macon, Ga.: Smyth & Helwys, 1997), p. 55.
14. Teresa of Avila, pp. 144–145.

Author

BRUCE DEMAREST is currently a professor at Denver Seminary, where he teaches courses in theology, Christian spirituality, and mentoring. In the past, he has served as a missionary educator and university student worker in both Africa and Europe and has also taught at Trinity Evangelical Divinity School in Deerfield, Illinois.

Dr. Demarest earned his B.S. in science from Wheaton College, his M.A. in New Testament from Trinity Evangelical Divinity School, and his Ph.D. in biblical and historical theology from the University of Manchester.

A retreat and seminar leader in the field of Christian spirituality and mentoring, Dr. Demarest is the author of *Integrative Theology* (Zondervan), *Who is Jesus?* (Victor), and *The Cross and Salvation* (Crossway).

Dr. Demarest and his wife, Elsie, have three grown children: Starr, Scott, and Sharon. They live in Littleton, Colorado, and enjoy hiking, camping, and skiing in the great Rocky Mountain outdoors.

General Editor

DALLAS WILLARD is a professor in the school of philosophy at the University of Southern California in Los Angeles. He has been at USC since 1965, where he was director of the school of philosophy from 1982 to 1985. He has also taught at the University of Wisconsin (Madison), where he received his Ph.D. in 1964, and has held visiting appointments at UCLA (1969) and the University of Colorado (1984).

His philosophical publications are mainly in the areas of epistemology, the philosophy of mind and of logic, and on the philosophy of Edmund Husserl, including extensive translations of Husserl's early writings from German into English. His *Logic and the Objectivity of Knowledge*, a study on Husserl's early philosophy, appeared in 1984.

Dr. Willard also lectures and publishes in religion. *In Search of Guidance* was published in 1984 (second edition in 1993), and *The Spirit of the Disciplines* was released in 1988.

He is married to Jane Lakes Willard, a marriage and family counselor with offices in Van Nuys and Canoga Park, California. They have two children, John and Rebecca, and live in Chatsworth, California.

Editor

David Hazard is the editor of spiritual formation books for NavPress. He is also the editor of the classic devotional series *Rekindling the Inner Fire* and writes the monthly column "Classic Christianity" for *Charisma* magazine.

For more than seventeen years, David has held various positions with Christian publishing houses, from editorial director to associate publisher. As a writer, he has contributed numerous internationally best-selling books to contemporary Christian publishing, some of which have been published in more than twenty languages worldwide. As an editor, David has developed more than two hundred books.

For the past twelve years, his special focus and study has been in the classic writings of Christianity, the formation of early Christian doctrine, and Christian spirituality.